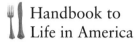

Handbook to
Life in America

Volume VII
The Great Depression and World War II
1929 to 1949

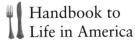

Handbook to
Life in America

Volume VII

The Great Depression and World War II
1929 to 1949

Rodney P. Carlisle
GENERAL EDITOR

Facts On File
An imprint of Infobase Publishing

Handbook to Life in America: The Great Depression and World War II,
1929 to 1949
Copyright © 2009 Infobase Publishing

Facts On File, Inc.
An Imprint of Infobase Publishing
132 West 31st Street
New York, NY 10001

Library of Congress Cataloging-in-Publication Data
Handbooks to life in America / Rodney P. Carlisle, general editor.
    v. cm.
Includes bibliographical references and index.
  Contents: v. 1. The colonial and revolutionary era, beginnings to 1783—v. 2. The early national period and expansion, 1783 to 1859—v. 3. The Civil War and Reconstruction, 1860 to 1876—v. 4. The Gilded Age, 1870 to 1900—v. 5. Age of reform, 1890 to 1920—v. 6. The roaring twenties, 1920 to 1929—v. 7. The Great Depression and World War II, 1929 to 1949—v. 8. Postwar America, 1950 to 1969—v. 9. Contemporary America, 1970 to present.
  ISBN 978-0-8160-7785-4 (set : hc : alk. paper)—ISBN 978-0-8160-7174-6 (v. 1 : hc : alk. paper)—ISBN 978-0-8160-7175-3 (v. 2 : hc : alk. paper)—ISBN 978-0-8160-7176-0 (v. 3 : hc : alk. paper)—ISBN 978-0-8160-7177-7 (v. 4 : hc : alk. paper)—ISBN 978-0-8160-7178-4 (v. 5 : hc : alk. paper)—ISBN 978-0-8160-7179-1 (v. 6 : hc : alk. paper)—ISBN 978-0-8160-7180-7 (v. 7 : hc : alk. paper)—ISBN 978-0-8160-7181-4 (v. 8 : hc : alk. paper)—ISBN 978-0-8160-7182-1 (v. 9 : hc : alk. paper) 1. United States—Civilization—Juvenile literature. 2. United States—History—Juvenile literature. 3. National characteristics, American—Juvenile literature. I. Carlisle, Rodney P.
  E169.1.H2644 2008
  973—dc22
                            2008012630

Contents

Volume VII
The Great Depression and World War II
1929 to 1949

*"Economic depression cannot be cured by
legislative action or executive pronouncement."*
— President Herbert Hoover

THE FLAVOR OF daily life in previous eras is usually only vaguely conveyed by examining the documents of state and the politics of the era. What people ate, how they spent their time, what entertainment they enjoyed, and how they related to one another in family, church, and employment, constituted the actual life of people, rather than the distant affairs of state. While governance, diplomacy, war, and to an extent, the intellectual life of every era tends to be well-documented, the way people lived is sometimes difficult to tease out from the surviving paper records and literary productions of the past.

For this reason in recent decades, cultural and social historians have turned to other types of physical documentation, such as illustrations, surviving artifacts, tools, furnishings, utensils, and structures. Statistical information can shed light on other aspects of life. Through examination of these and other kinds of evidence, a wholly different set of questions can be asked and tentatively answered.

This series of handbooks looks at the questions of daily life from the perspective of social and cultural history, going well beyond the affairs of government to examine the fabric and texture of what people in the American past experienced in their homes and their families, in their workplaces and schools. Their places of worship, the ways they moved from place to place, the nature of law and order and military service all varied from period to period. As science and technology advanced, the American contributions to those fields became greater and contributed to a different feel of life. Some of this story may be familiar, as historians have for generations commented on the disparity between rural and city life, on the impact of technologies such as the cotton gin, the railroad and the steamboat, and on life on the advancing frontier. However in recent decades, historians have turned to different sources. In an approach called Nearby History, academic historians have increasingly worked with the hosts of professionals who operate local historical societies, keepers of historic homes, and custodians of local records to pull together a deeper understanding of local life. Housed in thousands of small and large museums and preserved homes across America, rich collections of furniture, utensils, farm implements, tools, and other artifacts tell a very different story than that found in the letters and journals of legislators, governors, presidents, and statesmen.

FRESH DISCOVERIES
Another approach to the fabric of daily life first flourished in Europe, through which historians plowed through local customs and tax records, birth and death records, marriage records, and other numerical data, learning a great deal about the actual fabric of daily life through a statistical approach. Aided by computer methods of storing and studying such data, historians have developed fresh discoveries about such basic questions as health, diet, life-expectancy, family patterns, and gender values in past eras. Combined with a fresh look at the relationship between men and women, and at the values of masculinity and femininity in past eras, recent social history has provided a whole new window on the past.

By dividing American history into nine periods, we have sought to provide views of this newly enriched understanding of the actual daily life of ordinary people. Some of the patterns developed in early eras persisted into later eras. And of course, many physical traces of the past remain, in the form of buildings, seaports, roads and canals, artifacts, divisions of real estate, and later structures such as railroads, airports, dams, and superhighways. For these reasons, our own physical environment is made up of overlapping layers inherited from the past, sometimes deeply buried, and at other times lightly papered over with the trappings of the present. Knowing more about the many layers from different periods of American history makes every trip through an American city or suburb or rural place a much richer experience, as the visitor sees not only the present, but the accumulated heritage of the past, silently providing echoes of history.

Thus in our modern era, as we move among the shadowy remnants of a distant past, we may be unconsciously receiving silent messages that tell us: this building is what a home should look like; this stone wall constitutes the definition of a piece of farmland; this street is where a town begins and ends. The sources of our present lie not only in the actions of politicians, generals, princes, and potentates, but also in the patterns of life, child-rearing, education, religion, work, and play lived out by ordinary people.

VOLUME VII: THE GREAT DEPRESSION AND WORLD WAR II

The era from 1929 to 1949 was dominated by the two major historic developments that shaped the "Greatest Generation": the Great Depression and World War II. Alongside these two worldwide economic and military crises, the daily family life and material culture of Americans evolved, continuing trends already established, but also marking transitions that only later could be seen as deep-seated changes.

The stock market crash of October 1929 heralded a steep downturn in worldwide economic conditions. In the United States, the failure of financial institutions soon proliferated into the failure of hundreds, then thousands of local banks and thrift institutions. With reduced buying power, consumers pulled back, leading to industrial cutbacks, plant closings, and widespread unemployment. The cycle seemed to continue inexorably lower through the remaining years of Herbert Hoover's administration (1929–33), and only worsened in the years of Franklin Roosevelt's first administration (1933–37). Farmers across the central plains, particularly in Oklahoma and Kansas, faced a combination of falling farm prices, arid summers, and Dust Bowl conditions in the face of fixed mortgage payments. The fixed payments and declining income soon led to foreclosures and abandonment of small family farms. Migrating to California and Oregon, the economic refugees from the heartland often found a hostile reception as they sought jobs and a new life.

Despite a wide variety of reforms and relief measures, economic conditions worsened in 1937–38, only to begin to recover with vast government expenditures on weapons and war material procurement, beginning in 1940. During World War II, more than 16 million U.S. citizens served in the military, of whom some 400,000 died either in battle or from other causes. Considering that the U.S. population in 1940 was about 132 million, that meant that about one out of every eight persons in the country served in the military. In this fashion, the war directly touched nearly every family.

Wartime conditions on the home front meant shortages of some products and commodities (such as nylon and silk, used in parachutes), high prices, and a system of rationing gasoline and meat. Civil defense drills, air-raid warning tests, and black-out drills when all lights had to be turned off or dark shades drawn, brought the sense of war into the home.

The Depression and World War II years affected life in deeper ways, often not visible at the time, but with lasting effects. With economic hardship and then the separation of husbands and wives brought on by the war, millions of couples postponed having children, and the birthrate declined from 1929 through the end of the war. With the return of veterans and the coming of some modest prosperity in the immediate post-war years, the Baby Boom began in 1946. In later years, as the generation born between 1946 and 1961, "between the Bomb and the Pill," came to maturity, they would define the consumer generation of that later period.

The psychological and social impact of the Depression and the war were hard to assess at the time and later. Some observers believed that the generation of adults who experienced those crises generally came to respect the authority and leadership of government more than prior or succeeding generations. Americans had come to rely on the government to provide economic relief and regulation to offset the effects of the Depression, and then, to provide the necessary leadership and economic planning that brought the United States to a clear victory over the nation's enemies in 1945.

Although Americans had often claimed to represent a "melting pot" of cultures, the Depression and war years further accelerated the amalgamation process for many. As African Americans continued to leave the south for cities in the north and west, the disparity between the racial segregation of public facilities in the south and the more open access to such facilities in the north and west became more striking. Indications that change was in the air could be seen. By 1949, legal challenges to segregation of colleges and universities were underway. Courts also began to rule against the exclusion of black voters from access to the polls.

The disparity between rural and small town life and life in the large cities continued in the period, slowly shrinking under the impact of transportation and communication. With many rural communities still outside the electric grid, rural households through the 1930s were often lit by kerosene lamps, and outdoor "privies" remained a common sight. Federal rural electrification programs and the Tennessee Valley Authority worked to bring electric power to such isolated regions through the 1930s and 1940s.

Developments already underway in the fields of technology and scientific progress continued through these decades, profoundly shaping life. In the realm of media and entertainment, two developments of the 1920s led the way. The first full-length motion pictures with sound tracks had been introduced in 1927, and the first Technicolor productions were produced in 1933. By the mid-1930s, the movies had become a cheap and popular escape from the cares of the period, and as in the prior decade, movie stars became popular idols, instantly recognized across the country and around the world. Through the late 1930s and into the war years, radio broadcasting of news, quiz shows, band and orchestra music, comedy acts, and radio dramas provided home entertainment. As with the movies, and later with television, nationwide distribution of the same material by radio and cinema further welded American culture into a homogeneous popular form, continuing the process of reducing regional and sectional differences.

With less immediate impact on popular culture, scientific work in nuclear physics led to the development in the 1940s of the first nuclear reactors and, by 1945, an atomic bomb. Through World War II, behind security fences that helped keep the secret, massive weapons development and production facilities were built at Los Alamos, New Mexico; Hanford, Washington; Oak Ridge,

Tennessee, and at other locations across the country, launching the atomic age that would shape weapons policy and the military stance of the United States in future years. Technical progress in rocketry, electronics, explosives, and in more mundane systems such as diesel engines, all helped ensure the eventual victory of the United States and the Allies in the war.

Medicine, education, and public health were all affected by advances during the war years. The development of the "wonder drugs" penicillin and sulfa profoundly affected the course of medicine in the postwar years. A generous program that offered federally funded college education to returning veterans led to great expansion of colleges and universities, as "G.I. Bill" students flocked to higher education 1946–50. Rapid technical training in trades and academic fields during the war provided lifetime careers for many in the postwar decades.

Wartime industries producing rockets, aircraft, ammunition, autos, tanks, trucks, and ships flourished between 1941 and 1945, providing vast new employment opportunities, and bringing overnight prosperity to cities from Seattle, Washington, to San Diego, California, and across the south and west. Alongside the new industries, housing projects sprouted up. Many were quickly and poorly built, with "temporary" housing deteriorating to near-slum conditions after the war. Yet other communities saw rapid expansion of small homes and apartment structures that continued to provide medium and low-cost housing into the postwar decades.

The dislocations of Depression and war further advanced changes that had already affected the status of women. With husbands off at the war, and with industries and trades seeking women employees, hundreds of thousands of women were taken on as employees in jobs formerly held only by men, such as welding, construction, machinery operation, assembly line work, driving of trucks and buses, and other trades. To some small extent, the lifting of the gender barrier also affected employment in managerial, technical, and administrative positions. However, at the end of the war, a drive to re-employ men, and to emphasize the domestic role of women re-emerged. The myth of domesticity emerged full-blown in the early postwar years, creating frictions that would emerge more clearly in the women's movement of the 1950s and 1960s.

The surviving members of the "Greatest Generation" who had faced the horrors of war in Europe and the Pacific returned to a burgeoning and thriving postwar nation that began to reap the rewards of prosperity. Millions of Americans now successfully pursued the goals of homeownership, family stability, education, and regular employment, which had seemed so endangered during the Great Depression.

RODNEY CARLISLE
GENERAL EDITOR

Chapter 1

Introduction

"Freedom from want . . . will secure to every nation a
peacetime life for its inhabitants—everywhere in the world."
—President Franklin Roosevelt

THE 1930s BEGAN for Americans as a period of uncertainty and dread. After nearly a decade of economic growth, the stock market crash of 1929 signaled the beginning of a frightening period of global economic decline—a Great Depression that would last throughout the decade. Rising unemployment, bank failures, and farm foreclosures brought millions of Americans to the brink of financial ruin. Hundreds of thousands did, in fact, lose everything, with many becoming nomads roaming around the country, looking for a fresh start.

The administration of Franklin Delano Roosevelt tried a number of schemes to improve the economy and get people back to work. The New Deal produced some remarkable public works projects and alleviated some of the stress of the Depression years, but the economy remained stubbornly resistant to growth, and even slipped into a fresh recession in 1937.

Economic salvation came in the form of cataclysmic war. Although America at first tried to stay out of the conflicts raging in Europe and the Pacific, on December 7, 1941, the Japanese launched an attack on the naval base at Pearl Harbor, Hawaii. Over the next four years, millions of American men would go off to fight, while on the home front, everyone from Hollywood stars to humble home gardeners did their part for the war effort. World War II would be remembered as the Good War, a fight where the goals were simple and

1

noble and the country was unified. Still, there was a dark side: over 100,000 Japanese Americans were thrown into isolated "internment camps" simply on the basis of their ethnicity.

THE GREAT DEPRESSION

Economic historians still debate the causes of the Great Depression. Perhaps the most basic description is that the period of consumer and manufacturing growth that exploded from 1922 to 1929 was insupportable over the long haul. The underlying weakness of the system was hidden by speculation in the stock market by hundreds of thousands of small investors who drove up stock prices and created an economic "bubble" that could not help but burst.

The crash came in October 1929. After days of heavy losses on the New York Stock Exchange, on October 27—Black Tuesday—a record 16.4 million shares were traded on a single day, a volume not seen again until 1969. Stock value plummeted by $16 billion by the end of the month, with fortunes wiped out overnight. Even those Americans who did not directly invest in the market were impacted, since many banks had invested in the stock market and were suddenly facing catastrophic margin calls. An estimated 10,000 banks failed during the 1930s, wiping out the life savings of countless average citizens.

Unemployment was the hallmark of the Great Depression. Between 1930 and 1932, the unemployment rate jumped from 3.2 to 24.9 percent. That was just the overall rate; it could be much higher depending on the area. The mostly African-American community of Harlem experienced 50 percent unemployment by 1932. Manufacturing regions in the midwest suffered 75

Unemployed people wait in a bread line at the McCauley Water Street Mission under the Brooklyn Bridge in New York City in the early 1930s.

New Deal Programs for the Ages

Most New Deal programs were designed to meet short-term goals, and the majority were abolished when the economy began to rebound in 1943. However, the long-term goal of the New Deal was to provide the most vulnerable Americans with a safety net should hard times come again, and several programs are still operating:

1) The Social Security Administration (from the Social Security Act of 1935) provided financial assistance for the elderly and disabled.

2) The National Labor Relations Board (from the National Labor Relations Act of 1935) protects American workers' rights to form and join unions and engage in collective bargaining with employers.

3) The Fair Labor Standards Act of 1938 created the minimum wage, overtime pay, other worker rights, and abolished "oppressive" child labor.

4) The Securities and Exchange Commission (from the Securities Exchange Act of 1934) oversees stocks and financial transactions and requires securities designed for sale to the public to be registered with the government and backed up by publicly available information.

5) The Tennessee Valley Authority (TVA) of 1933 was designed to modernize navigation, flood control, and electrical generation in the Tennessee Valley. The TVA brought electricity to the desperately poor rural communities of the south, and still exists today to maintain the structures built during the period.

6) The Federal Deposit Insurance Corporation (FDIC) of 1933 sought to regain public confidence in the banking system after the vast number of bank failures during the Depression. The FDIC insures deposits in American banks, assuring people that if their bank collapses, their individual savings are not lost.

percent unemployment before 1935. In 1933 alone, 15 million people were out of work. Even the three in four Americans who held on to their jobs saw their hours or wages cut, and the average household income dropped from $2,300 a year to $1,500 a year. Consumer activity stalled. Soup kitchens and shanty-towns, called Hoovervilles, cropped up in all major urban areas, and the suicide rate climbed.

THE DUST BOWL

Farmers on the Great Plains faced a two-pronged crisis during the Depression years: falling global commodity prices and the environmental disaster known as the Dust Bowl. The decades before 1930 had been unusually wet

A father and his young sons run for cover as a dust storm approaches in Cimarron County, Oklahoma, in April 1936 in a famous photograph by Arthur Rothstein. About 15 percent of Oklahoma's population left during the Dust Bowl.

across the Plains, leading farmers to plant crop after crop of wheat, without rotating their fields to replenish the soil. When drought began in 1931, the depleted topsoil dried up and blew away. A seemingly endless series of wind storms from 1933 to 1938 took off a good three to four inches of topsoil during the Dust Bowl. Dust piled up to the windowsills of farmhouses; housewives tried to keep the fine dust out of the house by hanging damp sheets in the doorways. The biggest storms created fearsome "black blizzards," tossing dust 10,000 feet into the atmosphere and blotting out the light. A single storm in March 1935 devastated five million square acres of wheat. At the height of the drought, there was so little growing that people in Amarillo, Texas found a crow's nest made entirely of scraps of barbed wire, the only building material the bird could find.

Pneumonia and other lung diseases became widespread during those years. People tried to escape the fine dust by wearing masks during the worst storms, but it inevitably ended up in the lungs, leading to sometimes fatal illnesses. Decades later, one woman could still vividly recall her mother giving her drops of turpentine in sugar to help break up congestion in her lungs; a man remembered the stench of the skunk-fat grease his mother rubbed on his chest. Others remembered the anguish of their mothers when a sibling died, or how defeated and depressed their fathers were at not being able to provide food for their families.

Black blizzards and other disasters left 500,000 Plains residents homeless in the 1930s, and at least 2.5 million had moved out of the region by 1940. Among them were the "Okies," poor Oklahomans who pulled up stakes and headed for California during the drought. In all, about 15 percent of the state's population moved out of state between 1935 and 1940.

THE NEW DEAL

For the first three years of the Depression, President Herbert Hoover and his administration did little to aggressively counter the impact of the slowing economy on people's lives. Hoover's administration was unable to come up with an aggressive plan to counter the downward spiral. Few Americans today remember that Herbert Hoover had helped feed and clothe millions of Europeans during and after World War I, and his reputation as a humanitarian was what had propelled him into the White House. Instead he is unfairly remembered as the president who let Americans starve and suffer during the Depression.

Disappointment with the Hoover administration carried Democratic candidate Franklin Roosevelt into office in the 1932 elections. Promising "a new deal for the American people," Roosevelt entered office with great ambition, but few concrete plans. New Deal policies and programs arose out of a desire to meet the "the Rs": relief, recovery, and reform. They felt their role was first to help the people most in need, then to support economic growth, and finally, to remake the system to protect average Americans from economic hardship in the future. This last aspect of the New Deal was the most controversial: it was a revolutionary shift in the relationship between the federal government and the people.

There is considerable debate as to how effective many New Deal programs actually were. Employment projects like the Civilian Conservation Corps, the Works Progress Administration, and the Tennessee Valley Authority got people into jobs and created lasting legacies of public works. In that sense the programs were very effective. But even such dramatic acts as shutting down the nation's banking system until the solvency of each bank could be determined and removing the currency from the gold standard did little to stimulate the economy. There was a secondary recession in 1937 that brought new financial hardship to Americans who were just beginning to get back on their feet.

WORLD WAR

In the end, it was World War II that salvaged the American economy. The mobilization of massive military forces around the globe created a lucrative market for war material, from planes and battleships to uniforms and bullets. Most American manufacturers switched over to war production by 1942.

The four years of war were among the most united in U.S. history. Everything in society was reoriented toward the war. People were asked to save, reuse, recycle, grow their own food, and accept rations on consumer goods like gasoline, sugar, and meat. Most did so willingly. There was remarkably little outcry when the government expanded the income tax and began direct withholding from worker's paychecks. Americans seemed willing to endure the extraordinary in the name of victory.

POPULAR CULTURE IN THE 1930s AND 1940s

The Depression and war years were not all gloom-and-doom. People needed distractions, and low-cost diversions were particularly popular. It did not cost money to play parlor games or cards with friends. Traditional board games like checkers and chess were joined by new games like Chinese checkers. *Monopoly* was issued by Parker Brothers in 1935 and quickly become one of the best-selling games in history. In the 1940s, more child-friendly games like *Chutes and Ladders*, *Candy Land*, and *Clue* came onto the market. *Scrabble* was first available to a wide audience in 1949, although it did not become popular until years later.

Outdoor pursuits gained popularity. Children were the outdoor innovators: stickball and other street games were perennial favorites, but even kids in rural areas learned how to make do with whatever they could find. In more urban areas, miniature golf was popular, with 30,000 courses opened across the country by 1935. The Civilian Conservation Corps improved national parks and wilderness trails for those who wanted to commune with nature. Skiing gained popularity after the 1932 Winter Olympics in Lake Placid, New York, but would not really come into its own until the 1950s. For those who preferred their communion with nature at the track or the ballpark, spectator sports were the way to go: attendance at baseball games and horse races was high.

Spectator sports, including boxing, were well-suited to another popular pastime: gambling. People were always looking for ways to add to their meager supply of cash, even if that meant risking it. Poker, dice, and other games of chance were always likely to find players.

Eighty percent of American households owned at least one radio by 1939. The 1930s are considered the golden age of radio by historians, with audiences enjoying a truly staggering array of entertainment choices. Comedy, drama, classical and Big Band music, plays, and variety shows were popular. The Lone Ranger made his radio debut in January 1933. Serial daytime dramas—also

War and Peace

By the winter of 1941, Europe had been at war for two years, and hopes for an immediate peace had dimmed. Most Americans believed the United States should let Europe fight their own battles. President Franklin Roosevelt, on the other hand, was doing everything he could to help the Allies, including providing Britain with destroyers in exchange for long-term leases of bases located in British colonies in the Caribbean and Atlantic. Roosevelt and his advisors were negotiating with the Japanese, and everyone was well aware that the situation was volatile. Americans were still taken by surprise when the Japanese attacked the U.S. naval base at Pearl Harbor, Hawaii, on December 7, 1941.

Many people were just waking up when the Sunday morning attack began, and others were still asleep. A band on the U.S.S. Nevada continued to play the "Star-Spangled Banner" as planes roared overhead. At 7:58 A.M. a radio message was received at the base, "Air raid, Pearl Harbor, this is no drill." Orders to "man your battle stations!" blared over public address systems. In the air above Pearl Harbor, Japanese Commander Mitsuo Fuchida triumphantly relayed a message to headquarters announcing that the attack had been successful, "Tora! Tora! Tora!" In all, 2,433 Americans were killed at Pearl Harbor, and another 1,178 were wounded.

On December 8 the United States declared war on Japan with only one dissenting vote in Congress. Roosevelt would not live to see the end of the war. Less than a month after he died on April 12, 1945, Germany surrendered unconditionally. When Japan refused to surrender, President Harry Truman ordered atomic bombs dropped on the cities of Hiroshima and Nagasaki. Five days after the second bomb, Japan surrendered unconditionally. By that time 400,000 Americans had been killed or were missing, and another 300,000 had been wounded.

The Soviet Union used its role as an Allied power to dominate countries in Eastern Europe. The erstwhile alliance of the war broke apart as the Soviet government launched a campaign to spread Communism throughout the world. Led by the United States, Great Britain, and France, democratic nations determined to prevent such an occurrence; the resulting Cold War continued until the late 1980s.

Sergeant John Boone calling home while on training in 1942, not long after America entered the war.

A 1936 Hudson automobile. During the Great Depression, many people suddenly found themselves unable to afford the monthly payments on cars they had bought in better times.

known as soap operas, since most were sponsored by soap companies and targeted toward a female audience—got their start during the decade. *The Guiding Light* began in January 1937 and continued as a television drama in the 1950s. It holds the record for the longest story ever told, having been broadcast five days a week almost nonstop for 70 years.

Radio was also an important source of news and information during the era. President Roosevelt's Fireside Chats, a series of 20 radio broadcasts 1933–44, gained particular importance. Beginning with "On the Banking Crisis" on March 12, 1933, Roosevelt used his radio time to lay out the problems the country faced, and the steps his administration was taking to fix them. He also sought to assure Americans that they were not alone in their individual struggle for survival, and that the economic crisis was not beyond fixing. "It is your problem no less than it is mine," he assured them. "Together we cannot fail."

One of the most unusual events of the era began with a radio broadcast. On October 30, 1938, *Mercury Theater on the Air* presented an adaptation of H.G. Wells's 1898 novel *The War of the Worlds*. A young performer named Orson Welles cleverly modernized the story of a Martian invasion as a series of mock bulletins for the first half-hour of the show. For those who listened in from the beginning of the program or into its second half-hour, it was very clear that this was a fictional story, but in the days following the broadcast, newspapers reported that hundreds of thousands of Americans had tuned in midway through and actually believed there was a Martian invasion. There were stories after the fact of worried citizens running panicked in the streets, which historians now believe to be largely urban legends. *The War of the Worlds* broadcast went down as one of the great "hoaxes" of the 20th century, but it was never intended as a hoax or a trick—just as a good Halloween story.

During World War II, a small radio was part of the soldiers' Buddy Kits (or B-Kits). Armed Forces Services Radio began in 1942, and by 1945 was producing 20 hours of original programming for soldiers, to augment re-broadcasts of popular Stateside shows.

Movies were another source of diversion in the 1930s and 1940s. While overall box office receipts took a hit during the Great Depression and production budgets were slashed during the war, Hollywood churned out hundreds of feature films between 1930 and 1949, and audiences flocked to see them. As with radio, the period was later seen as a golden age of film, with some of the all-time classic pictures, such as *Gone with the Wind, The Wizard of Oz*, and *Mr. Smith Goes to Washington,* produced at the end of the 1930s.

The stars did their part for the war effort, joining in war-bond drives, participating in celebrity fundraisers, and producing propaganda films for the government. Others went a step further, among them Jimmy Stewart, who joined the Army Air Force, attaining the rank of colonel; Tyrone Power, who joined the Marines and fought in the Pacific; and Clark Gable, who—despite being past enlistment age—joined the Army and fought in Europe, rising from the rank of private to captain. While there was still plenty of light entertainment produced during World War II, the darker *film noir* genre found a willing audience, as did gritty war dramas. *Casablanca* and *Citizen Kane* also appeared during these years.

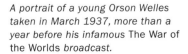

A portrait of a young Orson Welles taken in March 1937, more than a year before his infamous The War of the Worlds *broadcast.*

The Four Freedoms

On January 6, 1941, with continental Europe under Nazi occupation, England reeling under the German blitz, and Japan grabbing territory in the Pacific, U.S. President Franklin D. Roosevelt addressed Congress and the nation. The United States was not yet in the war, but it was preparing for war and helping its global allies as much as it could. In his address, FDR outlined what would become the moral center of America's coming war effort. His address became known as the Four Freedoms speech.

"We look forward to a world founded upon four essential human freedoms," said Roosevelt. "The first is freedom of speech and expression—everywhere in the world. The second is freedom of every person to worship God in his own way—everywhere in the world. The third is freedom from want—everywhere in the world. The fourth is freedom from fear—everywhere in the world."

The speech stirred Americans and helped them come to grips with the likelihood of war. It also gave rise to some enduring, iconic American images. Illustrator Norman Rockwell created a series of four paintings that depicted rugged, everyday Americans illustrating the four freedoms. "Freedom of Speech" shows a man expressing his thoughts at a local town meeting; "Freedom of Worship" shows Americans of different ages and races worshiping together; "Freedom from Want" (perhaps the most classic of the set) shows grandparents setting out a full Thanksgiving table; "Freedom from Fear" shows two parents tucking their child safely into bed.

The popular magazine *Saturday Evening Post* published the paintings as covers, and they caught Americans' attention. Capitalizing on the popularity of Rockwell's series, the federal government used them for war bond drives beginning in 1943 to remind Americans why they were fighting. The paintings remain some of Rockwell's most recognizable works.

LITERATURE

Literature flourished during the Great Depression: this was the height of the careers of novelists Ernest Hemingway, John Dos Passos, Thornton Wilder, and John Steinbeck; poets Carl Sandburg, Wallace Stevens, Ogden Nash, and Dorothy Parker; and playwright Eugene O'Neill. Erskine Caldwell's *Tobacco Road* and Richard Wright's *Native Son* were groundbreaking looks at racial and social injustice among the nation's poor, while John Steinbeck's *The Grapes of Wrath* dramatized the plight of farmers forced to leave their homes in the Dust Bowl for a new life in California.

Among the most important events in publishing during the period was the rise of the paperback book. Starting with Penguin Books in England in

The display of hardcovers in this bookstore window in New York City in 1941 includes the expected, such as romances, a memoir by Winston Churchill's secretary, and stories of wartime Europe, but also an advertisement for Adolf Hitler's follow-up to Mein Kampf, *at top.*

1935, the $0.25 paperback "democratized" reading in Europe and the United States over the next four decades, bringing literature into the price range of the average consumer. Not all of this was high-brow stuff; pulp fiction was as common as Hemingway and Fitzgerald. Traditional hardcover publishers turned up their noses at paperbacks until the profit motive became too strong; by 1944, most major houses had their own paperback divisions. In 1943, the U.S. government introduced Armed Forces Editions, providing popular books to soldiers in the field (specially formatted to fit in uniform pockets). By the time the division closed in 1947, Armed Forces Editions had produced 123 million copies.

EDUCATION
The Great Depression even had an impact on public education. As state revenues fell, there was less and less money to devote to the nation's schools, while an increasing number of parents found it difficult to scrape up the money to

The Presidents

Franklin Roosevelt (right), on the way to his March 4, 1933, inauguration. At left sits the unpopular outgoing president, Herbert Hoover.

Three distinctly different men served as president of the United States in the 1930s and 1940s. Republican Herbert Hoover (1929–33) was much admired in the early days of his presidency. Hoover had served as Food Administrator during World War I and had been in charge of the American Relief Commission, which offered direct aid to Europeans after the war. When the stock market crashed in 1929, Hoover believed the best thing to do was allow it to right itself. He informed Americans that "Economic depression cannot be cured by legislative action or executive pronouncement." Despite repeated assurances that the economy was on the upswing, banks and business continued to close. Numerous Americans lost their jobs and homes. The president was blamed for creating the Depression and for not being able to stop it.

Hoover lost the 1932 election to Democrat Franklin Roosevelt, who assured Americans in his First Inaugural Address that "This great Nation will endure as it has endured, will revive and will prosper" and asserted his "firm belief that the only thing we have to fear is fear itself..." Unlike Hoover, Roosevelt was a charismatic leader. In his First Hundred Days in office, FDR turned the United States into a social welfare state, sponsoring legislation that ranged from the Federal Emergency Relief and National Recovery Acts to the Emergency Conservation Work Act. The only president in American history to be elected four times, Roosevelt led the United States out of the Depression and into World War II after Japan attacked Pearl Harbor on December 7, 1941. His Four Freedoms became the cornerstone of the United Nations Charter.

When Roosevelt died unexpectedly in April 1945, it was left to his successor, Harry Truman, to oversee the end of the war. On the day he became the 33rd president, Truman implored reporters, "Boys, if you ever pray, pray for me now." Truman made the most difficult decision of his presidency when he determined to use the atomic bomb to force a Japanese surrender. In the early postwar years, Truman replaced the New Deal with the Fair Deal, determined to make the United States a more equitable nation. He instituted civil rights and fair housing policies and promoted national health insurance and unemployment compensation.

provide their children with the clothing, books, and supplies needed to get through a school year. Administrators in some schools noticed a troubling uptick in discipline problems among their students. One Chicago principal told a congressional committee that he told his teachers to ask a child who was acting out if he had had breakfast that morning, "which usually brings out the fact that he has had nothing at all." By 1933, about 200,000 teachers were out of work and 2.2 million children had dropped out of school. At least 2,000 rural schools never reopened. The schools that did stay open tried a number of schemes to stay that way: shortening the school day and the school year to save on operating costs, and slashing teachers salaries. In some places, teachers were lucky to receive $40 a week.

Colleges also felt the economic pinch in the initial years of the Depression, although enrollments rose by close to a half-million from 1935 to 1940 as the government began to offer student financial aid for the first time. This turned out to be a short-lived period of growth, as millions of college-aged men joined the armed forces or went to work in the defense industry during World War II. But with the passage of the Servicemen's Readjustment Act of 1944—more commonly known as the G.I. Bill—millions of former soldiers became eligible for tuition assistance of up to $500 a year for any academic program they chose to enter. While that seems like a small amount today, in 1946 the annual tuition at Harvard was just $400. While not every eligible soldier ended up in the Ivy League, millions enrolled in programs all over the country, overwhelming college admissions staffs and causing a shortage of on-campus housing and facilities. Colleges that a decade before were faced with the prospect of closing their doors were suddenly awash in cash and embarked on a massive building spree to cope with their newly expanded student bodies.

CONCLUSION

When World War II came to an end during the spring and summer of 1945, the true horror of Nazi extermination camps was finally uncovered, while on the other side of the planet, America ushered in a frightening new era with the dropping of atomic bombs on the Japanese cities of Hiroshima and Nagasaki. But all of that seemed secondary to the joy of watching the soldiers come home from the battlefield and resume their lives. As the decade came to an end, there was a new sense of optimism in the air, perhaps best represented by the bumper crop of babies born in 1946 and beyond—a Baby Boom that would have a profound impact in the years to come.

HEATHER K. MICHON

Further Readings

Barber, James David. *The Presidential Character: Predicting Performance In The White House*. Upper Saddle River, NJ: Prentice-Hall, 1992.

Brinkley, Alan. *The Unfinished Nation: A Concise History of the American People*. New York: McGraw Hill, 2004.

Dodds, John W. *Life in Twentieth Century America*. New York: Putnam's, 1973.

Farrell, Robert H. *Harry S. Truman and the Modern Presidency*. Boston, MA: Little, Brown, and Company, 1983.

Fausold, Martin L. *The Presidency of Herbert C. Hoover*. Lawrence, KS: University of Kansas Press, 1985.

Friedrich, Otto. "Day of Infamy." *Time*. (December 2, 1991).

Glennon, Lorraine, ed. *Our Times: The Illustrated History of the 20th Century*. Atlanta, GA: Turner Publishing Inc., 1995.

Gregory, Ross. *Modern America 1914 to 1945*. New York: Facts on File, 1995.

Harris, Jonathan. *Federal Art and National Culture*. New York: Cambridge University Press, 1995.

Kaledin, Eugenia. *Daily Life in the United States, 1940–1959: Shifting Worlds*. Westport, CT: Greenwood, 2000.

Lerner, Michael A. *Dry Manhattan: Prohibition in New York City*. Cambridge, MA: Harvard University Press, 2007.

Miller, Edward D. *Emergency Broadcasting and 1930s American Radio*. Philadelphia, PA: Temple University Press, 2003.

Miscamble, Wilson D. *From Roosevelt to Truman: Potsdam, Hiroshima, and the Cold War*. New York: Cambridge University Press, 2007.

Phillips, Cabell. *The 1940s: Decade of Triumph and Trouble*. New York: Macmillan, 1975.

Richardson, K.D. *Reflections of Pearl Harbor: An Oral History of December 7, 1941*. Westport, CT: Praeger, 2005.

Schlesinger, Arthur M. *The Coming of the New Deal*. New York: Houghton Mifflin, 1958.

Shlaes, Amity. *The Forgotten Man: A New History of the Great Depression*. New York: Harper Collins, 2007.

Ward, Geoffrey C. *The War: An Intimate History, 1941–1945*. New York: A.A. Knopf, 2007.

Young, William H., and Nancy K. Young. *Music of the World War II Era*. Westport, CT: Greenwood Press, 2008.

Chapter 2

Family and Daily Life

"The most important work you and I will ever do will be within the walls of our own homes."
—Harold B. Lee

AFTER THE ECONOMIC boom of the 1920s, the Great Depression hit Americans particularly hard. On Black Thursday, October 24, 1929, the stock market dropped an unprecedented 40 points in a single day. Unemployment stood at 3.2 percent for 1929, but within a year it had climbed to 8.9 percent. At least seven million Americans were out of work. On December 11, 1930, New York's Bank of the United States closed its 60 branch offices, and the accounts of 400,000 depositors were wiped out in the largest bank closure in American history. By 1933, more than a fourth of the workforce was unemployed. Americans were plunged into despair as prices on food and other necessities continued to rise. In the face of an economic crisis such as the United States had never known, Americans were uncertain of where the future would take them.

Support for President Herbert Hoover declined because of his reluctance to acknowledge the catastrophic impact of the declining economy. Hoover's reputation was further damaged when he failed to respond to demands of disabled World War I veterans who insisted on jobs and previously promised benefits. In the summer of 1932, when the Bonus Army of 15,000 veterans showed up in Washington, D.C., with their families, Hoover refused to meet with them. Instead, he asked Congress to allot money to pay passages home and ordered General Douglas MacArthur to destroy the shanties and tents in which the Bonus Army was camping. A three-month-old boy was killed when federal troops used tear gas to force evacuation, and the media joined the public in vilifying the president.

Americans responded to Hoover's declining popularity by giving Democrat Franklin D. Roosevelt a victory of 22.8 million to 15.8 million votes in the November election. The message was even clearer in the electoral college, with a vote of 472 to 59. Roosevelt famously assured Americans they "had nothing to fear but fear itself," and set about repairing the economic system, which he believed had been destroyed through reckless speculation and ruthless competition.

FAMILY LIFE DURING THE DEPRESSION

Life changed drastically for families during the Great Depression. One-half of all families earned less than $1,000 a year, and others had no income at all. Because they were paid less, women and children often replaced male wage earners on the job. Three million children between the ages of seven and 17 left school for the workplace in 1930 alone. Schools, particularly in rural areas, closed for lack of money and students. The children of Mexican immigrants were put into the fields to work as soon as they could perform simple tasks. Children worked in mills and factories for 50 to 60 hours a week, earning two to three cents an hour. Scores of children were sent to live with relatives or placed in foster care because their parents could not feed them.

The Roosevelt White House received three times the mail garnered under previous presidents. During the first year, Eleanor Roosevelt received 300,000 pieces of mail. A Massachusetts youngster asked the First Lady for old clothes for her mother, who was wearing "a thin thin coat with two sweaters all torn." A 17-year-old from Missouri wrote that she and her sister (15 years old) were trying to care for her ailing mother. She said, "sometimes I think I'll kill myself, but that wouldn't solve anything for the others."

Except for farm families who grew their own food, meals often consisted of basic foods; some of those were handouts from soup kitchens and bread lines. Rural families were more fortunate because there were berries, fruits, and nuts available in addition to food grown in gardens. Clothes were patched rather than replaced, and shoes were "mended" with cardboard or newspaper.

Children were particularly vulnerable. In the early years of the Depression, 250,000 children were homeless. One in five was hungry and lacked adequate clothing. In coal-mining regions, as many as 90 percent of children suffered from malnutrition. Government and charity groups provided aid, but there was never enough money and resources to feed all the hungry children and young people. When testifying before a congressional subcommittee, Clarence E. Picket, the secretary of the American Friends Service Committee, admitted that they "hit the worst spots first" based on the weight of children. In 1932, a report compiled by Grace Abbot, Chief of the Children's Bureau, warned that "malnutrition sufficiently prolonged and widespread will defi-

A young resident of a central Ohio Hooverville, or shantytown, glares into the camera in a photograph taken by Ben Shahn in the summer of 1938.

nitely reduce resistance to disease . . ." Abbott noted that Alabama and Arkansas were already reporting increased evidence of pellagra, and rickets was common among New York City's poor.

Teenagers were also in crisis during the Depression. Some depended on handouts to survive. "Blink," a teenager living in Oakland, California, called it a "good day" when he "made 80 cents helping a guy build a fence." He spent five cents on ice cream and ten cents on a movie before going to sleep under a loading platform. Some 250,000 teenagers were traveling the country by 1932, looking for work and/or handouts. Eighty-five percent of whites and 98 percent of African Americans said they were looking for work, according to one study.

Many teenagers "rode the rails." Weaver Dial of Seattle told of riding the rails at the age of 12, where he and others with "large packs on their backs, with sleeping gear and cooking pots" had to climb a nine-mile hill to catch another train after being thrown off by a railroad "bull." Nobody managed to catch the next train because it "roared by" with "a fireman [waving] from the engine cab, and [showing] us a mouthful of teeth, giving us the old Wyoming horse laugh." The teenagers had to make the long walk back down the hill. After finally catching a train, they were rounded up at gunpoint, and their wallets were rifled for valuables. Dial recalled, "Four bucks was my entire bankroll. I was given one $2.00 ticket on the first passenger train that stopped." Another stowaway was stripped of $40 of the $80 he was taking home to his family after working a harvest. Leslie E. Paul remembers leaving home at the age of 18 in the summer of 1933 because he felt he was a burden. His mother gave him 72 cents; it was all she had in her purse. He left his mother with "tears stream[ing] down her face," carrying a black satin bag because the family did not own a suitcase. Sixteen-year-old Henry Koczur, who was in a similar situation, recalls lighting a match whenever the train stopped at night "just to see what was growing in the fields."

THE NEW DEAL AND RECOVERY
Through a series of bills collectively known as the New Deal, President Roosevelt began to put people to work for the government and provide relief for the hungry, the unemployed, and the elderly. He also improved wages and conditions for the working class while increasing taxes on wealthy Americans. The New Deal set the United States on the road to economic recovery, which was completed with the prosperity brought on by World War II in the following decade.

The low point of the Depression had occurred in 1933. Between that point and 1940, average annual earnings steadily increased, rising from $754 to $1,289. As conditions improved, the number of Americans on relief declined, dropping from 3.2 million to 2.1 million between 1938 and 1939. The Gross Domestic Product rose by 60 percent, and Americans living below the poverty line dropped from around 50 percent in 1940 to approximately one-third in 1944. Despite the prosperity, in 1947, one-third of American homes had no running water, two-fifths had no flush toilets, and three-fifths lacked central heating. African Americans, rural families, and those living in the deep south continued to lag behind other Americans economically.

At a time when comedians Bob Hope and Jack Benny were garnering less than a third of radio listeners, more than 70 percent of Americans regularly tuned in to hear the president's Fireside Chats. Roosevelt used this venue in 1944 to introduce his concept of freedom to the American public. In his "Second Bill of Rights," Roosevelt declared that "Freedom from fear is eternally linked with freedom from want." While Roosevelt was not universally popular among Americans, he was the only president in history who won four presidential elections. The Twenty-Second Amendment, ratified in 1951, limited all future presidents to no more than two full terms.

THE WAR YEARS
On September 1, 1939, Adolf Hitler's Nazi forces invaded Poland, plunging the world into war. Two days later, Great Britain and France declared war on Germany, and other European nations were forced to choose between sup-

porting Britain and France and ceding their sovereignty to the Axis powers. Even nations such as Switzerland, which had issued formal statements of neutrality, were not immune to Hitler's war machine. In the United States, where conservatives had succeeding in convincing large segments of the population that Democratic President Woodrow Wilson had engineered World War I to promote his own interests, isolationism was the order of the day.

President Roosevelt bypassed Congress to help the Allies in all ways possible, rendering assistance through sales of American military equipment, food, and supplies. He also engineered Lend-Lease deals, whereby American bases were established in Allied nations in exchange for financial assistance. In 1940, a peacetime draft was established, and approximately 16 million American males reported for duty to prepare the United States for the war that Roosevelt and his advisors viewed as inevitable.

As World War II raged in Europe, American daily life was represented at the New York World Fair in 1940 in a meticulously designed Town of Tomorrow. For one week, two families deemed by newspapers to represent the average American family lived in Federal Housing Authority model homes. Predictably, both families were made up of a mother, a father, and two children. Only white, middle-class, American-born families were considered proper symbols of American life in the 1940s.

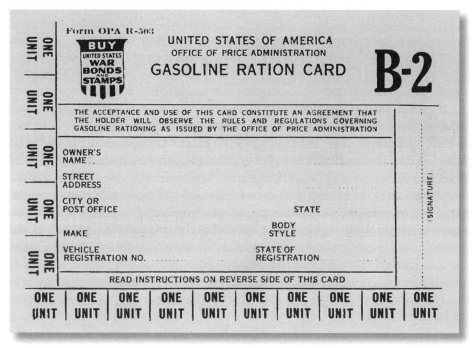

By December 1942, nationwide gas rationing was in effect. Cards such as this granted additional units of fuel for those who could prove their occupations required more driving.

The government attempted to prepare the public for further attacks with air raid drills, blackouts, and media like this poster from 1943.

The United States entered World War II after the Japanese bombed military bases at Pearl Harbor, Hawaii, on December 7, 1941. With the country at war, daily life for most Americans changed drastically. Price controls were established. Gasoline and food were rationed. Blackouts became common and were rigorously monitored, particularly in coastal cities. Air raid drills were held regularly, and families were encouraged to engage in emergency drills. Makeshift shelters were erected to provide protection from possible enemy attacks. Travel was restricted. First aid stations became common sights in American communities, and the Red Cross conducted training in public schools. Americans who were used to virtually unlimited freedom of speech were forced to submit to government censorship. Celebrities sold war bonds, entertained the troops, and performed in films promoting democracy and the American way of life. Although some 33,000 Japanese-American males served in the military, Roosevelt ordered 120,000 Japanese-Americans living on the Pacific Coast interned in camps in California, Arizona, Idaho, Wyoming, Colorado, and Arkansas. Polls indicated that large percentages of Americans initially supported Roosevelt's decision.

Using extensive emergency powers granted by the crisis, the national government established a gasoline curfew in 17 eastern states, forcing all gas stations to shut down between 7 P.M. and 7 A.M. In November 1942, Americans were forced to seek substitutes for coffee, which was rationed. By December, nationwide gas rationing was in effect. Under the auspices of the Office of Price Administration, rent ceilings were established, and wages and prices were frozen. Sales of all new automobiles and trucks were prohibited. Civilian use of rubber declined by 80 percent in order to save the material for war use. In early 1943, shoes, canned goods, meat, fats, and cheese were added to the list of rationed items. Ration books, identifying individuals by name, address, age, sex, weight, and occupation, were distributed to maintain tight control of rationing activities. Salvage drives became increasingly important, and schoolchildren collected tin cans, rags, and other materials. In 1943 alone, salvage drives netted 255,513 tons of tin cans, 43,919 tons of fat, six million tons of waste paper, and more than 26 million tons of scrap iron and steel.

Between February 9, 1942, and September 30, 1945, Daylight Savings Time was replaced with national War Time. Opponents refused to change their clocks, opting to adhere to "God's time." When the American Federation of

In 1943, scrap drives netted more than 26 million tons of iron and steel for the war effort. These Chicago children turned in salvaged scrap metal and tires at a civilian defense office in 1942.

The Miyatakes, a Japanese-American couple, were raising their children in a roughly constructed apartment in the barracks at the Manzanar internment camp in California in 1943.

Labor came out in support of the five-day, six-hour workday, American families had more time for enjoying leisure activities. By the fall of 1941, the 40-hour work week was in effect, as stipulated by the Fair Labor Standards Act of 1938. In 1943, workers employed in work deemed essential to the war effort were banned from leaving their jobs.

In the spring of 1944, with the end of the war in sight, meat rationing ended. The booming economy led to a 29 to 30 percent rise in the cost of living. On June 22, Roosevelt signed the Servicemen's Readjustment Act, establishing the G.I. Bill. Factories began manufacturing consumer goods for the first time since 1941. On November 7, 1944, Roosevelt won an unprecedented fourth term. The national government instituted a national dim-out on January 15 to alleviate wartime fuel shortages, and the following month, all establishments providing public amusements were placed under midnight curfew. In the midst of a national restoration of confidence, the president suddenly died at the Little White House in Warm Springs, Georgia, on April 12, 1945. Vice President Harry Truman was propelled into the presidency. It was left to Truman to make the difficult decision to drop atomic bombs on the Japanese

Christmas

Even during the Great Depression, Americans continued to celebrate Christmas by bestowing gifts on family and friends. In 1929, merchants reported that Americans spent $48 million during the season. By 1941, Christmas spending had risen to $54 million. During World War II, Christmas began to reach its modern-day significance. Profits that had declined during the Depression rose in response to Roosevelt's New Deal. Roosevelt responded to merchant complaints that the season was not long enough by signing an executive order moving Thanksgiving from the last day of November to the 23rd of the month, extending the shopping period by one week. Two years later, Congress officially changed Thanksgiving from the last Thursday to the fourth Thursday in November.

Profit-seeking merchants used the lengthy Christmas season to promote the holiday. Robert L. May of Montgomery Ward created Rudolph the Red-Nosed Reindeer as an advertising gimmick in 1939. Marshall Fields was the first department store to use the Santa Claus figure from Clement Clark Moore's *The Night before Christmas* (1823) as a Christmas symbol. By 1948, other stores had followed suit. Marshall Fields created Uncle Mistletoe and Aunt Holly who lived in Cloud Cottage on the eighth floor of the store.

Music and film were strongly intertwined with the Christmas spirit. In 1942, the film *Holiday Inn* introduced Irving Berlin's song "White Christmas." Bing Crosby's record sold over 30 million copies, and *White Christmas* became the best-selling record in the history of the world. Although it was not critically acclaimed at the time it was introduced in 1946, Frank Capra's film *It's A Wonderful Life*, starring Jimmy Stewart and Donna Reed, later became standard viewing during the American Christmas season. The following year another classic, George Seaton's *Miracle on 34th Street*, starring Maureen O'Hara, Edmund Gwenn, and a young Natalie Wood, was released.

Tree trimming at a Christmas Eve party in Washington, D.C., in 1943.

cities of Hiroshima and Nagasaki in August to force the Japanese into surrendering in order to bring World War II to a conclusion.

By 1945, rationing was lifted on selected items, and inflation spiraled. On October 26, 1949, an increase in the minimum wage from 40 to 75 cents an hour proved a boon for many American families. American newspapers were filled with stories about efforts to rebuild war-torn Europe and the founding of the United Nations. Politically, the postwar period was marked by a growing fear of communism. At the same time, the military-industrial complex grew increasingly more powerful. Americans developed a strong sense of their own importance as the United States dominated global politics. Religion continued to play a large role in American lives, and a new spiritual awakening occurred.

CHANGING DEMOGRAPHICS

The Baby Boom of the postwar years affected virtually every aspect of life in the United States. In 1929, the population of the United States had been 122 million. That same year, Margaret Sanger opened America's first birth control clinic in New York, but family planning was still in its early stages. Because of the Depression, between 1932 and 1940, the American fertility rate, defined as live births per 1,000 women aged 15–44 years, dropped from 81.7 to 79.9 per 1,000. Nevertheless, population figures rose as life expectancy increased, climbing from 58.6 years for whites and 46.7 years for non-whites in 1929 to 66.8 years for whites and 57.7 years for non-whites in 1945. Although the United States trailed many industrialized nations in infant mortality, fewer babies and birthing mothers were dying during the war years. In 1946, the fertility rate was 101.9 per 1,000 women aged 15–44 years. The rate peaked in 1957 at 122.7 per 1,000, and remained above 100 until 1965, when it dropped to 96.6. Americans born between 1946 and 1964 became known as Baby Boomers, a group that would significantly affect life in the United States for years to come.

By 1945, one in 10 Americans lived in a different county from that in which they had been born. Some 13.5 million Americans had moved to a different state, mostly in search of jobs and prosperity. New England, the Plains States, and the south, except for Florida and Texas, continued to lose residents to the industrial areas of New York, New Jersey, Washington, D.C., and the Pacific Coast. Whites made up 90 percent of the American population. By the 1940s, more than half the population lived in urban areas. The prosperity of the 1940s allowed large numbers of Americans to move into the middle class. In 1937, only seven million American families were earning more than $2,000 a year. That number had risen to 28 million by 1947.

Before 1940, African Americans were heavily concentrated in the rural south, where they generally subsisted as tenant farmers or sharecroppers. It was not uncommon for a black family to clear less than $100 for a year's

The Plight of the Elderly

The Great Depression hit older Americans extremely hard. As conditions worsened, Americans over the age of 60 were disproportionately laid off. Many were in poor health and had no way to obtain medical care. A 76-year-old African-American male from West Point, Georgia, wrote to President Franklin Roosevelt on July 31, 1934, asking for help because he had "Labored hard all my days until Depression came on, and i had no job in three years." City officials were threatening to take his home away because he owed $15 in back taxes. He noted that he could not find work with the Civil Works Administration because they "wanted younger men."

Even those who had been comfortable before the Depression found it hard to get by once disaster struck. A 69-year-old architect/builder from Lincoln, Nebraska, wrote to Eleanor Roosevelt on May 19, 1934, in support of a proposed pension for the elderly, "Seemingly everybody has been assisted but we the Forgotten Man these 60 years or more." He wrote that after carrying the load to assist others, "calamity and old age has forced itself upon us."

A male from Webbville, Kentucky, wrote to the First Lady, "I have almost lived out my three score and ten and have bin (sic) in ill health for over two years . . . [I] have no income at all [and] a wife and two children." An 80-year-old wrote to the First Lady on December 4, 1934, declaring that "there are thousands of aged women in this great and rich country who are facing the poor house . . . It is not their fault that they are poor and too old to work." Many letters to the Roosevelts were from grown children who lacked resources to care for elderly parents while supporting themselves.

Even after the Social Security Act was passed in 1935, it did not help all of America's elderly poor. It excluded farm laborers and domestic workers, two groups that had been hard hit by the Depression. Benefits were based on length and volume of contributions into the system, and many elderly had retired without paying benefits. Those who retired between 1937 and 1940 received a small lump sum, but no funds were available for those who had retired earlier. In 1940, the average benefit was $22.50 per month. Many Americans did not support the Social Security system because they believed it smacked of charity.

work after accounts with landowners were settled. In 1940, blacks began migrating to northern industrial areas in large numbers. Although black families faced less overt discrimination outside southern and border states, they continued to labor in low-status jobs at low wages. World War II provided greater employment opportunities for African Americans, but these opportunities sometimes caused tensions in the workplace. On June 20, 1943, for

A Quonset hut with a front porch addition in postwar Hawaii.

instance, race riots broke out in Detroit, Michigan, where 300,000 new workers had been employed. Over a two-day period, 35 people were killed and more than 500 workers were injured. Some 300 white workers were arrested.

The postwar period gave rise to an emergent civil rights movement as African-American soldiers led the way in demanding equal treatment before the law. Black soldiers returned to their homes refusing to accept a designation as second-class citizens. Some 200 racial incidents involving blacks and Hispanics were reported in the United States in 1943 in 45 cities. Even though new employment opportunities opened for African Americans, after the war they remained concentrated in low-paying jobs, and they continued to be openly discriminated against in many states.

During World War II, the marriage rate climbed, rising from 10.1 per 1,000 people in 1929 to 12.1 in 1945. After the war ended in 1945, the expanding marriage rate, coupled with the Baby Boom, increased the demand for affordable housing. In 1947, six million American families lived with relatives or friends. Another 50,000 lived in low-cost temporary housing built during the war, or in Quonset huts. In 1949, Congress agreed to subsidize five million low-income homes in urban areas. Cities responded to the housing shortage in a number of innovative ways. In Atlanta, Georgia, for instance, the government bought 100 abandoned trailers to be used by veterans and their families. In Chicago, the government converted 250 trolleys into family residences. In North Dakota, families lived in grain bins. In New York, a family moved into a department store window for two days to call public attention to their plight. Between 1944 and 1950, construction of housing units jumped from 114,000 to 1.7 million. In 1932 during the Great Depression, there were 250,000 non-farm foreclosures. By 1951, foreclosures had dropped to 18,000.

ENTERTAINMENT

During the 1930s and 1940s, toys came to be perceived as essential to children's developing intellectual and imaginative abilities. Movies, books, and radio programming were designed especially for young audiences. Cartoons made up a major part of children's entertainment. Media giant Walt Disney first appeared on the scene in 1930. Over the next nine years, a new Disney cartoon appeared every three weeks. Approximately half of those starred Mickey Mouse, who became the symbol of Disney's entertainment empire. Between 1932 and 1939, Disney won every single Academy Award given to cartoon shorts. In 1938, the Disney studio produced *Snow White*, the first of a long series of full-length animated movies that would entertain generations of children over the coming decades.

Adult entertainment also underwent major changes in the 1930s and 1940s. By 1930, vaudeville had been relegated to history. Popular performers such as Buster Keaton, Al Jolson, W.C. Fields, Fanny Brice, the Marx Brothers, Phil Silvers, Ed Wynn, and Jimmy Durante turned to night clubs before new opportunities opened in radio, film, and television. Because sponsors bore the cost of programming, radio broadcasts were generally available even to the poorest Americans. The number of radio stations climbed from 696 in 1929 to 919 in 1945. The number of radios in American homes grew from 12 million to 40 million between 1930 and 1938. Rural electrification projects expanded the radio audience by providing access to rural families.

Throughout the United States, the most popular radio shows of the day were the *Jack Benny Show*, *Fibber McGee and Molly*, and *Amos 'N' Andy*. The latter, which portrayed stereotypical African Americans speaking in crude dialects and exhibiting little common sense, generated strong protests from African Americans. Other popular entertainers of the Depression and World War II era included Rudy Vallee, Eddie Cantor, Ed Wynn, George Burns and Gracie Allen, Jack Benny, Fred Allen, Al Jolson, Bing Crosby, Edgar Bergen and Charlie McCarthy, Kay Kayser, Bob Hope, Walter Winchell, Red Skelton, and Abbott and Costello.

Because they were produced in large part by manufacturers of detergents who targeted homemakers, serial dramas such as *Ma Perkins*, *My Gal Sunday*, and *Pepper Young's Family* were known as "soaps." In 1931, there were three serial dramas on the radio. Within eight years, that number had climbed to 61. The "soaps" gradually made the leap from radio to television, becoming a staple of daytime programming.

At an average cost of 25 to 35 cents, movies provided an affordable means of entertainment for American families. Weekly attendance averaged 95 million in 1929. The gangster films that were audience favorites in the 1930s mirrored the rise of organized crime in the United States during Prohibition. By 1945, movie attendance had climbed to 100 million. Mickey Rooney, star of the Andy Hardy series and a number of

By the late 1940s over 90 percent of American homes had a radio.

A woman waiting in front of a sensational movie poster in Cincinnati, Ohio, in October 1938. During the Depression and World War II, weekly movie attendance often approached 100 million.

light-hearted musicals, was a top box office draw. Other favorites included comedians Bud Abbott and Lou Costello and leading man Clark Gable. In 1939, the film version of Margaret Mitchell's best selling Civil War novel, *Gone with the Wind*, starring Vivian Leigh and Clark Gable, debuted in Atlanta. The film carried home the Academy Award for Best Picture for that year, and Hattie McDaniel who played Mammy also became the first African American in history to win the coveted award, for Best Supporting Actress.

After 1941, movies such as *Mrs. Miniver* (1942) and *The White Cliffs of Dover* (1944) dealt directly with the effects of the war, but escapist films such as *State Fair* (1945) also attracted large audiences. Television was still in its infancy, but some visionaries were already predicting its potential effects. In 1941, only two television stations existed, and American families owned less than 5,000 television sets. By 1944, six stations offered Americans programming choices.

Newspapers, which kept families up-to-date on the economy and the war, were considered essential reading. Large newspapers such as the *Chicago Tribune* became known for their concentrated attempts to affect public opinion.

Americans became engrossed in stories of the day, including the sensational news of the kidnapping and death of one-year-old Charles Lindbergh, Jr., the antics of gangster Al Capone, and the opening of the Empire State Building in New York.

Entire families read together, enjoying such books as Pearl Buck's *The Good Earth* (1931) and Marjorie Kinnan Rawling's *The Yearling* (1938). Religion continued to be a popular topic in books, as illustrated by the success of Franz Werfel's *The Song of Bernadette* (1942) and Lloyd C. Douglas's *The Robe* (1943). Westerns were perennially popular, and in 1929 the most popular book was Edna Ferber's *Cimarron*. The following year the most popular book was Erich Maria Remarque's World War I novel *All Quiet on the Western Front*. The German veteran's antiwar epic was made into a film the same year and won the 1930 Academy Award for Best Picture. Other successful publications included Betty Smith's *A Tree Grows in Brooklyn* (1943), which offered a portrait of American parents who wanted their children to do better than they had done.

On stage, *I Remember Mama* (1948) showcased a Norwegian-American family that existed from week-to-week on a meager income without ever losing hope because Mama's mythical "bank account" provided a cushion against despair. In 1947, Elia Kazan's *Gentleman's Agreement* introduced the concept of anti-Semitism to American audiences.

During the Depression and World War II, music became increasingly important in American families. The focus of the music scene shifted from jazz to swing between 1930 and 1940, with Big Bands dominating the charts. Tommy Dorsey, Benny Goodman, Glenn Miller, Guy Lombardo, and Lawrence Welk became household names. Black jazz musicians, including Louis Armstrong,

These shelves display detergents and other household products typical of the 1930s and 1940s. Makers of such products became major sponsors of television programs with female audiences.

Dorothy Langdon, a former movie actress, took on work in an airplane factory in Detroit in 1942, working 48-hour weeks inspecting engine parts.

Count Basie, Cab Calloway, Duke Ellington, and Dizzy Gillespie gained in popularity. Families preferring classical music listened to opera on the radio and at various concert halls. On October 5, 1930, Columbia Broadcasting began offering regular Sunday night radio concerts performed by the New York Philharmonic. Music, like movies, mirrored the nation's concentration on war in the 1940s, and Americans listened to "The Last Time I Saw Paris" (1940), "The White Cliffs of Dover" (1941), and "This Is the Army, Mr. Jones" (1942).

After the war, Americans continued their love affair with musicals, standing in line to buy theater and movie tickets for hits such as *Brigadoon, Kiss Me Kate,* and *South Pacific.* Serious books and movies also had a strong following, as evidenced in 1948 by the popularity of movies such as *Oliver Twist* and *Hamlet.* Books bought after the war signaled a new interest in world affairs, religion, and human rights.

Sports, particularly baseball, were an important form of entertainment for many American families. The first all-star game was held on July 6, 1933, at Chicago's Comiskey Park. Some 49,200 fans watched the American League defeat the National League 4-2. The World Series was regularly covered in newspapers and later broadcast on radio. Golf gained in popularity after the first Master's Tournament was held in Augusta, Georgia, on May 25, 1934. Horton Smith won the tournament by beating Craig Wood by one stroke. American families also followed football, hockey, ice skating, tennis, horse racing, auto racing, and boxing. In 1947, Jackie Robinson joined the Brooklyn Dodgers, becoming the first African American to play in the major baseball leagues.

WOMEN'S ROLES

The lives of women changed during the Depression and war years, affecting family patterns in major ways. Women's roles in the work world were redefined as they were forced to help support their families during the Depression and take up the slack as American males joined the military during World War II. Rosie the Riveter became a strong symbol of the new American woman.

Women drove tractors and operated cranes, grinders, drill presses, and large equipment. They worked in factories, mills, shipyards, defense plants, and government offices. Even though they were not allowed to fight, some women joined the military, flying transport planes, nursing in combat zones, and serving as supply and clerical workers. In 1930, women had been barely a fifth of the total workforce. When the war ended in 1945, they made up 29.2 percent of the workforce. However, by the 1950s many of the women who had joined the workforce in World War II had left those jobs, which were often filled by returning male veterans, and returned to working only in the home.

TECHNOLOGY AND DAILY LIFE
In 1929, American families owned 20,068 telephones. During the Depression, ownership declined, but rose again with the outbreak of war in 1941. By 1945, 46 percent of American families had telephones. Lessons learned in the war had opened up ways of adding convenience to daily lives. In 1929 alone, manufacturers sold $160 million worth of electrical household appliances. As methods of preserving food became more advanced, purchases of frozen food rose accordingly. Between 1934 and 1944, the sale of frozen products climbed from 39 million pounds to 600 million pounds. By the mid-1940s, most American families owned radios, refrigerators, toasters, vacuum cleaners, washers, and electric irons.

Kitchen designs were symbolic of changing lifestyles. Built-in cabinets with increased storage space replaced free-standing cabinets of the past. Ubiquitous white was replaced with a rainbow of colors on walls, floors, and appliances. General Electric, for instance, offered products in Petal Pink, Canary Yellow, Cadet Blue, Turquoise Green, and Woodstone Brown. Kitchens were modernized with easy-to-clean linoleum or tiled floors. Porcelain counters and table tops were added, along with work areas for cooking and improved lighting. Many homes included small breakfast nooks. The refrigerators of the 1940s featured freezer compartments. Windows were added or enlarged for increased ventilation. Living rooms with large picture windows were placed at the rear of houses to allow mothers to supervise small children at play.

CONCLUSION
While the memory of the Great Depression has been vivid and lasting through the generations that followed, World War II may have done more to make family life what it is today. The necessity of war gave women both the opportunity and the social acceptance to enter the workforce and work in previously male-dominated occupations. After a postwar interlude, it would take the women's movement to carry this another step further. But the change in family structure and in life expectations had already begun.

ELIZABETH R. PURDY

Further Readings

Abbott, Grace. "Children and the Depression: A National Study and Warning." *New York Times* (December 18, 1932).

Chapman, Tony. *Gender and Domestic Life: Changing Practices in Families and Households.* New York: Palgrave, 2004.

Cohen, Robert. *Dear Mrs. Roosevelt: Letters from Children of the Great Depression.* Chapel Hill, NC: University of North Carolina Press, 2002.

Kaledin, Eugenia. *Daily Life in the United States, 1940–1959: Shifting Worlds.* Westport, CT: Greenwood, 2000.

Kalish, Mildred Armstrong. *Little Heathens. Hard Times and High Spirits on an Iowa Farm during the Great Depression.* New York: Bantam, 2007.

Kyvig, David E. *Daily Life in the United States, 1920–1940: How Americans Lived through the "Roaring Twenties" and the Great Depression.* Chicago, IL: Ivan R. Dee, 2004.

Lingeman, Richard R. *Don't You Know There's A War On?: The American Home Front, 1941–1945.* New York: Perigee, 1980.

Living History Farm. "Riding the Rails." Available online: http://www.livinghistoryfarm.org/farminginthe30s/water_07.html. Accessed October 2008.

McElvaine, Robert S. *Down and Out in the Great Depression: Letters from the "Forgotten Man."* Chapel Hill, NC: University of North Carolina Press, 1983.

Myers-Lipton, Scott J. *Social Solutions to Poverty: America's Struggle to Build a Just Society.* Boulder, CO: Paradigm, 2006.

Pante, Ellen M. *The American Kitchen 1700 to the Present: From Hearth to High Rise.* New York: Facts on File, 1995.

Restad, Penne L. *Christmas in America: A History.* New York: Oxford, 1995.

Smith, Judith E. *Visions of Belonging: Family Stories, Popular Culture, and Postwar Democracy, 1940–1960.* New York: Columbia University Press, 2004.

Thompson, Kathleen and Hilary MacAustin, eds. *Children of the Depression.* Bloomington and Indianapolis, IN: Indiana University Press, 2001.

Williamson, John B. and Fred C. Pampel. *Old-Age Security in Comparative Perspective.* New York: Oxford, 1993.

Yalom, Marilyn. *A History of the Wife.* New York: HarperCollins, 2001.

Chapter 3

Material Culture

"Use it up, wear it out, make do or do without."
—L. Reid

THE TWO MAIN historical events that dominated the 1930s and 1940s shaped the material culture produced during those decades. The consumer revolution of the 1920s ended with the financial devastation of the Depression and the rationing and shortages imposed during American involvement in World War II. Housing, household furnishings, and fashions all reflected the conservatism of wartime America. Comfort, function, affordability, and availability all guided consumer choices. The material culture of the decades would also reflect the growth of mass production, modern technology, and new materials in the machine age. A new modern aesthetic emphasizing simple styles and clean lines guided and inspired many American designers, architects, and consumers.

COMMERCIAL ARCHITECTURE
In the 1930s and 1940s modern architecture began to look to the future, eliminating most nonessential decorative elements in an attempt to create a simple, futuristic, streamlined look. Such simple structures were more economical to build and more useful, based on the earlier ideas of architects such as Louis Sullivan, who famously noted "form follows function." Modern styles such as Art Deco and Art Moderne (International), which originated in Europe, marked a new direction for American architecture. The new styles grew

33

from the inspiration of the machine age and utilized the new technologies and materials of the times. They would influence not just commercial architecture, but domestic architecture, furniture, jewelry, clothing, fine arts, and household products as well. Commercially, they would most notably change the growing cityscapes of America's major urban areas.

Art Deco, the popular architectural style of the 1920s, carried over into the 1930s and has remained popular ever since. While sometimes borrowing design elements and motifs from past cultures, Art Deco had a decidedly futuristic, modern approach. Art Deco made use of new building and decorative materials, such as Bakelite and aluminum, as well as new types of electric and neon lighting. Art Deco buildings often emphasized vertical lines, streamlined forms, showy designs, and bright colors. Polychromy, the use of multiple colors, was popular. The walls and other surfaces were usually smooth stucco, stone, or metal. Decorative themes borrowed from both the past and the future, including elements of Far and Middle Eastern, Greek, Roman, and Egyptian designs, natural and geometric patterns, and shapes based on machine and automobile parts. Sunrises, ziggurats, zigzags, and chevrons are examples of popular motifs.

Another modern architectural style popular in the 1930s and 1940s, similar to Art Deco, was alternately known as International Style, Streamline Moderne, or Art Moderne in the United States. The Bauhaus movement of architecture begun in Germany was a primary inspiration behind the movement. A number of noted Bauhaus architects fled Nazi Germany to the United States during this time period, including Walter Gropius, whose Gropius House in Massachusetts is a National Historic Landmark. Much of its design inspiration was also drawn from modern machines, especially the airplane. Architects who worked in the Moderne style designed simple buildings that typically featured asymmetrical facades, flat roofs with an absence of cornices or eaves, rounded corners, a horizontal design emphasis, and little to no decorative or-

A glass block wall at the 1938 Gropius House in Lincoln, Massachusetts.

namentation. Geometric forms, such as cylinders or cube-shaped houses, were popular. Hardware, window and door trim, and balustrades were made of polished metals, including nickel, chrome, aluminum, and stainless steel. Glass block windows that often wrapped around walls in horizontal rows that gave the illusion of movement distinguished many Moderne style buildings. Moderne style buildings featured open floor plans and smooth interior walls, usually painted white or grey.

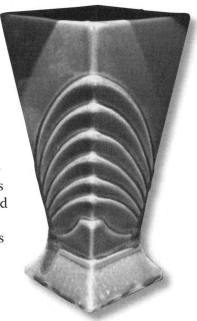

This 1945 Art Deco McCoy vase is an example of the spread of such designs from architecture to furnishings.

Art Deco and Moderne style buildings first began appearing in urban areas of the United States. Skyscrapers of glass and stone with steel frames began to radically alter and dominate the major U.S. cityscapes. Architect Pietro Belluschi designed the 12-story Equitable Savings and Loan Building in Portland, Oregon. Other well-known examples from the time include New York City's iconic Chrysler Building, the Empire State Building, and Rockefeller Center. In 1930 automobile manufacturer Walter Chrysler commissioned the Chrysler Building, one of the last skyscrapers constructed in the Art Deco style, in a race against the then Bank of Manhattan to be the tallest building in the world. It featured car ornament-shaped gargoyles and a spire shaped like an automobile radiator grille. The spire, which raised the building's final height to 1,045 feet, was constructed in secret to ensure victory. The architectural firm of Shreve, Lamb, and Harmon created the Empire State Building one year later, in 1931. It features Art Deco style and its 102 floors rose 1,252 feet above the city streets, surpassing the Chrysler Building. Raymond Hood designed the series of buildings and sunken plaza with iconic ice rink known collectively as Rockefeller Center with the assistance of a number of other designers and firms. The modern buildings were constructed between 1932 and 1940 and have remained midtown landmarks ever since.

DOMESTIC HOMES AND HOUSEHOLD FURNISHINGS

Like commercial architecture of the 1930s and 1940s, domestic homes and their furnishings showcased new materials and technologies. Noted architects like Ludwig Mies van der Rohe and Frank Lloyd Wright brought the modern aesthetic to domestic dwellings. Van der Rohe's famous Farnsworth

Mies van der Rohe conceived of the steel and glass Farnsworth House in 1946, and felt it could be a prototype for all glass buildings.

House, also called the Glass House, constructed in 1951, near Plano, Illinois, featured steel and glass design with transparent glass walls that emphasized its relation to nature. The Farnsworth House remains one of most famous examples of modern domestic architecture.

Frank Lloyd Wright practiced organic architecture, which united form and function as well as integrated a building with its time period and location. His houses were constructed of simple materials and were characterized by long, low planes, horizontal emphasis, and interior design featuring overlapping rooms and shared spaces. Some of his most well-known designs and sites include his homes Taliesin and Taliesin West, Falling Water, the Prairie house, and the Usonian house. Wright would influence many young architects over his lengthy career through lectures and books, as well as through his Wright studios and apprentice program known as the Taliesin Fellowship.

The economic devastation of the Great Depression and Dust Bowl forced many Americans out of their homes and off of their farms. People roamed the country looking for work, living in hastily erected shantytowns on the outskirts of many cities. These so-called Hoovervilles consisted of tents and rough shelters constructed from packing crates, cardboard boxes, and sheets of scrap metal. Lack of housing continued into the World War II era, but for different reasons. When the United States entered World War II, military

The Legacy of Charles and Ray Eames

Charles Ormond Eames, Jr. (1907–78) and his second wife Ray (Kaiser) Eames (1912–88) are among America's most well-known and influential architects and furniture designers. Charles Eames was interested in engineering, drawing, and architecture and was greatly inspired by the renowned Finnish architect Eliel Saarinen. Eliel's son Eero would later become Eames's partner and friend. Eames studied architecture at Washington University in St. Louis, Missouri, on scholarship, but the faculty soon dismissed him, claiming that his ideas were too modern. Ray Kaiser was an artist, designer, architect, and filmmaker who had met Charles Eames while both were studying at the influential Cranbrook Academy of Art in Bloomfield Hills, Michigan. Charles and Ray Eames married and moved to Los Angeles in the early 1940s. Later that decade, *Arts & Architecture* magazine sponsored a case study program in which the Eames participated. They built a manually constructed cliff house (Case Study House #8) along the Pacific Coast to serve as their private residence. The Eames House, made of prefabricated steel parts and finished in only days, is considered a modern architectural landmark.

During World War II they worked with the federal government and top private businesses to develop molded plywood products for use by the U.S. military. These experiments and the technology developed during wartime would later carry over into their highly successful and innovative furniture business. The Eames's office, located in Venice, California, remained in operation from 1943 until Ray's death in 1988. The Eames worked with renowned furniture companies such as Herman Miller, Inc. to create functional, comfortable furniture that could be mass produced at affordable prices.

In 1940 Charles Eames, in partnership with the Saarinens, won first place for a chair entered into an organic design competition held at the Museum of Modern Art in New York. This design became the basis for their first chair, introduced in 1946. Their seating relied on shaped surfaces and flexible materials, rather than cushioned upholstery to provide comfortable support. Materials used included molded plywood, fiberglass-reinforced plastic, wire mesh, and cast aluminum. Among their many designs were tables, storage units, and office furniture. Variations of their designs are still in production, and many original Eames pieces are now collector's items.

This fiberglass and metal "DAR" Eames armchair is based on a 1948 design.

men and their families quickly occupied all available housing near military installations, leading to housing shortages. Thus many families spent the World War II and postwar periods in temporary trailers or Quonset huts. A Quonset hut was an all-purpose prefabricated structure of wood and corrugated metal that was designed to be lightweight and portable. The U.S. military commissioned a number of the structures for a variety of military purposes, with the surplus stock sold to the public after World War II ended in 1945. They were used as temporary housing and as commercial space. Some Quonset huts are still in use today.

The average American family of the 1930s and 1940s lived in a one-level ranch style house, the popularity of which would soar in the coming decades. The older one and a half story Cape Cod style house, a style that dates back to colonial New England, remained popular, as did other Colonial Revival style dwellings. Those with more modern preferences resided in Art Deco or other modern-style houses. Families took great pride in owning neat single-family dwellings with green well-manicured lawns. Suburbs and planned communities began to appear in the postwar period, a trend that would sweep the country in the 1950s. Despite Henry Ford's pioneering mass-production techniques of the 1920s, many Americans still could not afford an automobile, but they were beginning to appear in front of more and more houses.

The interior decor of the typical 1930s and 1940s American home emphasized spaciousness and functionality. Modern and Art Deco styles were as popular for furnishings as for architecture, and began to appear in American homes beginning in the late 1920s. Modern style furniture often featured streamlined designs without unnecessary ornamentation, and bold color choices. The style began among the urban wealthy and slowly diffused throughout the country. Key modern furniture designers of the period included Charles and Ray Eames; Paul Frankl, known for his Skyscraper and Speed furniture influenced by the New York City skyline; Kem (Karl Emmanuel Martin) Weber; Wolfgang Hoffman; Donald Deskey; Gilbert Rohde; Eugene Schoen; Russel Wright; George Sakier; and Wallace Nutting. Companies such as Herman Miller Company, Knoll

This glazed pitcher is from the Fiestaware collection, which was introduced in 1936.

Rural electrification and new appliances changed the lives of farm families in the 1930s and 1940s. This farm woman is cooking on a new electric stove.

Associates, Inc., Barker Brothers, Higgins Manufacturing Company, Meyers Company, Berkey & Gay, Hakelite Manufacturing, S. Karpen & Brothers, Noha Furniture Company, Lloyd Manufacturing Company, and the Howell Company often made furniture to order for their customers. Mass production and standardization became common in furniture production.

Technological innovation affected the material possessions of American families as well. The 1930s were the golden age of radio, and many American living rooms featured a radio in a place of prominence where the family would gather to listen to music, news, or other entertainment. Most homes also had phonographs and records, inexpensive mass-produced paperback books, and increasingly popular board games such as *Monopoly*, introduced by Parker Brothers in 1935. The Radio Corporation of America (RCA) produced the first home television sets in 1939, and the five-inch black-and-white screens began appearing in a limited number of American homes when commercial television became available to the public in 1947.

Some kitchens began to feature innovations such as the refrigerator, aluminum foil, and Tupperware, introduced by Earl Tupper in the mid 1940s. Demand for Tupperware would rise steeply in the coming decades. Products made of Bakelite, the first synthetic plastic, began appearing in everything from jewelry and kitchenware to radios and children's toys. Many Bakelite products are now collector's items.

CLOTHING AND FASHION

The economic devastation of the Great Depression and the enforced shortages and rationing of World War II forced Americans to choose their clothing based on practicality, availability, and simplicity. Thrift was a necessary virtue. Fashion, along with designer labels, became a luxury that most Americans could not afford. Only the wealthiest wore the latest couture fashion from the renowned Paris designers of the time. For most Americans in the 1930s, conservative clothing suitable for work replaced the flapper style and the Jazz Age looks of the roaring 1920s. Everyday apparel emphasized a neat and polished appearance with few decorative embellishments. Clothing with zipper closures became common for the first time, as they were less expensive than other options such as buttons. Women wore simple skirts and blouses or simple print dresses. Women's shoes were comfortable, with lower and broader heels, and dark neutral colors such as black, maroon, and navy were featured. Pastels and brighter colors began appearing in women's shoes by the end of the decade. Small hats and clutch style handbags rounded out a typical outfit. Sandals, sneakers, and beachwear all became more common during this period.

Practicality continued into the design of some evening looks, with women's suits designed to go from daytime to evening with the removal of the jacket. On the other hand, day and eveningwear became truly separate fashion categories with their own styles during the 1930s. Designers used different hemlines to distinguish day and evening skirts and dresses. Daywear reached mid-calf, while eveningwear featured longer looks. The long, flowing evening gowns also featured flashy or more luxurious materials such as metallic lamé. Evening shoes also had more elaborate, glamorous styles and higher heels. Evening looks of the 1930s

A 1940s dress with relatively simple lines typical of the decade.

Clothing as Cultural Statement: The Zoot Suit Riots of 1943

African Americans and Mexican Americans first popularized the Zoot Suit in the 1930s and 1940s. The Zoot Suit was characterized by excessively baggy trousers with a high waist and tight cuffs, and an oversized jacket with wide lapels and padded shoulders. A button-up shirt and short tie were worn under the jacket. A duck tail hairstyle, felt fedora or tando hat with a feather, suspenders, flashy shoes, and a dangling key chain often completed the ensemble.

The Zoot Suit's origins are unclear, as various men have been credited with its development and introduction, including Chicago clothier and trumpet player Harold C. Fox, Memphis tailor Louis Lettes, and Detriot retailer Nathan (Toddy) Elkus. The Zoot Suit was most often associated with the urban jazz culture of the 1930s and 1940s and such jazz musicians as Cab Calloway. Scholars trace the name to the jazz slang term *zoot*, meaning an exaggerated style or performance. The suits were usually reserved for special occasions such as parties, and many wearers saw them as a symbol of their ethnic or racial identity.

When the federal government's War Production Board began restricting the amounts of fabric that could be used in garments, the excessively-sized Zoot Suits clashed with the wartime mentality of conservatism and conservation. Many tailors stopped producing the suits, but continuing demand led to a black market where others still continued their manufacture and sale. Many people viewed the suits' wearers as unpatriotic individuals who were openly flouting the federally-imposed wartime restrictions.

Tensions developed and in early June 1943, those tensions erupted into a series of clashes in Los Angeles, largely between the young white servicemen stationed there and the young Mexican Americans and African Americans wearing the Zoot Suits in the city streets. The riots soon spread to other military towns along the Pacific Coast, as well as the large cities of Detroit, Philadelphia, Pittsburgh, and New York and smaller cities in Texas and Arizona. The riots soon died down, but would leave a lasting impact on the affected areas. Los Angeles County even passed legislation preventing the wearing of Zoot Suits within its borders. The Zoot Suit riots would also help shape the future careers of civil rights activists Cesar Chavez and Malcolm X.

were inspired by the growth of the Hollywood film industry and the popularity of glamorous stars such as Bette Davis and Greta Garbo.

Men's fashion of the 1930s featured traditional three-piece suits with increasingly boxy jackets, vests, and wide-cut pants with high waists. Jackets

Economic conditions in the 1930s and rationing in the early 1940s made Americans frugal and self-reliant. This wife of a serviceman darned worn socks at home in 1943.

were commonly double-breasted, with wide lapels and padded shoulders. A more casual version of the men's suit replaced the vest with either a knitted waistcoat or a sleeveless pullover sweater. Most well-dressed men wore hats, and brogues were the most common male footwear, with loafers beginning to appear with some regularity during this period. A more daring look popular among young African Americans and Mexican-American immigrants was the Zoot Suit, which featured oversized padded jackets and excessively wide trousers with tight cuffs at the bottom. Their popularity became a social statement when World War II began and the federal government placed restrictions on the amounts of fabric allowed in the production of suits, leading to the infamous Zoot Suit Riots of 1943.

Wartime rationing and restrictions ensured that the practicality and conservatism that had been hallmarks of 1930s fashion would continue into the mid-1940s. The wartime economic boom meant that unemployment dropped and more families had money to spend on clothing, but the shift to military production and the federal government's War Production Board restrictions meant that there was less clothing available. Nazi Germany's occupation of Paris, the haute couture fashion capital of the world, temporarily disrupted the Paris fashion shows that had inspired many American fashion designers. Fashion remained a luxury, although now for different reasons. American consumers received ration coupons for a variety of goods, including clothing items. For clothing manufacturers, the federal government placed limits on the amount of fabric, pockets, and buttons to be used in each garment. Many American women began once again sewing their own garments from patterns or remaking older outfits, rather than purchasing new ones.

Fashion of the 1940s was restrained and conservative, with looks designed for comfort and to last multiple seasons. Designers began to produce coordinating separates that would increase the flexibility of a woman's wardrobe. Skirts and jackets became shorter due to restrictions on the amounts of material allowed in individual pieces. Dungarees and trousers became acceptable wear for the many women who joined the workforce during the war. Pin-up girl Rita Hayworth, popular among many American servicemen, popularized the wearing of sweaters. Many American fashion designers emphasized the development of sportswear, and the United States soon became a world leader in that fashion category. Short, sheath-style evening dresses replaced the long, glamorous evening gowns of the 1930s. Manufacturers created shoes designed for walking as a way to save gasoline, another rationed product. The restrictions on the use of leather and other fabrics led to the use of alternatives such as reptile skin. Platform shoes and wedges were popular choices. The shortage of nylon stockings made ankle socks and bare legs a common look. Many women instead sought to create the illusion of stockings by drawing a straight line along the back of the leg with black eyeliner to mimic the seams common on the stockings of the day. During World War II, it was quite common to see military personnel in their service uniforms, even when off duty or at social functions such as parties and dances.

When World War II ended, femininity and glamour quickly began to reappear. After the hardships of the Great Depression and World War II, many American women looked forward to the return of fashion and softer, more feminine clothing. They had more time and money to devote to their appearance in the postwar period. Wearing two separate undergarments, a bra and girdle, became common, with the bras often featuring wire lining. The end of wartime restrictions meant the return

Nylons like these with seams were in high demand during the war when silk and nylon were needed for parachutes.

Christian Dior and the New Look

Many fashion historians credit French haute couture fashion designer Christian Dior with the reintroduction of Paris as the fashion capital of the world in the post-World War II period. Dior's first designer collection, called his Corolle line, swept the fashion world in 1947. The fashion press of the day dubbed the glamorous, ultra-feminine style the New Look. It was considered a symbol of the postwar youth culture. Unlike the conservative, sleek wartime look, the New Look featured numerous yards of opulent fabrics such as satins, wools, and taffetas with decorative embellishments and embroidery. Initially critics complained that the new style was wasteful excess in times when shortages and rationing still existed in many places. Feminists claimed that its use of corsets and crinolines returned women back to the days when they were merely decorative objects whose burdensome garments restricted their every movement.

Dior's New Look consisted of long, full, bell-shaped skirts with drawn-in waists, topped by a fitted jacket with an emphasized bust and rounded shoulders. Most women wore the jacket without a blouse, instead wearing just an undergarment, or gathering a satin scarf or dickey at the neck. The evening New Look substituted the jacket with a strapless boned top. High heels, cosmetics, and softly curled hair worn high in the front and long in the back completed the classic New Look. This romantic style would remain a dominant force in women's fashion for almost a decade, and Dior continued to rise in the world of haute couture afterward, becoming one of the most well-known and respected fashion designers in the world.

of nylon stockings, fuller, longer skirts, puffy-sleeved blouses with Peter Pan or pointed collars, and decorative additions such as peplums, ruffles, bows, and lace. Leather was once again available for shoe production and leather platform shoes and matching purses studded with nail heads became a postwar fashion trend. New synthetic fabrics like rayon began to appear alongside cotton and silk garments. The liberation of Paris meant the return of that city's designers to the top of the haute couture world. French designer Christian Dior's first collection, debuted in the mid-1940s, would quickly revolutionize the postwar fashion world.

CONCLUSION

Experimentation with the new materials and technologies of the 1930s and 1940s provided Americans with glimpses into the imagined future, and would continue to influence American material culture for decades to come. World

War II had fueled military technology that found civilian uses in the postwar period, while bringing the country out of the Great Depression. Innovative products, such as the RCA television set that made its debut at the New York World's Fair in 1939, would become commonplace in the next few decades. The first computers, weighing many tons, would be replaced with smaller models accessible to American consumers in the not too distant future. A new consumer revolution was just around the corner.

MARCELLA TREVINO

Further Readings

Brouws, Jeffrey T. *Readymades: American Roadside Artifacts*. San Francisco: Chronicle Books, 2003.

Byrde, Penelope. *A Visual History of Costume: The Twentieth Century*. New York: Drama Book Publishers, 1987.

Dubrow, Eileen. *Styles of American Furniture, 1860–1960*. Atglen, PA: Schiffer Publications, 2007.

Emmanuel, Muriel. *Contemporary Architects*. New York: St. Martin's Press, 1980.

Farrell-Beck, Jane and Jean Parsons. *Twentieth Century Dress in the United States*. New York: Fairchild, 2007.

Gould, Richard A. and Michael B. Schiffer. *Modern Material Culture: The Archaeology of Us*. New York: Academic Press, 1981.

Hall, Lee. *Common Threads: A Parade of American Clothing*. Boston, MA: Little, Brown, 1992.

Hunt, Marsha. *The Way We Wore: Styles of the 1930s and '40s and Our World Since Then*. Fallbrook, CA: Fallbrook Publishers, 1993.

Kuchler, Susanne and Daniel Miller. *Clothing as Material Culture*. New York: Berg Publishers, 2005.

LeBlanc, Sydney. *Twentieth Century American Architecture: 200 Key Buildings*. New York: Whitney Library of Design, 1993.

Leone, Mark P. and Neil Asher Silberman. *Invisible America: Unearthing Our Hidden History*. New York: H. Holt, 1995.

Martin, Richard and Harold Koda. *Jocks and Nerds: Men's Style in the Twentieth Century*. New York: Rizzoli, 1989.

Mayo, Edith. *American Material Culture: The Shape of Things Around Us*. Bowling Green, OH: Bowling Green State University Press, 1984.

Schlereth, Thomas J. *Cultural History and Material Culture: Everyday Life, Landscapes, Museums*. Charlottesville, VA: University Press of Virginia, 1992.

Susman, Warren I. *Culture as History: The Transformation of American Society in the Twentieth Century*. New York: Pantheon Books, 1984.

Welters, Linda and Patricia A. Cunningham, eds. *Twentieth Century American Fashion*. New York: Berg Publishers, 2005.

Wilcox, R. Turner. *Five Centuries of American Costume*. Mineola, NY: Dover, 2004.

Chapter 4

Social Attitudes

*"We must learn to spell the word RESPECT. We must respect
the rights and properties of our fellow man."*
—Jesse Owens

THE AMERICANS WHO reached adulthood in the 1930s were the first generation born into an America that was more urban than rural. Those who reached adulthood in the 1940s were the first to be born into a truly modern America, one where nationwide culture and media had outgrown—if not yet displaced—their regional versions, and where the United States was a major and prosperous player on the international stage. Compared to their parents, both generations had remarkably different conceptions of their country and their national identity.

In this period and the decades leading up to it, the United States was busy absorbing the massive waves of immigrants who had arrived in the heretofore primarily Anglo, Irish, French, and German melting pot; adjusting to its newly strengthened role on the international stage; incorporating the Great Migration of blacks to the Midwest and North; and growing into the new social climate created by the Progressive Era's reform movements and the Third Great Awakening's extraordinary amount of religious innovation. In the 1920s, the influx of immigration and the rise of Catholicism and Judaism inspired the formation of a new Ku Klux Klan. The victory in World War I and recovery from earlier economic troubles led to the prosperity of the Roaring Twenties for urban Americans. Reactionary movements against those Progressive social and religious reforms also picked up speed, as Conservative and Orthodox

47

Women's Roles in World War II

Mrs. Virginia Young (right), a Pearl Harbor widow, went to work as a supervisor of women workers at the Naval Air Base in Corpus Christi, Texas, in 1942.

With American males at the front, women were actively recruited during World War II. Rosie the Riveter became the symbol of the modern American woman. Rosie posters were displayed throughout the United States, proclaiming "We can do it!" Jan Angell, who was employed by Seattle's Boeing Aircraft Plant, states that in the beginning she "was trying to learn to become a riveter when no one seemed to know [how]." Hazel Owensby Harper, who worked on the atomic bomb in Oak Ridge, Tennessee, remembers the tight security at the plant: "We were only allowed into our specific work area, [and] guards were everywhere." Dorothy Lewis reminisces that young girls worked 10 hours a day, five days a week, for 50 cents an hour. Kate Grant Moore was extremely proud of her work at the Richmond Shipyards in California, where "one time we built a Liberty Ship, start to finish, in an astounding four and one-half days."

Labor leader Elizabeth Gurley Flynn told American women in 1942 that women's work included "industry, civilian defense, politics, [and] the labor unions" and assured women that they had a role to play as "trained auxiliaries to the armed forces." Women of all races and classes heeded the call to duty. African-American women established the Negro Women in National Defense organization. Other women enlisted in military auxiliaries by the score. Elizabeth R. Pollock was one of the first women to train for the Army Auxiliary. During a four-week training course in the summer of 1942, Pollock ruminated in a letter to her mother on the reasons women enlisted: "With some, it was because they were separated from their husbands, with others because they had gotten in a rut in their jobs." Others, she noted, were recruited. In the military, women served as accountants, bakers, bookkeepers, chauffeurs, clerks, cooks, librarians, photographers, telephone operators, waitresses, and X-ray technicians. Women also served on the front lines as airplane pilots, Red Cross workers, nurses, war correspondents, and even spies. Some 200 military nurses died while serving their country.

Judaism formed in response to Reform Judaism. The advent of Christian fundamentalism and its appeal to conservative Americans led to the Scopes Monkey Trial. Finally, a desire for normalcy and respectability propelled the presidencies of Coolidge and Hoover.

That was the climate of the United States when the Great Depression hit in 1929, precipitated by the Black Tuesday stock market crash, worsened by the income inequality 1920s prosperity had created, and compounded by the inherent unsustainability of the credit-driven boom. Combined with the drought of the early 1930s that turned the American prairies into the Dust Bowl, the effect on American farmers and those who depended on them was especially devastating, forcing millions of Americans to leave their homes—not only searching for work

By the time the war ended in 1945, 45.7 percent of all working women were married—a change in expectations this government poster encouraged.

in other parts of the country, but fleeing the dust storms that raged for as long as six years in some places, leading to darkened skies, dust pneumonia, and air so dirty that as far away as New England, the snow fell red.

Democrats and liberals, continuing the Progressive thread from earlier decades, considered big business at fault for much of the Depression, and Franklin Roosevelt's 1932 election was achieved on a wave of this sentiment. The "new deal for the American people" Roosevelt promised dominated the rest of the decade. It reflected American attitudes during and after the Depression: the emphasis was on the government's responsibility to help the needy, especially by providing work opportunities and completely reforming the agricultural sector in order to enable farmers to prosper and support their families in the modern age. Business and banking interests were limited in order to prevent them from prospering too greatly at the expense of others.

THE HAYS CODE AND "SIN CITY"

While many of the New Deal reforms survive, other reforms of the day have fallen away and may seem odd now—as Prohibition undoubtedly does. It was repealed in 1933, in no small part in response to the Depression, as well as to the obvious mounting power of organized crime, which profited from the boozy black market. But there were moral reforms as well. Best known of those is the Hays Code, formally known as the Motion Picture Production Code of 1930, perhaps the first major instance of institutionalized censorship in the United States. There had always been local and state laws regarding appropriate material, and obscenity laws both in the books and inherited from the body of common law—but obscenity laws are purposefully vague, allowing the standards of the day to be enforced. In a departure from this, the Hays Code was specific.

The Supreme Court had ruled in 1915 that movies were not covered by the free speech provision of the First Amendment, a ruling that should seem shocking now (as it should have then). Throughout the 1920s, the drug-related deaths of several actors, the revelation of director William Taylor's bisexuality (brought to light after his unsolved murder), and the manslaughter trial of Fatty Arbuckle all led to Hollywood's Sin City reputation. The Motion Pictures Producers and Distributors Association, precursor to today's Motion Picture Association of America (MPAA, the body responsible for movie ratings), took on conservative Midwestern lawyer William Hays

Movie billboards in Atlanta, Georgia, in 1936 in a photograph by Walker Evans. The Hays Code meant movies could be refused approval simply because of their advertising campaigns.

Charles Lindbergh and Isolationism

After the 1932 kidnapping and murder of his son, Charles A. Lindbergh and his wife, Anne Morrow, left the United States for Europe to escape the publicity surrounding their family. While in Europe Lindbergh toured Germany and in 1938 accepted a decoration from the German government. Upon his return to the United States in 1940 Lindbergh began to make speeches in support of isolationism and eventually became a spokesman for the America First Committee and its opposition of the war. Excerpted below is the speech Lindbergh made in New York on April 23, 1941.

I know I will be severely criticized by the interventionists in America when I say we should not enter a war unless we have a reasonable chance of winning. That, they will claim, is far too materialistic a viewpoint. They will advance again the same arguments that were used to persuade France to declare war against Germany in 1939. But I do not believe that our American ideals and our way of life will gain through an unsuccessful war. And I know that the United States is not prepared to wage war in Europe successfully at this time. We are no better prepared today than France was when the interventionists in Europe persuaded her to attack the Siegfried Line. . .

I do not blame England for this hope, or for asking for our assistance. But we now know that she declared war under circumstances which led to the defeat of every nation that sided with her, from Poland to Greece. We know that in the desperation of war England promised to all those nations armed assistance that she could not send. We know that she misinformed them, as she has misinformed us, concerning her state of preparation, her military strength, and the progress of the war.

In time of war, truth is always replaced by propaganda. I do not believe we should be too quick to criticize the actions of a belligerent nation. There is always the question whether we, ourselves, would do better under similar circumstances. . .

It is not only our right but it is our obligation as American citizens to look at this war objectively and to weigh our chances for success if we should enter it. I have attempted to do this, especially from the standpoint of aviation; and I have been forced to the conclusion that we cannot win this war for England, regardless of how much assistance we extend.

as its head. Hays was responsible for the first morality clauses enacted by studios—giving them the right to fire a star or director for immoral off-set behavior, a clause still often included in modern contracts—and assembled a proposed list of standards he felt the movies should abide by in their subject matter, in order to clean up the industry's image.

CENSORSHIP THEN AND NOW

The advent of talkies increased the potential for "inappropriate material" to show up in movies, and just as Prohibition was repealed in response to the Depression, so too did the movies become a little racier. Movies and radio were the main forms of distributed entertainment in the country, and the radio was federally regulated, with the risk of a license being taken away—but then, as now, the movies enjoyed greater leeway than broadcast media. The Barbara Stanwyck movie *Baby Face* was a little more suggestive than previous American movies had been (though tame even by the standards of family sitcoms today). Several foreign films were denied distribution in the United States for reason of content—most famously, the Hedy Lamarr movie *Ecstasy*, which became somewhat of an underground sensation through private screenings. Studios began to worry—with good reason—that if they did not police themselves, the federal government would begin doing so. Local censorship boards already had considerable clout. If a movie could not play in New York, it was considered financially doomed. Yet under the Roosevelt administration and after the Progressive reforms of the previous few decades, the mode of the day was to shift things from the local to fed-

The Legion of Decency

The National Legion of Decency—originally called the Catholic Legion of Decency and often still referred to that way—was founded in 1933, during the period when the Hays Code had been formulated but not yet enforced by the studios. A church-based response to the growing concerns over the morality of the movies, the Legion was founded by John McNicholas, Archbishop of Cincinnati, after a prolonged discussion about the effect of the cinema on the nation's youth. The still-growing motion picture industry was absorbing much of the old vaudeville and burlesque scene, and sly, raunchy actress Mae West was a frequent object of contempt among Catholic authorities. Her movies were among those that were the final straws on the Hays camel's back.

The early Legion was actually multi-denominational, despite the name. It issued ratings for movies, before the MPAA adopted their official rating system, dividing movies into A (morally unobjectionable), B (morally objectionable in part), and C (condemned by the Legion). A-rated movies were further rated according to whether they were suitable for general audiences or adults only. Among the movies condemned by the Legion were *Forever Amber* (a historical romance with many steamy scenes and references to abortion); *Black Narcissus*, for its portrayal of nuns; *Design for Living*, which includes a divorce; and *The Scarlet Empress*, which starred Marlene Dietrich as Catherine the Great.

eral level. One thing Hollywood could not afford was to cede control of its content to a national government.

So the Hays Code was strengthened in 1934. There had been no way to enforce it before; it was little more than a list of suggestions. Yet now every Hollywood picture would need to be approved by the Production Code Administration and given a certificate of approval. The Hays Code persisted for 30 years in various forms, with few movies distributed in the United States without that approval. The days of independent film were far off, and even today the MPAA operates in much the same way, enforcing different standards. Then, as now, when a movie did not meet the required standards, suggestions might be made for its alteration.

Obscenity was the Hays Code's biggest concern. Partial nudity was edited out of several movies, while others were refused approval simply because of their advertising campaigns. Because there were no movie ratings, and because of the usual structure of exhibition (a feature-length movie would be shown after a number of short cartoons, featurettes, news reels, and other short subjects, which encouraged mixed audiences) all movies were treated the same, without consideration for their prospective audience. The phrasing of the Hays Code's provisions highlights the fact that the concern was principally moral. One can imagine how differently things would be phrased today. For instance, these are the three General Principles of the Hays Code, quoted here in their entirety:

1. No picture shall be produced that will lower the moral standards of those who see it. Hence the sympathy of the audience should never be thrown to the side of crime, wrongdoing, evil or sin.

2. Correct standards of life, subject only to the requirements of drama and entertainment, shall be presented.

3. Law, natural or human, shall not be ridiculed, nor shall sympathy be created for its violation.

From there, the Code becomes more specific: Crimes must not be portrayed in a way that will encourage or instruct the audience to commit them (this is still a concern today, with various details in *Fight Club* changed in order to prevent audiences from making explosives at home); violence cannot be portrayed too graphically; illegal drugs cannot be portrayed at all; rape (which the Code groups in with "seduction") must not be explicitly referred to, only suggested; adultery can be presented only in a negative light; "sex perversion" (which would include homosexuality) can never be mentioned; sexual or romantic relationships between blacks and whites are not allowed; and both obscenity ("the F-word" and its cousins) and profanity (taking God's name in vain, but also the use of words like *Hell, damn,* and *S.O.B.*) are forbidden. While some of that may sound typical of the standards of evening television today, in practice much of it was far stricter. For instance, an actor could not say the word *pregnant* in a movie. Priests and other religious figures could not be used as villains or made objects of ridicule. Filmmakers were discouraged from showing bedrooms, mentioning prostitution ("the sale of a woman's virtue"), or portraying surgery in their films.

Much of this led to the "exploitation" film genre, in which salacious material like sex, drugs, and violence are presented in a story claiming to be a cautionary tale about the consequences of immoral behavior. The *ABC After-school Special* of the 1970s and 1980s and the slasher film genre both descend from exploitation films (there is a reason the survivor of a slasher movie was always a virgin).

The Hays Code is one reason why the film industry continues to have the reputation of being a "lesser medium" compared to novels and plays, despite the fact that the medium has no limitations not also shared by the theater. For 30 years, just as talkies arrived and should have enabled movies to offer a fuller portrayal of human life than they had in the previous decades, American movies (and foreign movies seeking wide distribution in the United States) were limited not only in what they could show and what words they could use, limitations that most art can live with, but also in what content they could treat, which for narrative art is as constricting as a straitjacket. The novels of the day, even the lesser ones we have forgotten about now, vastly outpaced the cinema in the sophistication of their material, while the country's most popular writers—with a readership as large as the movie audiences—regularly published stories that would have been forbidden had they been screenplays.

From a historical perspective, the interesting thing about censorship is not just when, where, and why it is enforced. It is the change in what is acceptable. So, keeping in mind everything the Hays Code was keeping out of the public eye during this era and well into the 1960s, we now note that during this same period, the famous "Censored Eleven" cartoons were produced.

THE CENSORED ELEVEN

The talkies had led to the Golden Age of Animation, with Warner Brothers (producers of *Merrie Melodies* and *Looney Tunes*, and hence Bugs Bunny, Daffy Duck, Porky Pig, and so on) more or less neck and neck with the Disney studio when it came to cartoon shorts. Disney dominated early on in animated features, and would cede little ground on that front until the 21st century. The Censored Eleven are 11 Warner Brothers cartoons that, beginning in the late 1960s, were removed from circulation—essentially a voluntary ban. They continue to remain "in the vault," with no legal release in any country. In that 30-year period—less than that, in some cases—standards had changed, and Warner Brothers no longer found these cartoons appropriate, largely because of their portrayal of blacks.

Marian Anderson

African-American opera singer Marian Anderson was considered one of the greatest contraltos in the world when she agreed to perform at Constitution Hall in April 1939. Noted Italian musician Arturo Toscanini contended that "a voice like [Anderson's] occurs once in a hundred years." In February the Daughters of the American Revolution (DAR), who owned Constitution Hall, refused permission for Anderson's performance. First Lady Eleanor Roosevelt responded by resigning from the DAR. In her resignation letter dated February 26, Roosevelt decried the DAR's actions, chiding them for passing up "an opportunity to lead in an enlightened way" and declaring that "it seems to me . . . your organization has failed." The following day the First Lady used her *My Day* column to call public attention to the matter.

Marian Anderson singing for the crowd of 75,000 gathered at the Lincoln Memorial in April 1939.

Anderson's manager Sol Hurok ripped into the DAR, proclaiming that they "have not yet begun to understand the true meaning of American democracy." Hurok applauded the First Lady, calling her a "woman of courage and excellent taste" who had provided African Americans with "one of the most hopeful signs in these troublesome times for democracy." On March 19, the American Institute of Public Opinion announced that 67 percent of the public approved the First Lady's actions.

With Eleanor Roosevelt's support, a new venue was arranged, and Marian Anderson's concert took place on Easter Sunday, April 9, 1939, on the steps of the Lincoln Memorial in Washington, D.C. The audience of 75,000 included Supreme Court Justices, members of Congress, and the Roosevelt Cabinet. Anderson opened the half-hour open air concert with "My Country 'Tis of Thee." Other numbers included Schubert's "Ave Maria" and Donizetti's "O Mio Fernando." Because Anderson considered her voice a gift from God, she included three gospels in her program: "The Gospel Train," "Trampin'," and "My Soul Is Anchored in the Lord."

Americans throughout the country heard the concert on national radio. Marian Anderson later stated, "I forgave the DAR many years ago. You lose a lot of time hating people." She believed that music transcended race, declaring that "When I sing, I don't want them to see that my face is black. I don't want them to see that my face is white. I want them to see my soul. And that is colorless."

A segregated United Service Organizations (USO) dance for African Americans, who took on important roles in the war despite ongoing discrimination.

The Censored Eleven include some of the most popular cartoons of their day, most notably Bob Clampett's "Coal Black and De Sebben Dwarfs." Released in 1943, six years after Disney's *Snow White* feature, "Coal Black" is a retelling of the fairy tale with an all-black cast and a jazz soundtrack. The characters are drawn as "darky" caricatures, as was common in cartooning in this period, with exaggerated features—thick lips, overly dark complexions like that of burnt-cork blackface, often (though not in the case of "Coal Black") wild hair and bestial, animalistic features to suggest that the black character is "less evolved" than whites. Nevertheless "Coal Black" is considered a technically and artistically excellent cartoon, often included by animation historians in their lists of the greatest of the Golden Age. It is unfortunate that it suffered from the ills of the day, and the insensitivity toward race concerns that so marked the era. Clampett's intent certainly was not racist, and by all accounts the cartoon was first inspired by a conversation with jazz musician Duke Ellington, and black actress Dorothy Dandridge's sister Vivian voiced the main character.

Other cartoons have simply been edited in their release. In addition to racist imagery being removed, many cartoons have been edited for television to reflect the fact that the primary demographic of cartoons is now children, whereas the original *Looney Tunes* were widely enjoyed by adult audiences. As a result, repeatable behavior like the accidental ingestion of poisons is often removed—and many of these early cartoons have been criticized for their violence, something we can surmise the Hays Commission had little objection to because of the lack of realism in its presentation.

RACE RELATIONS AND JAPANESE INTERNMENT

Little of the New Deal reforms dealt with racism at all. Anxious to keep the support of the Dixiecrats, Roosevelt refused to sign anti-lynching legislation or ban the poll tax, though he decried both in speeches. The period saw some growing clout by black leadership. The National Association for the Advancement of Colored People (NAACP) successfully mounted a campaign to stop the appointment by Herbert Hoover of Judge John J. Parker, a member of the KKK, to the Supreme Court. The Roosevelt administration did appoint several black administrators to federal positions, such as Mary McLeod Bethune, as Director of Negro Affairs in the National Youth Administration. Black leaders, such as NAACP attorney Thurgood Marshall, fought against segregation in higher education through the courts. Others, including labor leader A. Phillip Randolph, pressured the administration to insist on employment quotas for blacks on government defense contracts. Such advances toward racial justice, however, were minor compared to later achievements in the administrations of Harry Truman and Lyndon Johnson. At the policy level, racism was simply not a concern of the Roosevelt administration—nor, we can assume, many of its white constituents.

When World War II broke out, that indifference to race concerns and old nativist paranoias combined, and the internment camps resulted, one of the darker episodes in recent American history. In addition to the German and Italian resident aliens who were forcibly interned, 100,000 Japanese citizens and their children were sent into camps by the U.S. government—and it is no coincidence that of those nations with which the United States was at war, the worst treatment was reserved for those who were most racially different from the typical American.

After the Japanese attack on Pearl Harbor, some Americans

The sign on this boarding house was one of many such warnings prevalent in the atmosphere of fear and paranoia brought on by the war.

expressed concern that the Japanese and Japanese Americans living in the United States represented a threat—that they might feel a greater loyalty to the country of their birth (or their parents' or grandparents' birth) than their country of residence. The State Department prepared a secret report on the matter, and found that Japanese-American communities posed no threat. More than half of the ethnically Japanese individuals living in the United States had been born there and were full citizens. Though they might enjoy cultural ties to Japan, it was ludicrous to assume that a significant number of them would feel loyalty to a government with which they had had no contact.

At first, the Japanese were treated no differently. Like all foreigners, resident Japanese aliens were required to submit to fingerprinting after the 1940 Alien Registration Act, during a time when the United States was neutral in the war but feared aggressive actions by the Axis powers. Perhaps reasonably, a widescale attack was expected after the surprise of Pearl Harbor—and that reasonable expectation led to the unreasonably paranoid assumption by many Americans that some, even many, Japanese Americans might be involved in such an attack. "A Jap's a Jap," Lieutenant-General John DeWitt told newspapers; he was in charge of the Western Defense Command, and oversaw the internment. Presidential proclamations were immediately issued to round up

Japanese Americans carrying their possessions as they transfer from a train to a bus at Lone Pine, California, on their way to the Manzanar internment camp in April 1942.

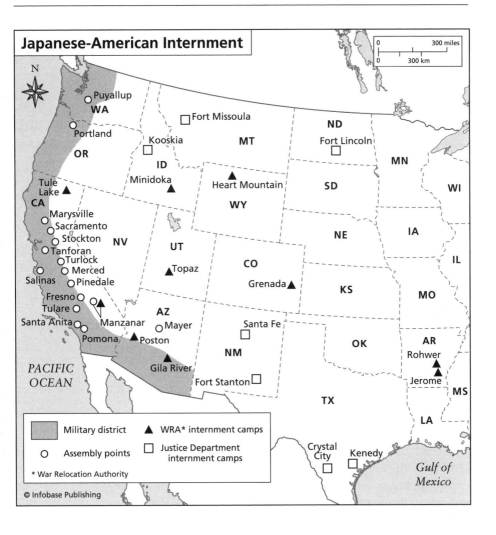

German, Italian, and Japanese aliens in order to remove them from strategic areas; most of them returned to their homes before long.

Executive Order 9066, signed by President Roosevelt on February 19, 1942, some two months after Pearl Harbor, allowed military commanders to designate "exclusion zones" from which anyone of the commander's choice could be excluded, according to whatever criteria they specified. Order 9066 was used primarily to exclude German Americans and Italian Americans—not just resident aliens—from about one third of the country.

Subsequent proclamations and orders allowed the government to seize property and freeze assets belonging to resident aliens, established a mandatory curfew for all ethnic Japanese, and eventually—in March and May 1942—confined all individuals of Japanese ancestry on the West coast (including orphans and adopted children with partial Japanese ancestry) to a

Ansel Adams took this photo of a street inside the Manzanar internment camp in California in 1943. Adams was not allowed to photograph the guard towers manned by military police with submachine guns.

particular area, from which they were then required to report to assembly centers so they could be moved to Relocation Centers—internment camps.

Internment was justified as a military necessity, but the language of the law and internal documents make it clear that a racial distinction was made between the Japanese and European enemy powers, and that Japanese Americans were seen as inherently untrustworthy in the eyes of those enforcing these policies. The camps were often referred to as concentration camps, until the end of the war, when that term came to be associated with the camps where the Nazis imprisoned Jews. Even among the resident aliens, the majority of these prisoners were permanent American residents who were unable to attain citizenship because of discriminatory laws. These were not visitors who may have been traveling back and forth between the United States and Japan. These were Americans—as American as they were allowed to be.

The camps were built all over the West, illegally occupying Native American reservation lands. Internees typically lived with their families, sleeping on cots in cramped barracks, sharing public toilets, given a daily food ration costing a few coins. Conditions were kinder than in many prisons, and the excess of land meant baseball diamonds could be hastily constructed at some camps for recreation. They had few of their personal belongings with them.

After two and a half years, the Supreme Court ruled that the camps were unconstitutional; the exclusion orders were rescinded weeks later, and internees were given $25 each and train tickets to return home. Few, at this point, argued in favor of the camps, though many insisted that they had been a necessary precaution at their inception. A formal apology was not issued by the U.S. government until 1976.

CONCLUSION

The New Deal inspired changes in American social attitudes during and after the Depression, and meant that the government would now be looked to more for poverty alleviation and support for farmers, and to rein in business and banking activities. World War II brought further change, reducing isolation and exposing many Americans for the first time to foreign cultures, but some areas of American life continued to follow old, destructive patterns. Bias toward nonwhites, epitomized by the internment of Japanese Americans during the war and by the ongoing oppression of African Americans, would mean decades more strife, even for an increasingly prosperous country now weary of conflict.

BILL KTE'PI

Further Readings

American Rosie the Riveter Association, *104 More Rosie the Riveter Stories: Stories of Working Women from World War II as Written by Real-Life Rosies.* Kimberly, AL: American Rosie the Riveter Association, 2005.

"Concert and Opera." *New York Times* (April 9, 1939).

Drinnon, Richard. *Keeper of Concentration Camps: Dillon S. Meyer and American Racism.* Berkeley, CA: University of California Press, 1989.

Flynn, Elizabeth Gurley. *Women in the War.* New York: Workers Library, 1942.

Goldstein, Richard, ed. *Mine Eyes Have Seen: A First Person History of the Events That Shaped America.* New York: Simon and Schuster, 1997.

Grossman, James R. *Land of Hope: Chicago, Black Southerners, and the Great Migration.* Chicago, IL: University of Chicago Press, 1991.

Lasalle, Mick. *Complicated Women.* New York: Thomas Dunne Books/St. Martin's Press, 2000.

Lewis, Jon. *Hollywood V. Hard Core.* New York: New York University, 2000.

Litoff, Judy Barrett and David C. Smith, eds. *American Women in a World at War: Contemporary Accounts from World War II.* Wilmington, DE: Scholarly Resources, 1997.

Mackey, Mik, ed. *Remembering Heart Mountain: Essays on Japanese American Internment in Wyoming*. Powell, WY: Western History Publications, 1998.

"Mrs. Roosevelt Indicates She Has Resigned from D.A.R. over Refusal of Hall to Negro." *New York Times* (February 27, 1939).

Redmond, Juanita. *I Served on Bataan*. Philadelphia, PA: J.B. Lippincott, 1943.

Roberts, Adam. *The History of Science Fiction*. New York: Palgrave Macmillan, 2006.

Robinson, Greg. *By Order of the President: FDR and the Internment of Japanese Americans*. Cambridge, MA: Harvard University Press, 2001.

Roosevelt, Eleanor. "Resignation Letter." Available online: http://www.fdrlibrary.marist.edu/tmirhfee.html. Accessed October 2008.

Wiebe, Robert. *The Search for Order*. New York: Hill and Wang, 1966.

Chapter 5

Cities and Urban Life

"A city is a place where there is no need to wait . . . to taste the food of any country [or] find new voices to listen to and familiar ones to listen to again."
—Margaret Mead

DURING THE 1920s, the United States had become a predominantly urban country for the first time. Entering the 1930s, the American city still featured a downtown central business district at its core, surrounded by nearby manufacturing, working-class neighborhoods, shopping and financial areas, saloons and restaurants, entertainment facilities, and cultural institutions and recreational facilities. Urban planning had become a noted feature of city life in the 1920s as more and more cities and municipal areas began adopting zoning ordinances by the decade's end. The U.S. Department of Commerce published its Standard City Planning Act in 1928, expanding city planning to the regional level. Urban population growth had begun to slow as new immigration laws imposed quotas on the numbers of new arrivals, and the mass production of automobiles fueled urban flight and decentralization. The economic distress of the Great Depression and the explosive growth of the suburbs in the post–World War II period would further slow urban population growth in the coming decades.

THE URBAN IMPACT OF THE DEPRESSION AND NEW DEAL
The Great Depression accelerated the decline of the golden age of the inner city. The economic devastation stopped the growth of many downtown businesses, especially in the older, industrial cities of the northeast and Midwest.

Urban businesses faced lessening consumer demand and cuts in production, often in a cyclical pattern as production cuts led to layoffs, which resulted in further decreased consumer demand, and so on. Despite their difficulties, businesses sought to keep people in the cities by providing aid through organizations such as the National Association of Community Chests and Councils. Urban governments faced declining property tax revenues, and increasing demands for social services. Cities offered individual assistance to the homeless and the unemployed, but limited funds meant that it often was not nearly enough for families to survive. The Great Depression magnified the problem of urban homelessness because of the stock market crash, high unemployment rates, and the migration of rural Americans seeking jobs or refuge from the Dust Bowl.

Urban residents faced widespread underemployment and unemployment, lowered wages, and foreclosures and evictions. Soup kitchens and bread lines swelled, and desperate peddlers selling apples or pencils on street corners became familiar sights. Observers noted people fighting for garbage scraps behind restaurants. People slept on street corners, in parks, beneath bridges, or in the shantytowns commonly referred to as Hoovervilles that sprang up on the outskirts of many cities. Public and private charities were quickly overwhelmed, and many people began to view the homeless as victims of economic circumstances, rather than of moral or character defects such as laziness or drunkenness.

These squatters' shacks in the Hooverville that sprang up along the Willamette River near the city of Portland, Oregon, were photographed in July 1936.

Urban reformers such as Chicago's Saul Alinsky sought to improve urban conditions through participatory democracy, grassroots political activism, and community organization. Cities also became the sites of protests as people began demanding that the federal government take a more active role in alleviating the suffering of the Depression's individual victims. The most well-known example was the 1932 Bonus Army of World War I veterans who marched on Washington, D.C., camping near the Capitol Building to demand early payment of a military bonus to be paid by Congress in 1945. Their suppression by U.S. Army troops would further hurt President Herbert Hoover's bid for reelection and boost Democratic candidate Franklin Roosevelt's campaign.

The federal government would become heavily involved in aiding urban recovery from the Great Depression with the 1932 election of Roosevelt and the implementation of his domestic agenda, known as the New Deal. The New Deal would provide programs to aid in urban planning, urban capital improvements and public works projects, low-cost housing and increased availability of home mortgages, and job creation to benefit the individual victims of the Depression that Roosevelt called the "Forgotten Man." The federal government provided loans to city governments for public works projects, such as the building or renovation of post offices, schools, public recreational facilities, roads, and court houses, that both modernized city life and created temporary jobs for the unemployed. One of the most famous public works projects of the New Deal was the construction of San Francisco, California's, famed Golden Gate Bridge. The National Recovery Administration (NRA) sought to aid businesses while various "Alphabet Soup" programs such as the Federal Emergency Relief Act (FERA), Civilian Conservation Corps (CCC), and Works Progress Administration (WPA) sent aid to state and local governments to help individuals or create temporary jobs. The Social Security Act of 1935 provided insurance for the elderly and the unemployed.

The federal government under the New Deal also sought to ease the burden on the housing industry and related businesses, such as construction, real estate, and home finance, while aiding individual Americans who wished to become homeowners. Under the earlier Hoover Administration, the Emergency Relief and Construction Act of 1932 had created the Reconstruction Finance Corporation (RFC) to provide loans to troubled corporations, state and local governments, and private institutions that provided housing for low-income families. The Federal Home Loan Bank Board (FHLBB) chartered federal Savings & Loan institutions that provided residential mortgages. The Home Owners' Loan Corporation (HOLC) followed in 1933, helping many Americans refinance their mortgages. Significant barriers to home ownership remained, however, as most mortgages required large down payments and short payback periods of three to five years, terms that most middle and lower class Americans were unable to meet.

Saul Alinsky and the Community Organization Movement

Saul David Alinsky (1909–72) was born to Russian Jewish immigrant parents in Carmel, California, in 1909 but was raised in a ghetto in Chicago, Illinois. He developed his political philosophy in the old stockyard neighborhoods of Chicago in the 1930s and 1940s. He earned a degree in criminology from the University of Chicago and, in 1938, found work researching gang behavior and the causes of juvenile delinquency at the Institute for Juvenile Research. He conducted his research in the Chicago neighborhood known as Back-of-the-Yards, which bordered the old Union Stockyards made famous in *The Jungle*, Upton Sinclair's 1906 novel exposé of the meat-packing industry.

Alinsky traced criminal behavior to a life of poverty and a feeling of powerlessness over one's circumstances and called for active mass grassroots political action as the cure. He believed that the poor could achieve democracy and social justice through the unification of all sectors of a community, including labor unions, various racial and ethnic groups, and churches. He began putting his beliefs into practice and would become known as the father of the community organization movement.

Alinsky began by organizing the old stockyard neighborhoods into the Back-of-the-Yards Council in 1939. His tactics included the use of pickets, strikes, and boycotts, many of the same tactics used by labor unions. Congress of Industrial Organizations (CIO) President John L. Lewis would come to serve as his mentor. In 1940, Alinsky founded the Industrial Areas Foundation to assist other communities in the founding of their own organizations. In 1959, he co-founded The Woodlawn Organization (TWO) in Chicago's South Side neighborhood to fight for civil rights. In 1969, he established a training institute for would-be community organizers.

Alinsky also published several books on community organization, including 1946's *Reveille for Radicals* and 1971's *Rules for Radicals*. He became a role model for young campus radicals in the 1960s, and for other community and labor organizers, including Ed Chambers, Cesar Chavez, Tom Gaudette, and Fred Ross. Alinsky's ideas were also instrumental in shaping the Community Action Program of the 1960s, part of President Lyndon Johnson's War on Poverty. Saul Alinsky died of a heart attack in 1972 at the age of 63.

The National Housing Act of 1934 created the Federal Housing Administration (FHA) to encourage private lending institutions to provide more widely accessible mortgage loans through government issuance of mortgage insurance to institutions that would issue FHA-approved mortgages to individual home buyers. The government required lending institutions to provide long-term, low-interest rate mortgages with little money required as an

Boys dressed for Easter pose with a car on the South Side of Chicago in April 1941, a few years after Saul Alinsky began his community organization work in the city.

initial down payment. The FHA removed the risk of lending at little cost to the government, as program expenditures were low and the construction and home finance industries rebounded. The federal government next issued the Housing Act of 1937 to benefit those still left out of the housing market by providing affordable public housing through the creation of the U.S. Public Housing Authority. The FHA also chartered the Federal National Mortgage Association, commonly known as Fannie Mae. Various reorganization acts between 1937 and 1949 provided for the creation of the National Housing Agency (NHA) and later the Housing and Home Finance Agency (HHFA).

City governments worked alongside the federal government during the New Deal to aid urban residents and modernize urban life. Urban voters were a central component of New Deal support and also elected a number of mayors supportive of New Deal urban policies, such as Fiorello La Guardia of New York City, Frank Murphy of Detroit, Michael Curley of Boston, and Edward Kelly of Chicago. Numerous mayors banded together to help lobby for direct federal aid to cities, forming the U.S. Conference of Mayors (USCM). The USCM maintained close ties to Roosevelt Administration aides such as Harry Hopkins. The crisis of the Great Depression led to the

Mayor Fiorello La Guardia and the Modernization of New York

Mayor La Guardia addressing a radio audience on March 23, 1940.

Fiorello La Guardia (1882–1947) was born in the borough of Manhattan in New York City to immigrant parents. He was elected a Republican representative from New York's fourteenth congressional district in 1916. After serving in World War I, where he rose to the rank of major, he returned to Congress. His progressive agenda included providing better social services for the poor and unemployed, as well as fighting for legislation against monopolies, inequality in immigration laws, and Prohibition. His work gained favor during the widespread economic devastation of the Great Depression, but as a Republican he lost his office in the Democratic landslide that brought Franklin Roosevelt to office in the 1932 presidential election. Despite his party affiliation, La Guardia supported Roosevelt's New Deal policies and he was elected mayor of New York City in 1933.

Fiorello La Guardia would serve as mayor of New York City for three terms, from 1934 until 1945. Mayor La Guardia's alliance with President Roosevelt helped modernize New York, which became a model city for urban New Deal policies. He inherited control of a city known for its corruption, financial difficulties, and lack of an overall plan for future development. He instituted a series of weekly Sunday radio addresses, similar to Roosevelt's Fireside Chats, to gain support for his vision. He utilized a team of skilled experts to centralize and streamline the city's municipal government. His New Deal ties helped bring in funds for public works, such as the construction of bridges, tunnels, sewer systems, parks, highways, schools, and hospitals. Noted projects completed during his administration include the Triborough Bridge and a Queens airport that would later come to bear his name. He also instituted a sales tax to raise funds, provided public housing, improved mass transit, and took action against gamblers and burlesques. Fiorello La Guardia became known as the father of modern New York City, and his work helped in the development of a national policy for urban development.

modernization and expansion of city governments, as they became involved in providing for their cities' economic development and the social welfare of their constituents.

THE DEVELOPMENT OF MODERN URBAN LIFE

The United States' entry into World War II in 1941 ensured full economic recovery from the Great Depression, as factories switched to the production of war materials, and civilian and military employment opportunities abounded. Cities that had large defense industries or heavy industrial bases that could switch to wartime production experienced population booms, as people migrated there in search of now plentiful jobs and high wages. Older industrial cities such as Detroit became known as Arsenals of Democracy as wartime production surged. Other defense cities were located on the West coast, accelerating a westward trend in urban growth that would continue into the postwar period with the rapid rise of cities such as Los Angeles, San Diego, and Seattle. Recruiters toured southern states with stories of widespread employment, high wages, and comfortable living. The numbers of women working outside the home also increased due to defense industry opportunities. Urban residents also contributed to the war effort through civil defense and Red Cross activities, scrap metal drives, war bond sales, and the planting of "victory gardens."

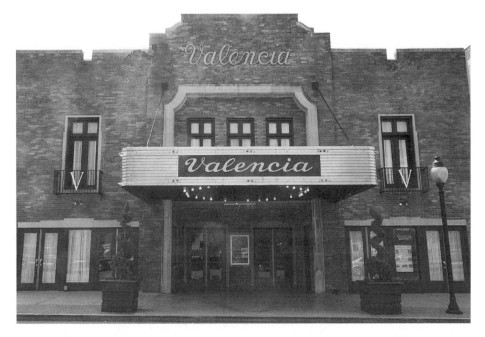

The Valencia ballroom in the small city of York, Pennsylvania, is an example of 1930s Art Deco urban architecture.

The economic boom of World War II brought employment and high wages back to urban dwellers, but also imposed a number of hardships on daily life. Mandatory rationing and the switch from consumer to military production meant that there was little on which to spend newfound money. The influx of defense workers and a temporary federal government moratorium on housing construction except for defense purposes limited housing options, resulting in overcrowding. Municipal services such as public transportation, utilities, education, and recreation struggled to meet with increased demand. The wave of anti-Japanese hysteria that swept the country after Japan's 1941 surprise attack on the U.S. Naval Base at Pearl Harbor, Hawaii, resulted in discrimination against Japanese Americans. A federal executive order forced their evacuation from key defense industry areas, including the West coast, to internment camps for much of the war. Other racial and ethnic tensions were exacerbated by the impact of the sudden population growth and the resultant competition for jobs and housing.

RACE RIOTS

Racism remained a constant presence, and racial tensions were fueled by the difficulty of enforcing desegregation in the workplace, although the country's armed forces remained segregated. In 1941, the Roosevelt Administration created the Fair Employment Practices Committee (FEPC), which prevented discrimination in defense industries. Many white workers resented the fact that they had to work alongside African Americans, particularly if African Americans received promotions. Work stoppages and slowdowns sometimes resulted, and groups such as the Ku Klux Klan made their presence known in many workplaces and communities. African Americans were excluded from many public housing projects. Those dedicated to them often featured houses in poor condition at higher prices than those in white projects. Complaints of police brutality and unfair treatment also remained.

The rapid influx of defense workers, and the resulting social and cultural upheavals in the metropolitan "Arsenals of Democracy" led to a series of race riots in cities across the United States in the summer of 1943, resulting in a number of deaths and arrests and millions of dollars of property damages. A race riot broke out in the Belle Isle park in Detroit on June 20, 1943. An earlier 1942 clash in the Sojourner Truth Project, a housing complex built by the Detroit Housing Commission for African-American defense workers in a predominantly white neighborhood, had already heightened existing racial tensions. After 36 hours of rioting, President Franklin Roosevelt sent federal troops in jeeps and armored cars to ride through the affected area with automatic weapons at the request of Detroit Mayor Edward Jeffries Jr. and Michigan Governor Harry Kelly. The 1943 Detroit Riots left over 30 people dead and close to 700 people injured. Close to 2,000 people were arrested. Riots also occurred in Los Angeles, Mobile, Philadelphia, Indianapolis, Baltimore, St. Louis, Beaumont

Skilled mechanic Zed W. Robinson tightening bolts on a cylinder barrel of a military aircraft engine at the Melrose Park Buick plant in Illinois in July 1942.

in Texas, the Harlem neighborhood of New York City, and Washington, D.C. Racial tensions persisted and the 1943 riots would prove to be forerunners of numerous other riots that would sweep urban areas in the 1960s.

OTHER DEVELOPMENTS

Air pollution had been present since the industrialization of cities, but had largely been considered a nuisance of urban life. A deadly cloud of smog that covered the town of Donora, Pennsylvania, in 1948 (the Donora Tragedy) brought the potential health hazards of pollution to nationwide attention and helped spur the future passage of clean air regulations. Home construction

City Life During the Depression

Between 1929 and 1933, incomes in American cities fell by one third. Born in 1935, Charles H. Trout, author of *Boston, the Great Depression and the New Deal,* grew up in the Depression years. He maintains that cities, which had been enjoying unprecedented prosperity in the 1920s "felt [the depression] first and longest." During the Depression, Boston was largely dependent on the textile and shoe industries to support its manufacturing sector. The unemployment rate was one of the highest in the United States.

Although city leaders repeatedly voted for Roosevelt, they believed the New Deal was tainted with "socialism." According to Trout, "men with self-inflicted wounds staggered into Boston City Hospital to get themselves three meals and a bed," while Boston women "slept at night on hard benches in Boston Common." One unemployed Bostonian wrote to the president, saying that he had not eaten "anything for two days" and was sleeping "on a ten-cent flop where there *is* 500 men," which is "worse than an insane isylam (sic)."

In Memphis, Tennessee, two-thirds of city residents lived in rented homes for which they paid up to $9 each month. Much of the housing was already substandard, and only grew worse. In 1930, industrial traffic along the Mississippi River began to shrink. Unemployment reached 7,000 in November and climbed to 10,000 over the following month. Breadlines formed outside hospital kitchens as residents waited to obtain surplus food. In 1929, the Salvation Army had provided meals to 1,700 people. By March 1931, that number had skyrocketed to 10,250.

So many people were jumping off the Harahan Bridge in Memphis that newspapers began printing contact information for local ministers. Then a minister jumped off the bridge. Even those who managed to hold on to jobs saw their work hours and wages slashed. The Fisher Body Company went under. School teachers were paid in scrip. When the Bonus Army of veterans arrived in Memphis in 1932 en route to their protest in Washington, D.C., it caused a panic in Memphis because there were no resources to feed the influx. The veterans were transported to Nashville by train where they became the responsibility of Nashville city officials. The Great Depression hit the South hard, and conditions generally worsened until mobilization for World War II brought new industrial jobs to urban areas.

would once again soar as postwar families sought the "American Dream" of a single-family house in the suburbs. The G.I. Bill of Rights, the 1944 federal authorization of the Veterans Administration (VA) home loan program, and the continued popularity of FHA-backed mortgages fueled the decentralization of urban areas and the explosive growth of the suburbs on their peripheries.

Municipal governments and downtown businesses began responding to the twin problems of urban flight and suburban sprawl even before the postwar period accelerated their development. Downtown businesses began banding together in associations. The National Association of Real Estate Boards and its affiliate, the Urban Land Institute, began studying the problem in the late 1930s. Recommendations for halting urban decay included improving mass transit, constructing highways linking the inner cities with the rapidly growing suburbs, building more downtown parking garages, and the urban renewal of the decaying inner-city neighborhoods that surrounded many central business districts. In 1949, the federal government would become involved in urban renewal with the passage of the Housing Act of 1949, which authorized the use of federal funds to aid in slum clearance and redevelopment.

During the war, urban residents were urged to grow some of their own food in "victory gardens."

CONCLUSION

The New Deal response to the Great Depression shaped America's urban areas in ways that are still visible today, especially in the vast amount of infrastructure built during those years. By the late 1930s, economic upheaval, increased restrictions on immigration, and the rise of the automobile meant that urban decay and suburban sprawl had already begun, though they were briefly halted by a temporary population boom for wartime production jobs in industrial centers. The postwar period also foreshadowed a number of trends that would impact urban development in the decades to follow, including the growth of suburbia and federal involvement in urban renewal programs.

Other developments during this period, such as worsening race riots and a growing tradition of urban activism, would resonate in the decades that followed. The Bonus Army march to Washington in 1932 set a precedent for similar marches later in the century, most notably the March on Washington in 1963 during the Civil Rights movement.

MARCELLA TREVINO

Further Readings

Bernard, R. *Snowbelt Cities: Metropolitan Politics in the Northeast and Midwest Since World War II*. Bloomington, IN: Indiana University Press, 1990.

Biles, Roger. *Memphis in the Great Depression*. Knoxville, TN: University of Tennessee Press, 1986.

Brandt, Nat. *Harlem at War: The Black Experience in World War II*. New York: Syracuse University Press, 1996.

Brodsky, A. *The Great Mayor: Fiorello LaGuardia and the Making of the City of New York*. New York: Truman Talley Books, 2003.

Findlay, John M. *Magic Lands: Western Cityscapes and American Culture After 1940*. Berkeley, CA: University of California Press, 1992.

Fogelson, R.M. *Downtown: Its Rise and Fall, 1880–1950*. New Haven, CT: Yale University Press, 2001.

Ford, L.R. *Cities and Buildings: Skyscrapers, Skid Rows, and Suburbs*. Baltimore, MD: Johns Hopkins University Press, 1994.

Foster, Mark S. *From Streetcar to Superhighway: American City Planners and Urban Transportation, 1900–1940*. Philadelphia, PA: Temple University Press, 1981.

Fox, Kenneth. *Metropolitan America: Urban Life and Urban Policy in the United States, 1940–1980*. New Brunswick, NJ: Rutgers University Press, 1990.

Goings, K.W. and R.A. Mohl, eds. *The New African-American Urban History*. Thousand Oaks, CA: Sage, 1996.

Horwitt, Sanford D. *Let Them Call Me Rebel: Saul Alinsky: His Life and Legacy*. New York: Alfred Knopf, 1989.

Isenberg, Alison. *Downtown America: A History of the Place and the People Who Made It*. Chicago, IL: University of Chicago Press, 2004.

Jackson, Kenneth T. *Crabgrass Frontier: The Suburbanization of the United States*. New York: Oxford University Press, 1985.

Katz, Michael B. *The "Underclass Debate": Views From History*. Princeton, NJ: Princeton University Press, 1993.

Melosi, M.V. *The Sanitary City: Urban Infrastructure in America From Colonial Times to the Present*. Baltimore, MD: Johns Hopkins University Press, 2000.

Monkkonen, E.H. *America Becomes Urban: The Development of U.S. Cities and Towns, 1780–1980*. Berkeley, CA: University of California Press, 1988.

Sugrue, Thomas J. *The Origins of the Urban Crisis*. Princeton, NJ: Princeton University Press, 1996.

Trout, Charles H. *Boston, the Great Depression and the New Deal*. New York: Oxford University Press, 1977.

Wright, G. *Building the Dream: A Social History of Housing in America*. Cambridge, MA: MIT Press, 1983.

Chapter 6

Rural Life

*"I want to get up again each morning as I hear the roosters crow.
I want to pick flowers while the dew is still on them."*
—John Sharp Williams

THE GREAT DEPRESSION affected rural people as well as urbanites. Conditions were arguably worse in the countryside than in the city, since agriculture had been in the doldrums since the end of World War I. The hardest-hit farmers were those caught in the Dust Bowl in the Great Plains, including the Dakotas, Kansas, Nebraska, Texas, Oklahoma, New Mexico, and Colorado. A severe drought that began in 1931 meant that millions of acres of crops failed in these states in the mid-1930s. The wages of rural people overall slipped from an average of 70 percent of factory workers' wages in 1929, to 50 percent in 1932.

While those in Dust Bowl states joined mass migrations to find jobs in other areas, rural people who were able to stay on their farms sought to decrease expenses. They shared farm machinery instead of purchasing new machinery that they could ill afford. Some farmers reverted to using horses and mules to save money that they otherwise would have had to spend on the operation and upkeep of a tractor. Rural people bartered goods and services instead of paying for them—rural doctors and lawyers might accept a chicken or butter in lieu of payment in cash. Many farmers could not afford to pay their property taxes.

Bereft of tax revenues, townships and counties reduced their services to rural Americans. Public schools struggled to stay open. Some could not afford to pay teachers, who left the classroom in search of remunerative work. Other schools issued teachers IOUs, but some banks refused to accept them, and others accepted them at a fraction of their face value. Schools relied on volunteers to teach, and when volunteers could not be found, closed their doors. Where schools closed, parents had no choice but to keep their children home. Even where schools remained open, some parents kept their children home to help on the farm. The most fortunate schools were those to which the Works Progress Administration assigned a teacher. Because the federal government paid the salaries of these teachers, a rural school could staff its classes without drawing upon its revenues. In addition to operating schools, a township or county needed to maintain roads and bridges, but absent tax revenues, it could do little upkeep. Consequently roads and bridges fell into disrepair.

Aware of their plight, but unable to offer concrete solutions, state agricultural extension agents advised rural people to be self sufficient because they would not need to spend money if they could meet all their needs at home. The necessity of self-sufficiency was not a noble undertaking, but rather an acknowledgment that rural people had little money to spend. The live at home movement, as the quest for self-sufficiency was known, was hard on rural women who already toiled under a heavy burden. Few rural homes had electricity in 1929, leaving rural women to clean lamps of grime every few days. Other chores included dusting surfaces, washing floors, walls, and windows, sweeping carpets, and making soap. Rural women scrubbed clothes by hand and ironed them under hot conditions, for the flatiron had to be heated on a stove and used on the spot. Although women might have welcomed the heat from the stove in the winter, it was very uncomfortable in the summer. At three to 12 pounds, the flatiron challenged the endurance of women who had a pile of clothes to iron.

In addition to these chores, rural women tended the vegetable garden, canned vegetables, raised poultry, kept dairy cattle for milk, and at times helped their husbands in the field. Men worked in the field, butchered hogs and cattle, and preserved meat. Farmers who had afforded the luxury of hiring a man to help in the field let him go during the Depression. Instead they depended on women and children to do extra work. Children gathered eggs, hoed the soil, and did whatever else their parents needed.

The Depression reversed the trend in population in the countryside.

Flat irons like this one stayed in use longer in rural areas lacking electricity.

Young people returning to farms during the early 1930s before widespread rural electrification would have found that much of the work, such as haying, had changed little.

Since the Industrial Revolution people had left the farm in search of work in the city. During the 1930s, however, people who lost jobs in the city returned home to the farm. In 1932 and 1933 alone 750,000 people migrated from city to countryside. Most of these were young people who had family in the countryside and who now returned to live with them. Many of the newly unemployed preferred work on the family farm, even if it paid little, to being on relief. The farmer was happy to have extra help, particularly during planting and harvest. Those who had returned to the farm had less to do during slack time, and underemployment plagued the countryside during the Depression.

In the South white landowners put black sharecroppers and tenants off the land. Sharecroppers and tenants were not alone in facing eviction. In 1930 more than 40 percent of farms carried a mortgage. Not only could farmers not afford property taxes, but they also had too little money to pay their mortgages, and so faced eviction. Even when farmers fell behind on their mortgage payments, some banks were reluctant to evict farmers from their land because the banks might have to sell the farms at a loss. Other banks did not hesitate to act and between 1929 and 1933 banks foreclosed on nearly one million farms.

Some banks, having repossessed a farm, hired the evicted family to labor on the land. No longer owner of the farm, the family suffered a loss in status. However, sometimes communities united behind an evicted family. When the bank auctioned a farm, the residents of a community agreed that only one of them would bid on the farm, and then only for a nominal sum. Having secured

A collection of headlines from the Dust Bowl era emphasizes the widespread effects and human toll of the drought and "black blizzards."

The Dust Bowl

A consequence of drought, the Dust Bowl was a series of dust storms on the Great Plains between 1931 and 1940. Climatologists blame the Dust Bowl on La Niña, a body of cool water along the Pacific Coast of North America that did not put water vapor into the stream of air across the Great Plains. Bereft of water vapor, clouds released little rain onto the plains, causing drought. Farming techniques contributed to the Dust Bowl. In plowing the land, farmers removed native grasses, whose roots had held the soil in place. Native grasses might have survived the drought, but it killed the crops, leaving nothing to anchor the soil in place. Drought, beginning in 1931, afflicted the Dakotas, Kansas, Nebraska, Texas, Oklahoma, New Mexico, and Colorado. So severe was the drought that more than 45 million acres of crops failed in these lands in 1935. Winds swept up the soil, which had neither crops nor indigenous grasses to hold it in place, turning it to dust. The wind often had so much soil that the sky turned black. Winds carried the soil as far east as Washington, D.C. In some years the wind deposited soil on the streets of Chicago and contaminated the snow that fell in New England. In 1933 winds eroded the soil from South Dakota farms, forming a large black cloud of dust. In May 1934 a two-day storm blew dust to Chicago, Buffalo, Boston, and New York City. Dust blew inside homes and settled on clothes and skin.

Of the 2.5 million people who left the plains, many migrated to California in search of work in the orchards and vegetable farms. The new arrivals found themselves in competition with Mexicans for jobs, each group willing to work for subsistence wages. Mobilized by the crisis, Congress created the Soil Conservation Service in 1935 to teach farmers to protect their land from erosion. The Resettlement Administration bought some 10 million acres of eroded land in the Plains, removing it from cultivation, and helped farmers move to other regions.

the farm for next to nothing, the community returned it to the original owner. Not all banks accepted these sales as legitimate. Some declared the auction fraudulent and sold a farm only when they could get a fair price.

EDUCATION

Nearly half of all children attended rural schools, and the other half attended urban schools, according to a 1944 survey. Rural schools spent $900 million per year on instruction, 40 percent of total expenditures in education. Admittedly rural schools had less money than urban schools and so lagged behind in expenditures per pupil. In 1944 rural schools spent on average $100 per student, whereas urban schools averaged $128 per pupil. Most rural schools had neither the teachers nor the money to offer kindergarten. Expenditures were higher in the rural North and West, where schools averaged $2,199 per classroom, and lower in the South, where schools spent on average $1,166 per classroom. Segregation was still the law in the South; rural black schools fared

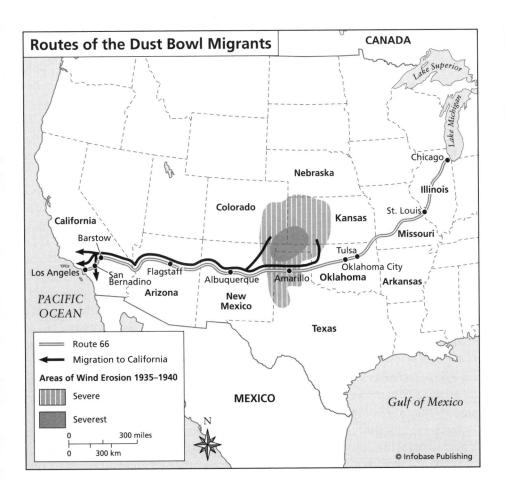

Routes of the Dust Bowl Migrants

worst at $477 per classroom. One sociologist rated rural black schools as "little more than shacks." In cases where black schools were too poor to own a school building, they held classes in a local church. Mexican Americans, an important group of farm laborers in the West, likewise attended segregated schools.

Not only did rural schools spend less per pupil and per classroom than did urban schools, but rural schools paid their teachers less. In 1944 rural teachers averaged $1,275 in salary compared to $2,215 for urban teachers. Some rural teachers earned as little as $400 per year, and black teachers fared even worse. As a rule rural teachers were less qualified than urban teachers. The comparatively high salaries that urban schools paid attracted the best teachers, whereas those with fewer credentials, unable to compete with highly qualified teachers, settled for a job in the countryside. Once they gained experience, teachers left rural schools for better paying positions. The average teacher spent one year at a rural school. Seldom did teachers spend more than five years teaching in the countryside. Ordinarily the profession of teaching carried status in rural communities, but the rapid departure of teachers led communities to regard them as outsiders, and as people uncommitted to rural life. The tendency of teachers to settle in a nearby village or town and commute to work, rather than to live in the countryside, further separated them from the rural community. As happened during the depression, schools that could not maintain a core of teachers or sufficient enrollment had little choice but to close, as they did by the hundreds during the 1940s. Others hired anyone willing to teach, regardless of qualifications.

ONE-ROOM SCHOOLHOUSES AND RURAL CULTURE

Another indicator of the poor quality of rural schools was the persistence of the one-room schoolhouse, prevalent in the South, particularly among black schools, in the Corn Belt, and in Appalachia. In an effort to rid the countryside of one-room schoolhouses, township and county government sought to unify several independent schools into a single district. In Lyman County, South Dakota, for example, one-room schoolhouses declined 58 percent between 1940 and 1945. Nevertheless rural people at times opposed the consolidation of schools for fear that they would lose influence over them. Rural notables were accustomed to serving on the school board, thereby deciding whom to hire to staff their schools. As they feared, consolidation transferred power from the countryside to the township or county. Consolidated schools settled in towns and bused children to them. The ranchers of Miles City in Custer County, Montana, for example, had two schools and a community college. Ranching communities like Custer County were too sparsely settled to support schools in the countryside. Rather a school in town served all rural children of a single county.

Despite their difficulties, rural schools continued in the 1930s and 1940s as a part of rural life. They remained sensitive to the rhythms of farm work, many of them holding classes for six weeks in the summer when rural children had time to devote to their studies. In autumn these schools took a hiatus so that the children could help with the harvest. Rural schools were also sensitive to the needs of local churches. In contrast to the mainline Protestant denominations, the new, often fundamentalist churches had no building of their own and so, where schools granted permission, they used the local school building for Sunday service and Sunday school.

Sensitive to the importance of farming to rural life, rural high schools offered vocational courses in agriculture and, for girls, home economics. In this context rural schools perpetuated the gender stereotype that men worked in the fields and women in the home. Dairy farmers were particularly eager to have their children take vocational courses, and they expected that their children would graduate high school. Some schools accommodated rural youth by maintaining stables for the horses that children rode to school. In addition to educating children, rural schools provided recreation for the community. Auditoriums hosted school plays, gymnasiums basketball games, and sports fields football games. Often all parents in a community attended these events, even if their children were not participants. In these close-knit communities, parents felt an attachment to all children, and cheered for them as they did for their own.

Students entering a segregated school in Destrehan, Louisiana, in September 1938. Rural African-American schools were only able to spend a paltry $477 a year per classroom.

Agricultural Adjustment Act

The Agricultural Adjustment Act (AAA) paid farmers to remove land from production and livestock raisers to reduce the size of their herds. In the 1930s farmers faced the problem of overproduction. For years they had heeded the advice of scientists to increase production as a way of raising income, but the reverse occurred. The more food farmers produced, the greater the surplus and the lower the price. In 1932, for example, farmers produced eight million bales of cotton, driving down the price to five cents per bale.

Aware of the farmers' plight, Secretary of Agriculture Henry A. Wallace wrote the AAA, which Congress enacted on May 12, 1933. The AAA aimed to limit the production of corn, wheat, oats, cotton, rice, peanuts, tobacco, pork, and milk. The AAA paid farmers to take land out of production and to slaughter a portion of their herds. In 1933 farmers slaughtered six million piglets and more than 200,000 cows. Cotton was already growing in the fields that year, leading farmers who participated in the program to plow under as much as one-quarter of their crop.

Farmers critical of AAA claimed the mules were smarter than the people who administered the AAA because the mules resisted plowing under the cotton. The public, horrified by the killing of so many pigs and cows, wondered how the federal government could pay farmers to diminish the production of food when so many American were hungry. Some Republicans were exasperated by what they perceived as an illogical program. At the same time as farmers were reducing the production of corn, the federal government was in 1933 importing 30 million bushels of corn. The federal government also imported oats while it paid farmers to cut their production.

The behavior of landowners in the Cotton Belt was more serious. By the terms of the AAA they were to share their payments with tenants and sharecroppers. In many cases landowners ignored the law, pocketing all the money and, because they had taken land out of production and so needed less labor to tend the remaining acres, they put tenants and sharecroppers off the land.

Other farmers, wanting to produce as much food as possible within the bounds of the AAA, removed their least productive acres, leaving the most fertile soils to produce crops. Despite its shortcomings, the AAA worked. Between 1933 and 1936 farm income rose 50 percent. In 1936, however, the U.S. Supreme Court invalidated the AAA. In lieu of the AAA the federal government, through the Soil Conservation and Domestic Allotment Act, continued to pay farmers, and in 1938 Congress passed the second Agricultural Adjustment Act.

A harrow resting in a field. By the early 1930s overproduction had reduced farmers' incomes significantly; however, once production was curbed, farm income rose 50 percent.

Low attendance and achievement plagued rural schools. In Appalachia children stayed home in autumn to help with the harvest and in winter when roads were covered with snow. Migrant laborers sent their children to school only sporadically. Southern whites and blacks were likewise apt to keep their children from school to help in the field and in the home. Others devalued education, instead urging their children to find a job at the earliest opportunity to bring money into the household. Among rural regions the South had the largest proportion of children truant and the largest proportion of illiterates. Only 64 percent of 12-year-olds attended school in the countryside, whereas 84 percent attended school in the city. Compared to urbanites aged 25 to 29, only half as many rural adults had graduated high school, and less than one-third as many had graduated college. In 1940 rural whites over age 25 averaged eight years of schooling but rural African Americans averaged only four years. Rural areas with the lowest levels of education had the highest birthrate and a high rate of juvenile crime.

RELIGION

Rural Americans, like their counterparts in the city, were overwhelmingly Christian. In the South, Baptist and Methodist denominations were the most numerous. In the West, rural people were predominantly Congregationalist and Presbyterian. Everywhere in the countryside were new churches that stressed emotion and a literal reading of the Bible. These churches appealed to rural people who wanted simple answers to questions of faith and who had a low tolerance for ambiguity. In 1936 the average rural church had only 93 members, and during the Depression membership declined. Sunday school attendance likewise sunk to low levels. In Culpeper, Virginia, for example, three-fourths of children were not enrolled in Sunday school in 1940. Moreover, half the children in Sunday school did not attend church services. As this example suggests, church attendance was not universal. Economic demarcations influenced who attended church. Landowners were faithful churchgoers, but tenants were less regular in their attendance.

Churches varied in what they offered members. Some concentrated on evangelism and offered few social services. Elsewhere churches held dinners, fairs, Christmas programs, and picnics. These were the churches that fostered recreation for both children and adults, and that viewed their function as social as well as religious. Many rural churches held a revival meeting during one week in the summer. At a revival, a minister aimed to intensify members' commitment to the church and to the doctrines he preached. A revival meeting also strengthened community ties, because in many places rural people attended in large numbers.

Much depended on the energy and commitment of a minister to his rural community. As was true of schools, rural churches had trouble attracting talent. In 1941 churches in rural North Carolina paid ministers as little as $122 per year, well below subsistence wages. By contrast urban churches paid as much as $3,728 per year. The graduates of divinity school took parsonages in the city, whereas clerics with little training settled for a job at a rural church. Some ministers took posts at two churches in order to earn a better income. Where one church was in town and the other in the countryside, a minister put his energy into the town church, which paid more than the rural church. Consequently the rural church suffered from neglect. A minister preached on Sunday, but otherwise left the congregation to tend to its needs. At some churches a minister delivered a Sunday service only once or twice a month. Some ministers doubled as part-time farmers to increase their income. Like the rural teacher, the minister viewed the rural church as a place to gain the experience necessary to advance, not as a place to sink roots.

HEALTH AND DISEASE

The idea that the countryside was full of sunshine, invigorating work, and robust health resonated with many Americans. This line of thinking held that cities were the repositories of disease and the countryside was rich in the curative powers of nature. In reality, however, malaria, hookworm, pellagra, mumps, chickenpox, whooping cough, and scarlet fever were more prevalent in the countryside than in the city. The tragedy was that many of these diseases, such as hookworm and pellagra, were easy to prevent, but poor habits

Life on Midwestern Farms

By October 1929, when the Great Depression began in the United States, farmers in the Midwest had been suffering economic decline for more than a decade. The impact of the Depression was intensified by the drought that lingered in both the East and Midwest. Even though most farmers continued to grow their own food, they were not always able to produce enough for the market. Joe Friederich, who grew up in St. Clair County, Illinois, during the Great Depression, recalls his family planting "lots of potatoes, watermelons, cucumbers, cantaloupes, tomatoes, green beans . . . sweet potatoes and peanuts." Even though life on Midwestern farms was generally harsh during the Depression, most farmers felt it was still "a better place to be than the street of a big city."

By 1933, the price of corn had dropped from 77 cents to 19 cents a bushel, and wheat fell from $1.08 to 33 cents. In "Seven-cent Cotton and Forty-cent Meat," Bob Miller sings of the misfortunes of the farmer:

How in the world can a poor man eat?
Poor getting poorer all around here,
Kids coming regular every year.

As the impact of the Depression deepened, more than half of all farm debts were in default. Many Midwestern farmers lost their homes and had to turn to tenant farming to survive. In Rockford, Illinois, May Lyford Davis described to her diary the pain that accompanied bank failures, dust storms, raging floods, and crop failures. In response to the drought and the Depression, the economies of small Midwestern towns began to fail, and town leaders were at a loss as to how they could provide basic services.

On January 8, 1934, a 16-year-old from Gettysburg, South Dakota, wrote to Eleanor Roosevelt, asking for help because "we are so poor we haven't hardly enough to eat . . . We haven't had a crop for eight years." A farmer's wife from Knoxville, Illinois, who was raising her dead daughter's three children, wrote the First Lady on March 29, 1934, asking for assistance because their crops had failed due to "the cinch bug and dry weather." The writer informed Eleanor Roosevelt that her family now had "to move if we can find a place. We do not know where." The following year, a farmer's wife from Goff, Kansas, asked for help in obtaining a spring coat because "every penny we can save goes for feed to put into crop."

and inertia allowed them to persist, particularly in the rural South. Public health campaigns emphasized that one could prevent hookworm merely by wearing shoes. A disease of dietary deficiency, pellagra was curable simply by eating foods rich in niacin. Rural schools played an important role in the campaign against hookworm and pellagra, sending home literature and culturing the hookworm in classrooms so that parents, touring the classrooms, could see the disease's culprit.

In the fight against disease, rural people enlisted the help of the country doctor. In the early 20th century doctors had been among the first to buy automobiles so that they could more easily visit their far-flung patients. In the 1930s and 1940s house calls became less frequent as doctors began to amass diagnostic equipment, for example an X-ray machine, that was not portable. The patient who needed to consult the doctor now had to visit him in his office. The country doctor was a general practitioner. Rural people with ailments that the country doctor could not treat had to seek a specialist in the city. The trip to the city, even with an automobile, was an all day affair, as many rural people lived far from the city. The ordeal of going to the city led nearly two-thirds of the inhabitants of one rural county in Missouri to wish that a hospital be built nearby. Perhaps because cities were so far away, 40 percent of residents in this county had never had anyone in their family in the hospital. With fewer visits to a physician or hospital, rural people spent less per person on medical care than urbanites.

In 1942 only 45 percent of rural women gave birth in a hospital, whereas that percentage nearly doubled for urban women. Among a minority of rural women, a midwife performed the functions of a physician, attending the labor of 12 percent of pregnant rural women in 1944. By contrast only 2 percent of pregnant urban women used a midwife. Dentists may have been scarcer than physicians in the countryside. The residents of one rural county in Missouri visited a dentist, in a town or city, only when decay had proceeded so far in a tooth that extraction was necessary. With physicians and dentists in shortage, many rural people relied on home remedies to treat ailments.

Despite the dearth of medical services in the countryside, rural people benefited from advances in public health. Pasteurization reduced the incidence of microbial infections from milk. The chlorination of water eliminated waterborne diseases that had once killed thousands of people. The use of antibiotics against bacterial infections saved countless lives. Penicillin, the first antibiotic, was available in large quantities after World War II. In 1943 microbiologist Selman Waksman discovered streptomycin, the first antibiotic effective against tuberculosis. Vaccines prevented several diseases. Rural people who made sensible decisions about their health lived longer, more productive lives than had rural people in the past.

ELECTRICITY, AUTOMOBILES, AND TRACTORS

At first a curiosity, electricity spread throughout the countryside in the 20th century. In the 1930s few rural people had electricity but the federal government aided the electrification of the countryside. The Tennessee Valley

Farmers socialize on the front porch of a combination store, gas station, and post office at a crossroads in Sprott, Alabama, in a well-known photograph by Walker Evans from around 1936.

Authority built dams along the Tennessee River and generated hydroelectric power for rural residents in the valley. In 1935 Congress created the Rural Electrification Administration to provide electricity to rural households. Electricity reduced the drudgery of housework and eased the operation of a farm, powering a range of appliances including vacuum cleaners, refrigerators, clothes washers, irons, and toasters. Electricity drove milking machines and

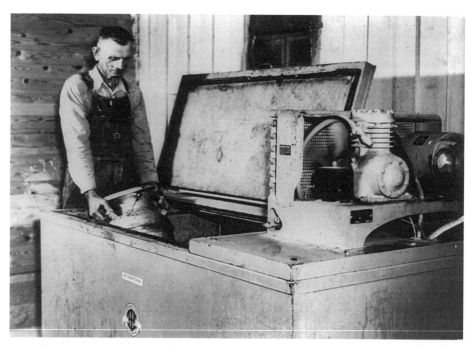

This photo created during the rural electrification program shows a farmer using the new refrigerators for milk storage. By 1945 more than half of rural people had electricity.

powered large refrigerators for storing milk. Thanks to the Rural Electrification Administration, by 1945 more than half of rural people had electricity.

The automobile likewise shaped rural life in the 1930s and 1940s. Rural people had eagerly adopted Henry Ford's Model T early in the 20th century, and by 1930 it was a fixture of rural life. Rural people used the automobile to travel to town to buy supplies, converse with friends and acquaintances, and enjoy the latest motion picture. In the era of the horse and buggy, the trip to town had been an ordeal. With the automobile, however, rural families thought nothing about driving to a city 100 miles distant, conducting business and recreation, and returning home the same day. Driving as much as they did, rural people spent more money on gasoline and on the upkeep of their car than urbanites. At the same time, however, the family car was a source of tension. Rural teens wanted the car to go parking or dancing, and parents, anxious about such behavior, put restrictions on its use, demanding, for example, that teens be home by 10 P.M. In some cases the father, regarding the car as his property, was reluctant to allow his children to drive it under any circumstances.

The counterpart to the automobile was the tractor, which became more common on farms in the late 1930s and 1940s. Farmers had forgone the purchase of a tractor during the Depression but as their finances improved many of them bought one. The number of tractors rose from 1.4 million in 1939, to 2.4 million in 1945, and 2.8 million in 1947. With a tractor a farmer could plant, cultivate, and harvest without the need for additional labor. With a tractor, a farmer no longer needed to keep a stable of horses. The absence of horses in turn allowed farmers to shift acreage from forage to crops, increasing the amount of food they could grow. Yet not everyone benefited from the tractor. Fruit and vegetables were too fragile to harvest by machine. Fruit and vegetable growers continued, as they had for decades, to employ laborers to pick the crop. Some farmers were too poor to afford a tractor, and even in the 1940s they harvested wheat with a cradle and threshed it by hand.

DAILY LIFE

Rural life was primitive in other ways. As late as 1945 only 28 percent of farmers, compared with 95 percent of city dwellers, had running water. Without running water rural people had a hard time keeping clean and were vulnerable to lice and ticks. In some rural counties only 7 percent of homes had

A woman washing clothes on a farm in the early 1940s. Electrification brought washing machines and other conveniences to some farms, but in 1945 over two-thirds still lacked running water.

a bathroom. The rest used an outhouse. Because hookworms were in feces, an outhouse that was not self-contained allowed them to spread through the ground. In addition to running water, many poor rural people lacked electricity and natural gas. They depended on a wood or coal-burning stove for heat in winter. The burning of coal deposited soot throughout the home, and its removal was yet another chore for rural women.

The farm family worked long days. Out of bed at 4:30 or 5 A.M., the father and children did chores while the mother prepared breakfast. Sometimes accompanied by his wife and older sons, the father worked in the field from 6 A.M. until noon, when the mother, having prepared lunch, served her family the midday meal. Some women who labored in the field expressed satisfaction with this work, at its progress and completion, whereas housework never ended. Back in the field at 1 P.M. the father and his older sons worked until 6:30 or 7 P.M. while the mother did her household chores. Dinner, again prepared by the mother, allowed the family a respite from a long day's work. Without fanfare the family went to bed at 8:30 or 9 P.M.

RECREATION

Recreation occupied an uncertain place in rural America. One line of thinking upheld hard work as a virtue and branded recreation as sloth. At best, recreation was a waste of time. At worst, it was immoral and therefore sinful. Rural ministers condemned gambling, which cost rural people money and threatened their livelihood, and dancing, which brought teen boys and girls together under lax supervision. From another perspective, however, recreation was a proper use of time. Rural advocates of recreation pointed to the creation story in *Genesis*, noting that God had rested on the seventh day. Likewise people, following this example, should devote a portion of their time to rest and recreation.

Often all members of a community attended the same rural church. After the Sunday service people talked with one another, sharing details about their lives. Church festivals and revival meetings strengthened ties among rural people. The people in a community likewise came together for the county fair and, in the Corn Belt, for the corn show. The county fair showcased the fruits of rural labor: a beautiful quilt or a large and perfectly round pumpkin. Aside from these collective forms of recreation, rural people pursued recreation of their own devising. Rural girls enjoyed reading and sewing, whereas boys liked to play baseball. Men and women turned to the radio for entertainment, women enjoying religious music, and men listening to country music. In 1945, 72 percent of rural households had a radio. In other ways music was a form of recreation. In the 1940s, 40 percent of rural families owned a piano, and mothers often taught their daughters to play. Rural families took fishing trips during the slack time of midsummer. Families in the Corn Belt went to town for a movie twice a week, whereas ranchers and rural Southerners viewed movies less often.

CONCLUSION

One of the defining images of the Great Depression is, for good reason, Dorothea Lange's 1936 "Migrant Mother." The woman and her family had failed to find work as pea pickers because of the failure of the crop when they were photographed in Nipomo, California. While urbanites also suffered greatly during the Great Depression, those rural people whose crops were ruined by drought or who were otherwise caught in the Dust Bowl may have had it worst of all, descending into a level of destitution not often seen in American history.

Florence Thompson, age 32 and the mother of seven children, in the photograph known as "Migrant Mother."

The recovery that followed the mobilization for World War II drew even more rural people away from farms with suddenly abundant manufacturing jobs. In spite of all this, those who did remain in rural areas emerged from this era hardier than ever, with many of their traditions based in churches and schools still intact.

CHRISTOPHER CUMO

Further Readings

Adams, Jane, ed. *Fighting for the Farm: Rural America Transformed*. Philadelphia, PA: University of Pennsylvania Press, 2003.

Bedford, Faith Andrews. *Country Living Barefoot Summers: Reflections of Home, Family, and Simple Pleasures*. New York: Hearst Books, 2005.

Castle, Emery N., ed. *The Changing American Countryside: Rural People and Places*. Lawrence, KS: University Press of Kansas, 1995.

Danbom, David B. *Born in the Country: A History of Rural America*. Baltimore, MD: Johns Hopkins University Press, 1995.

Kalish, Mildred Armstrong. *Little Heathens: Hard Times and High Spirits on an Iowa Farm during the Great Depression*. New York: Bantam, 2007.

Luloff, A.E. and Louis E. Swanson, eds. *American Rural Communities*. Boulder, CO: Westview, 1990.

McElvaine, Robert S. *Down and Out in the Great Depression: Letters from the Forgotten Man*. Chapel Hill, NC: University of North Carolina Press, 1983.

Meyer, Carrie A. *Days on the Family Farm: From the Golden Age through the Great Depression.* Minneapolis, MN: University of Minnesota Press, 2007.

Stewart, James B. and Joyce E. Allen-Smith, eds. *Blacks in Rural America.* New Brunswick, NJ: Transaction, 1995.

Taylor, Carl C. *Rural Life in the United States.* New York: Alfred A. Knopf, 1949.

Volanto, Keith J. *Texas, Cotton and the New Deal.* College Station, TX: Texas A & M University Press, 2005.

Walton, Gary M. and Hugh Rockoff. *History of the American Economy.* Fort Worth, TX: Dryden Press, 1998.

Chapter 7

Religion

"Some bright morning when this life is over, I'll fly away.
To that home on God's celestial shore, I'll fly away."
—Albert E. Brumley

THE ROARING TWENTIES were a time of great religious activity. On the one hand, in the wake of World War I, American religious bodies experienced greater ecumenism than ever before. The financial prosperity of the country led some, such as Bruce Barton, to articulate a gospel of wealth—claiming financial prosperity as a boon from God. Liberal theology and religiously motivated social reform continued to prosper in the wake of the Social Gospel Movement, and the philosophical realism of theologians such as William James grew in popularity.

The 1920s were also a time of religious controversy. Most notably the growing popularity of Pentecostalism and the rise of Christian Fundamentalism and its focus on the conversion of souls over the improvement of working and living conditions marked a change in the landscape of Christianity. The Fundamentalist controversies culminated in the 1925 Scopes trial concerning the teaching of evolution in the nation's schools. Though the fundamentalists won the battle in court, the scathing portrayal of this group by the media led to a decline in their popularity. Despite growing cooperation among religious groups, many Americans still harbored resentment and suspicion of the many immigrants that continued to arrive on American shores.

The Great Depression deeply challenged the religious enthusiasm and economic comfort prevalent in the 1920s. The economic downturn's effect on the everyday lives of Americans was immeasurable and led many to question the reason for such a tragic turn of events. On the one hand, the Depression led to extensive scapegoating and a return to the nativist sentiments prevalent at the turn of the century. On the other hand, the Depression also led to a religious revival as religious communities and individuals turned to religion to find solace, support, and resources in the face of economic disaster. Combined, these two trends led to a more diverse religious landscape and a newly articulated social conscience in America.

NATIVISM AND ANTI-SEMITISM

As at other points in American history, economic, political, and social strife could lead to scapegoating. Moreover the large numbers of immigrants to America in the late 19th and early 20th centuries added financial pressure and cultural conflict to an already tenuous situation in America's cities. The increasing prevalence of Catholics in the nation's courts and political parties caused anxiety among many. For example, in 1928, Roman Catholic Al Smith sought the presidential nomination, leading many to fear Vatican influence in the United States. These prejudices would only deepen as financial crisis hit America. The eventual defeat of Prohibition in 1933 led many Protestants to look to immigration as a contributing factor to what they saw as a moral decline in the country.

Ethnicity and religion often formed the basis for discrimination, anger, and sometimes violence between new and "native" Americans. Unsurprisingly, then, the Great Depression served to add fuel to the fire of these sentiments. For example, the Ku Klux Klan, revived during the 1920s, continued its blend of racism, anti-Semitism, and religion into the 1930s and beyond. Indeed, it was the Jews who faced the majority of religious discrimination and endured the most hate speech. The reasons were both religious and circumstantial. Though Jews had lived in America since the colonial era, their numbers were limited prior to the great immigrations around the turn of the 20th century. By the time of the Great Depression, Jews numbered over four million, and many had migrated westward to stem the growing overcrowding in eastern cities. After World War I, additional tension surrounded this population as the country tried to manage an influx of displaced Jews.

Latching onto the fears, anxieties, and concerns of Depression-era Americans, several charismatic leaders appealed to nativist ideologies in their rhetoric. In 1944, Gerald L.K. Smith, a Disciples of Christ candidate for the America First Party, attacked supposed Jewish conspiracies. Father Charles Coughlin, a Roman Catholic priest who issued regular radio broadcasts under the auspices of religious programming, espoused a similar rhetoric. However, over the course of the early 1930s, the message became increasingly anti-Semitic, anticommunist, and anti–New Deal. Appealing to American concerns over the state of the country, Coughlin blamed America's problems on a combination of godless communism and Jewish bankers. As he saw it, the American government, under Roosevelt, was merely playing into the hands of these foes.

Coughlin's support was mixed. His anti-Semitic statements were so provocative that even the anti-Catholic Ku Klux Klan supported his broadcasts. Coughlin put these ideas into action when he formed the National Union for Social Justice political party in 1934. Coughlin also published his ideas in the newspaper *Social Justice*. The church finally spoke out against him, insisting that he did not reflect Catholic social policy. In 1942 the church hierarchy asked Coughlin to either be quiet or resign the priesthood. He chose the latter option, but continued to write in opposition to both communism and, later, the changes brought about by Vatican II.

RELIGIOUS REVIVAL AND INNOVATION

During this period, religious rhetoric was not always so jarring and religion was not always used to such negative ends. On the one hand, due to the overwhelming financial, social, and political concerns of the Great Depression, many historians have characterized the era as secular in focus, and represent-

The Jewish Community Center of San Francisco, constructed 1932–33, was one of many built to help coordinate the work of charitable organizations. Such activities by the Jewish-American community influenced the rise of the profession of social work.

Father Divine

Demonstrating the innovation of Depression-era religion and the varieties of African-American religion, Reverend General Jealous Divine began the International Peace Mission movement and orchestrated its growth from a small, largely African-American group to a diverse and international church. Born a Baptist in the South and spiritually reborn through the Azusa Street Pentecostal Revival, his preaching emphasized equality and total desegregation of American society.

Father Divine's Peace Mission appealed to a broad spectrum of people. His followers were known for their austere lifestyle and were known for their insistence on economic self-sufficiency. Divine and his followers believed in the uniqueness of America as the eventual birthplace of the Kingdom of God.

Claiming to be the second incarnation of Jesus Christ, Divine's charismatic preaching and sometimes outlandish antics and political action led to several arrests and, at one time, commitment to a mental asylum. Father Divine garnered much fame after he was arrested in 1931 for "invading the country with his religious practices" such as allowing white women and black men to cohabitate. After Divine was sentenced to a year in jail by Judge Lewis J. Smith, Smith died suddenly. The press seized on this coincidence and widely reported that, when asked for comment on this turn of events, Divine replied, "I hated to do it."

In the wake of the Great Depression, 150 Peace Missions arose throughout the country, many in New York. By accumulating property and businesses, Father Divine and his mission were able to provide food, shelter, and jobs to many in cities, thus becoming rather popular in the Depression era. Mother Divine, Divine's second wife Edna Rose Ritchings, continued to carry on the work of Father Divine, conducting services to a decreasing congregation. The movement continues to have chapters in California, Pennsylvania, and New York, but lacks a centralized organization.

ing a challenge to and decline in religious life. However, though many fell away from religion as they questioned how a just God could allow such devastation, others found renewed faith and turned to religion for answers and hope.

This tendency led to what was in many ways a lay-driven movement in religion. The poorest of Americans felt religion was inextricably tied to their everyday lives, and it continued to be as they encountered itinerant preachers seeking to bring religious renewal, as they frequented soup kitchens run by religious groups, and as they gathered with their neighbors on Sunday mornings in prayer.

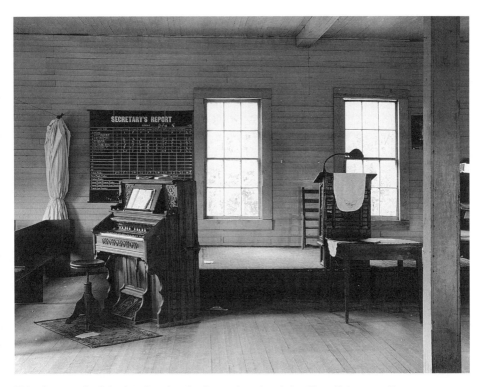

This photograph of the interior of a simple wooden church in either Alabama or Tennessee was taken by Walker Evans in 1936.

In addition to strengthening individual religious experience, the Depression also affected group religious experience. While the 1920s gospel of wealth had encouraged individual achievement and financial gain, the widespread devastation brought by the Great Depression led to the impulse of many to reach out to one another. New coalitions of those with similar religious, political, and social interests flourished, as did ecumenism among differing groups.

Growth was particularly steady in Fundamentalist, Holiness, and Pentecostal churches, largely due to their explicit attempts to appeal to those who were in need. While the mainline denominations of Christianity saw decreases in membership giving and growth as a result of the limitations of the Depression, certain Pentecostal denominations saw their membership numbers double or even triple. In this time of hardship, the sometimes dramatic, emotionally engaging Fundamentalist or Pentecostal worship often spoke to people's experiences in ways more staid denominations could not.

Mergers and the creation of new organizations reflected both disagreements and newfound cooperation among religious groups. On the one hand, continuing the controversies from the 1920s, many Fundamentalist churches openly opposed the supposed liberalism of the Federal Council of

Christian Realism

In response to the growing international role of the United States in World War I and to liberal Christian movements such as the Social Gospel Movement, a group of Christian scholars and theologians developed a different type of Christian theology, meant to be deeply and immediately relevant to the problems of the early- and mid-20th century. This group of young men shared similar life and faith experiences. Each had experienced a conversion experience and, while in college during World War I, had learned to approach their faith from an intellectual perspective. Their theology was focused on Christ and rejected both racism and nationalism—putting emphasis on God's kingdom, not the earth's. These giants of Christian theology—among them Karl Barth, Henry P. Van Dusen, Francis P. Miller, Paul Tillich, and Reinhold Niebuhr—produced numerous books throughout the 1920s and beyond that questioned the relevance of liberal Christianity to the challenges of their time.

These men and others met in a Theological Discussion Group 1934–35 to discuss the proper role of the church. This group saw the main opponents of Christianity in the world of the late 1930s to be Communism, Fascism, and even Democracy. Two groups arose from this discussion group, both focused on ecumenical work—Life and Work, which met in 1937 in Oxford, and Faith and Order, which met in Edinburgh in 1937. These two groups would later join as the World Council of Churches. According to Christian Realists, the Social Gospel focus on creating the Kingdom of God on Earth was false optimism and led Christians to disregard foreign threats and other concerns due to a belief that God would right all in the Second Coming.

In his most well-known text, *Moral Man and Immoral Society*, written in 1932, Reinhold Niebuhr distinguished between the morality of groups and individuals, arguing that the desire for power and the interplay of sinful personalities in group settings necessitate a realism not allowed by Christian idealism. Though man should seek the kingdom of heaven with all his heart, that kingdom was not possible on Earth. Instead, the responsible use of power and coercion was necessary to stem evil impulses and maintain some control over the evil forces in the world. Niebuhr's main goal was to replace love with justice as the achievable goal of Christianity. The Christian Realists advocated American involvement in World War II before Pearl Harbor, and published frequently to this effect in the journal *Christianity and Crisis*. After Pearl Harbor, the group worked to encourage roads to peace. While their influence declined after World War II, this group is notable not only as representing an important phase in Christian theology, but also as an important influential group in worldwide ecumenism within Christianity and as a model for religious involvement in social issues. For the Christian community of the time, they represented the difficulties many faced in reconciling their political pragmatism with religious idealism.

Churches and formed the American Council of Churches in 1940 and the National Association of Evangelicals in 1941. On the other hand, the Methodist denomination reunited its northern and southern segments in 1939, but continued to exclude African Methodist churches. As a result of mergers of several German churches in America, the Evangelical and Reformed Church was formed in 1934 and the Evangelical United Brethren Church was formed in 1946.

During this period, American Jews added significantly to their numbers. Their support of the New Deal and involvement in its programs as well as the arts catapulted Jews into the mainstream of American culture. Similarly, though Catholics had experienced a rocky American past with the scorn of nativists, internal controversies over modernism and Americanism, and the persistent concern of balancing assimilation with personal and religious integrity, they too began to enter the mainstream in this period. Having proven their loyalty through work in World War I, many Catholics had gained the cultural prestige and economic ability to influence larger society.

AFRICAN-AMERICAN RELIGIOUS MOVEMENTS

This era saw shifts and innovations in the African-American community as well. In the wake of the Great Depression, many African Americans chose to migrate from rural to urban areas and to the North where greater assistance was available to the poor and unemployed. This migration had religious effects, such as the spread of Gospel music. Blending jazz and blues with religious hymns, this genre flourished in the 1920s and into the 1930s. The combination of secular rhythms with religious ideals allowed many to find continuity in the different aspects of their lives. In the 1930s Tommy Dorsey, who has been called the father of gospel music, reached the pinnacle of his career. This music would help many African Americans through the struggles of World War II and the coming Civil Rights movement.

As in American religion in general, the difficulties of the Great Depression spawned a number of new religious movements in the African-American community. Eccentrics such as Father Divine claimed to provide easy answers and spiritual renewal to those struggling with economic and personal problems. Other previously existing movements proved popular during this time. The Moorish Science Temple of America, founded in 1913 by Timothy Drew, appealed to the lengthy history of Islam in the African-American population. Known by his followers as the Prophet Noble Drew Ali, Drew claimed to be called by Allah to use Islam as a means of liberation for black people. His call involved a rewriting of the Koran and a strict lifestyle and prayer regimen.

One extreme response to the difficulties posed by the Great Depression was the formation of the Nation of Islam. This religious group was founded in 1931 by Wallace D. Fard and Elijah Poole (later known as Elijah Muhammad). Only marginally connected to traditional Islam, the Nation of Islam was cre-

Elijah Muhammad (once known as Elijah Poole), one of the founders of the Nation of Islam, preaching at a podium in 1964.

ated as a religion for African Americans, and as a means of explaining the race's oppression in the past and present and of providing a way to escape this oppression in the future.

Elijah Muhammad taught his followers that Wallace D. Fard was, in fact, Allah, the Islamic monotheistic God. According to Muhammad, Allah had created the world through a big bang and created the first man black. Yakub, an evil scientist, bred lesser beings until they were lighter in color, yielding the white race. Muhammad claimed black superiority over whites, but held that whites had conspired against blacks with the devil, and suppressed them for 6,000 years. The primary tool for this conspiracy was the Bible, a corrupt book. Elijah Muhammad claimed to be called by Allah to restore the "Lost-Found Nation of Islam" out of this suppression.

The vast economic trauma and social upheaval caused by the Great Depression led many African Americans to seek an answer and an improved life condition. The Nation of Islam in particular appealed to criminals and the poor through its proposed solutions to sinful ways and difficult life. The movement grew slowly, experiencing early growth in cities such as Detroit and Chicago. It was in the 1960s, in the midst of the Civil Rights movement,

Dorothy Day and the
Catholic Worker Movement

A converted Catholic, Dorothy Day is best known as one of the founders of the Catholic Worker movement in 1932. Born in 1897 in Brooklyn, New York, and raised in Chicago, Day experienced firsthand the reality of poverty in America's cities. Through her early years, she increasingly focused on the plight of the working poor. After only two years in college, Day moved to New York to report for *The Call*, a socialist daily paper where she covered labor organizations, rallies, and demonstrators. Foreshadowing her later pacifist convictions, Day would continue her journalistic career by working for *The Masses*, a newspaper that spoke out against American involvement in European war. Her journalistic responsibilities led to personal involvement in many social movements and Day was arrested in 1917 for agitation for women's suffrage.

In 1918 Day decided to address social problems through a different avenue and began nurse training. It was during this period that Day, raised an Episcopalian, began to be attracted to Catholic ritual and spiritual discipline and saw church as particularly relevant for the poor and immigrants. It was when Day faced one of the biggest challenges of her life that she formalized her relationship to Catholicism. Unmarried, Day gave birth to a daughter, Tamar Theresa Day, in 1927 and had her baptized in the Catholic Church. She would join the church herself soon thereafter.

In 1932 Day visited Washington, D.C., during the Hunger March as a reporter for *Commonweal* and *American* magazines. During this visit she met Peter Maurin, who encouraged Day to begin a paper advocating Catholic social teaching and seeking to change society. On May 1, 1932, Day and Maurin published the first issue of *The Catholic Worker* and sold it for one penny. The paper quickly gained in popularity, and soon *The Catholic Worker* offices became a house of hospitality. By 1936 there were 33 Catholic Worker houses throughout the country that provided shelter, food, organizing space, and Catholic worship services for people in need. The Catholic Worker movement also experimented with communes and became most controversial through its expressions of pacifism.

In many ways analogous in theology and mission to the Protestant Social Gospel movement of several decades earlier, the Catholic Worker movement displayed an uncompromising optimism about their ability to improve the world and a commitment to addressing the basic needs of Americans before or while attending to their spiritual needs. The Catholic Worker movement would later expand its concerns beyond labor conditions of the working poor to support the Civil Rights movement. Day died in 1980 and, though never canonized, many regard her as a saint.

and with the support of Malcolm X and others, that the movement reached its heyday.

THE NEW DEAL AND REVIVAL OF THE SOCIAL GOSPEL

While religion evolved through the Depression era as both a catalyst for conflict between ethnic and racial groups and a tool for revival and innovation, it also served as a motivation for and organizing body for social reform work. The need for such work was great in the Depression era, as pre-existing resources for the poor and the unemployed were stretched beyond their limits. Harkening back to the Social Gospel movement of the turn of the 20th century and its focus on an improvable world and activist Christianity, many Christians mobilized their meager resources to improve the country's situation.

Politically, presidential styles and philosophies greatly influenced this work by religious groups. Throughout political rhetoric, one saw an increase in the appeal to morals. Even in the immediate wake of the Great Depression, then President Herbert Hoover called on Americans to seek assistance from community and religious resources such as the Salvation Army, Community Chest, and Red Cross. His strategy was to advocate the use of pre-existing social service organizations. In contrast, Roosevelt led a government reform and revival through his New Deal programs that created new resources for help. In many ways, the New Deal effectively took over many of the programs previously managed by religious groups.

Yet Roosevelt also saw the necessity of religious organizations and communities for renewing the country and for managing foreign policy. In fact, it was under his presidency that a formal Ambassador to the Vatican was announced. Roosevelt looked to religious organizations in particular to answer the refugee problems of World War II. The National Refugee Committee was established in 1939 and combined Protestant, Catholic,

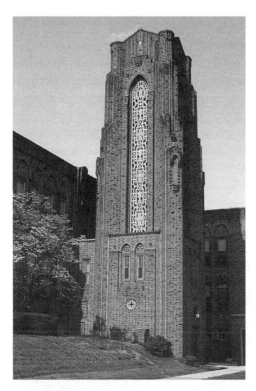

An Art Deco–influenced tower at a Catholic school built in 1930.

and Jewish leadership to manage private philanthropy overseas. They helped foreign refugees, many of them Jews, to find placement.

In the Catholic community, the teachings of the 1891 encyclical *Rerum Novarum* had articulated a concern for the worker and the poor—a concern reflected in Catholic activism for several decades. Perhaps the most famous manifestation of this social concern came in the Catholic Worker movement, founded in the 1930s by Dorothy Day and Peter Maurin. This group's Houses of Hospitality provided religious, economic, and social support for struggling workers in major cities. The group's publication, *The Catholic Worker*, became a mouthpiece for a liberal Catholic advocating of pacifism and labor reform.

Beyond the isolated work of the Catholic Worker movement, Catholics found a bit of fame and notoriety in other ways. One individual in particular, Father John Ryan, worked extensively with the National Conference of Catholic Charities and American Federation of Catholic Societies to improve labor conditions in the name of the dignity of the human person. When Pope Pius XI issued the encyclical *Quadragesimo Anno* recognizing the fortieth anniversary of *Rerum Novarum* in 1931, American Catholics found vindication for their commitment to religious social reform in America.

WORLD WAR II

All of the reform, revival, and conflict of American religious life in the interwar years would move to the backburner as the nation once again mobilized for a national war effort. Theologically many religious bodies turned to the morality of war itself as a pertinent question for the time. In the years following World War I, many of the American churches, and the nation as a whole, entered a period of self-examination and repentance. The virulent patriotism with which most Americans, and even most American churches supported the war caused many, in retrospect, to question the conflation of religious and political ideas. As World War II would show, this pattern was to be repeated.

Nevertheless, in the interwar years, the Great Depression heightened the feelings of disillusionment already prevalent among Americans when they thought of the war. Church leaders throughout the country condemned their own actions as well as those of the Christian community in general in having allowed themselves to become caught up in the war craze at the expense of Christian values. A pacifist sentiment prevailed.

As World War II came to a head, it was clear that not only was American involvement necessary, but also that the horrors of Hitler and Nazi Germany necessitated a religious response. The staunch pacifism advocated by most of the nation's denominations soon morphed into an enthusiasm and passion rivaling that of World War I. The rhetoric of the nation's leaders frequently used religious language to garner support—casting Japanese and Germans as devils and elevating the nation as an agent of the good and holy. The conflation of pacifist leanings with passionate convictions about this particular war led to

This photo of starving prisoners in the Mauthausen-Gusen concentration camp in Austria was taken by the U.S. Army's 80th Division, which liberated the camp on May 5, 1945.

a period of rich theological discussion and development, including the emergence of Christian Realism and Neo-Orthodoxy.

The attack on Pearl Harbor led to a dramatic change in religious sentiment about the war and a period of intense support of American involvement that would continue throughout the war years. Demonization of Japanese in both political and religious rhetoric led to mobilization of support and, later, rather conflicted and reserved reactions to the use of atomic bombs in Japan. Support for the war led many Christian churches in particular to support religious life overseas and with the troops, and pooled resources to dramatically increase the number of chapels and chaplains overseas.

Surprisingly, the Holocaust—the most notable religiously charged event of the war, received relatively little attention in America during the war. Whether this was simply due to governmental ignorance of the events taking place, or willful selectivity in dealing with a religious minority, religious and political publications and addresses were virtually devoid of mention of the Holocaust. Once Hitler's atrocities became clear, Americans found it easier than ever to compare Hitler to the devil, further advocating swift and decisive American action. In retrospect, Americans have questioned the extent to which the government did all it could have and whether American religious bodies spoke out as virulently as they should have. World War II and the Holocaust obviously had a significant impact on American Jews, many of whom had close relatives and friends die as a result of these events. In the wake of the war and the establishment of the state of Israel in 1948, an upsurge in Jewish self-consciousness and participation in activities occurred, but no real increase in synagogue attendance came until after the war. Even among American Jews, controversy ensued as to the extent to which the Jewish-American population had appropriately responded to the horrors of the Holocaust. New strands of Jewish literature, poetry, and other art expressions developed as Jews sought to understand and heal from the Holocaust tragedy.

CONCLUSION

After the war American Christianity faced a sense of regret at its militaristic embracing of American foreign policy similar to that of World War I, and many articulated pacifist philosophies once again. Moreover each religious community faced the challenge of welcoming home their soldier sons and ministering to their unique needs as veterans. Also echoing the effects of World War I, American religious groups demonstrated a renewed level of cooperation after having weathered the storm of war together. Within each religion and denomination came a renewal of piety, spurred by reflections on the wars and an increase in attendance and membership in religious bodies.

Having proven their loyalty through enthusiastic participation in both wars, American Catholics were able to back down from a defensive posture and develop a more mature, settled presence in the United States. With the publication of Thomas Merton's *The Seven Story Mountain* in 1948, an increased interest in monasticism, piety, and the contemplative life arose among the spiritual elite. Catholic scholars and theologians began to develop a distinctly American Catholic theology, as exemplified by the work of John Tracy Ellis and John Courtney Murray. The laity experienced increased religious enthusiasm and participation in the church. Such participation was encouraged by then Pope Pius XII, who increasingly stressed the role of the laity in Church work, and would be further emphasized in Vatican II. Among everyday American Catholics, nonliturgical devotions grew in popularity such as devotions to Our Lady of Fatima and to favorite saints such as St. Ann or St. Jude.

This renewal in Catholicism and the various trends of mourning and renewal in Judaism signaled a new era in American religion. Fueled by the unity that came through negotiating the difficulties and challenges of World War II, religions began to coexist more peacefully. Nativists and others could no longer claim America as a land of Protestants with unwelcome immigrant visitors. Rather the nation had become a diverse religious landscape and would only continue to become more so. This pluralistic demographic would become more salient in the 1950s as the nation's religious communities united against communism. Though new and different conflicts would arise, the land of immigrants had, through the experience of economic depression and war, found a level of unity in diversity.

ANN W. DUNCAN

Further Readings

Alhstrom, Sydney E. *A Religious History of the American People.* New Haven and London: Yale University Press, 1972.
Cavert, Samuel McCrea. *The American Churches in the Ecumenical Movement, 1900–1968.* New York: Association Press, 1968.
Day, Dorothy. *The Long Loneliness.* Chicago, IL: Saint Thomas More Press, 1993.
Flynn, George Q. *American Catholics and the Roosevelt Presidency, 1932–1936.* Lexington, KY: University of Kentucky Press, 1968.
Halsey, William M. *The Survival of American Innocence: Catholicism in an Era of Disillusionment, 1920–1940.* Notre Dame, IN: University of Notre Dame Press, 1980.
Lincoln, C. Eric. *The Black Muslims in America.* Grand Rapids, MI: W.B. Eerdmans, 1994.
McDannell, Colleen. *Picturing the Faith: Photography and the Great Depression.* New Haven, CT: Yale University Press, 2004.
Meyer, Donald B. *The Protestant Search for Political Realism, 1919–1941.* Berkeley and Los Angeles, CA: University of California Press, 1960.
Miller, William. *Dorothy Day: A Biography.* New York: Harper & Row, 1982.
Nichols, J. Bruce. *The Uneasy Alliance: Religion, Refugee Work and U.S. Foreign Policy.* New York: Oxford University Press, 1988.
Niebuhr, Reinhold. *Moral Man and Immoral Society.* New York: Scribner, 1932.
Piehl, Mel. *Breaking Bread: The Catholic Worker and the Origin of Catholic Radicalism in America.* Philadelphia, PA: Temple University Press, 1982.
Simon, Julius, ed. *History, Religion and Meaning: American Reflections on the Holocaust and Israel.* Westport, CT: Greenwood Press, 2000.
Sittser, Gerald L. *A Cautious Patriotism: The American Churches and the Second World War.* Chapel Hill, NC: The University of North Carolina Press, 1992.
Warren, Donald. *Radio Priest: Charles Coughlin, the Father of Hate Radio.* New York: Free Press, 1996.
Warren, Heather A. *Theologians of a New World Order: Reinhold Niebuhr and the Christian Realists, 1920–1948.* New York: Oxford University Press, 1997.

Chapter 8

Education

"Education is the mother of leadership."
—Wendell Wilkie

THE DECADES BETWEEN the Great Depression and World War II were turbulent and fraught with instability. Public education, though a priority in the country, took many hits as the Depression began to tighten its grip on the pocketbooks of the country. President Roosevelt used the reaches of the federal government to create organizations like the Civilian Conservation Corps (CCC), Works Progress Administration (WPA), and National Youth Administration (NYA), that worked in a manner that was parallel to educational institutions. This created an opportunity for the restructuring of and experimentation with education in America. The need for intervention on the behalf of African Americans and those who were disadvantaged was necessary during the depths of the Depression, not only due to economic woes, but also to social inequities.

Progressive educators were implementing the theories of John Dewey, an American philosopher and psychologist who influenced the very nature of education by focusing on pragmatism and the concept that children should be allowed to develop freely. Freedom and exploration with reflection would lead to inquiry and higher levels of learning. In addition, Dewey viewed education as a manner of promoting democracy as an equalizer for the masses. Though Dewey's theories were widely touted as revolutionary, many teachers resisted the change in structure from teacher-centered instruction to student-centered

107

A Typical Day for School Children

Schools of the era were typically constructed by community members to serve as both the local school and the church building. Many of the one-room schools that were in service in the 1930s were built in the earlier decades when supplies and labor were limited. In rural areas, a single building was used to educate students from grades one through eight. Rural areas did not always have access to indoor plumbing, relying on an outhouse instead. More populated areas may have had a central building, dedicated solely to academics, which had classrooms for each grade or grade group. The building was filled with wooden desks that were constructed as a single seat with a table attached to the back of the seat. The student behind would situate their seat so that it fit under the table of the desk they were facing. This configuration was usually repeated in rows on either side of a central heating unit. In one-room buildings, the heating unit was a wood or coal burning stove in the center of the room that had to be lit about an hour before students were to arrive. Populated areas with divided grades had access to more modern facilities and central heat sources. Students faced the front of the school room that typically had a large wooden desk for the teacher and a large blackboard. Students used individual slate boards to work on assignments at their desks, with the teacher traveling from group to group to review their work.

The day started with the ringing of a large bell affixed to the top of the school building. This bell was used to encourage students who were on their way to quickly report to the front of the building. A few minutes later, the teacher would emerge from the building and ring a hand bell that signified the start of the school day. Students lined up in order of age and filed into the room to stand by their desks and wait quietly for the morning activities to begin. The day would start with the students reciting the *Pledge of Allegiance*, singing, and moral lessons that relied heavily on the use of the Bible as a teaching tool. The remainder of the morning was focused on literacy activities. The day began with students reading aloud from their text at the appropriate level. Students would then be given a passage to memorize and recite to the teacher. Spelling and writing were practiced by repetitive writing on individual slates. The students were encouraged to focus on penmanship in addition to their writing and spelling drills.

Students typically had one hour for lunch and recreation. Most often, students brought their lunches from home in small pails. Lunches were cold and could consist of a biscuit left from breakfast, and a piece of ham or other cured and cooked meat. Lunch was taken in the school yard, weather permitting, where students could socialize and play. Games included kick the can, tag, baseball or stick ball, and fetch the bacon. Schools that could raise the funds purchased equipment like balls, or community-constructed equipment like seesaws and swings. When the school day resumed, the focus was then on geography, arithmetic, and history.

By the 1930s, every state had made school attendance compulsory up to age 16. This boy was attending a rural school in Williams County, North Dakota, in the winter of 1937.

learning. This was partly because the structure of schools, as well as the demands of the job were such that the teacher-centered approach helped the teacher ensure that students were learning what they needed to learn prior to promotion to the next grade.

Texts in the classroom centered around American culture and were written not only to teach students how to read or write, but also how to function in American society. Texts were filled with images of American heroes and passages from the Bible as well as American literature. Both the student's academic and moral virtues were targeted for development.

EDUCATION DURING THE DEPRESSION

The years after the Wall Street stock market crash of 1929 led to dramatic changes in the educational arena. Public education was funded by taxes and tuition, and both were hard to come by. To conserve funds, school terms were shortened to five months and by 1935, new teachers in some areas received an average of $40 per month for those five months of service, and per pupil expenditures dropped to just $78 per student. Teachers would not see a substantial increase in pay until the teacher shortages during the World War II era. In addition to clothing and shoes, parents had to furnish textbooks and supplies for their children. When parents could not find funding for those items, the children were not allowed to attend.

Many school districts were forced to declare themselves insolvent and closed their doors. States were forced to intervene. Due to the disparity in funding between affluent and poor districts, states were forced to mandate a minimum level of economic support for each district as a condition of receiving monies from the state. The federal government provided financial relief through a series of legislative acts that were designed to aid schools during financial instability.

SCHOOL REFORM

School reform in the previous era centered around concepts of social justice and social service. Because of the large number of immigrant students that were matriculating, the very nature of both the curriculum and the concept of assimilation were at the forefront of most debates. Those who were cultural outsiders, women and African Americans for example, were increasingly represented within the populations of schools, creating a focus on the need to cope with diverse issues.

One particularly heated debate revolved around schools becoming agents for assimilation or separation. By 1930, more than three million children had immigrated to the United States. Schools that had a focus on educating a diverse student body concentrated on creating one population that shared the same culture. Those who were immigrants or from culturally diverse backgrounds learned how to shed their cultural identities and conform to the norms that made up American existence. Those who favored separation based their position on the argument that children from certain cultures were so diverse that they would be better served in an educational setting that was tailored to their cultural and academic needs. Unfortunately this type of education generally reinforced the concept that students would remain segregated in their adult lives, living in segregated neighborhoods, working in segregated environments, and coexisting with other cultures only when forced. These students were regarded as culturally and academically inferior and not considered candidates for assimilation. Schools evolved into organizations with two major focuses, one to assimilate the majority of the population, and one to segregate the remainder of the population, which consisted of children of Mexican, Native-American, or African descent.

This *Marx Deluxe toy typewriter was made in 1930, around the time of a growing focus on vocational training.*

The Lemon Grove Incident

The Lemon Grove incident was the first challenge to segregation within schools. Because of the agrarian nature of Lemon Grove, California, it was a perfect place for Mexican Americans to settle and find work. Initially the school board began discussions about segregating students based on cultural heritage in 1930. The school board was determined to allow Anglo-American students to attend Lemon Grove Grammar School, a modern educational facility that was supported by state and local funds, including local taxes paid by all citizens. The Olive Street School was designed for Mexican-American students. Regardless of the nationality of the students, the vast majority of whom were U.S. nationals, all students labeled "Mexican" were sent to the segregated school. The Olive Street School was a converted barn that was on the "Mexican" side of town. In the era of schools that were designed for the purpose of Americanization of foreign-born students, Lemon Grove was no anomaly.

The parents of students with Mexican ties staunchly opposed the segregation. However, on January 5, 1931, Anglo-American students were permitted to enter the Lemon Grove Grammar School, while Mexican students were not allowed to enter the building. The Mexican students were sent to the converted barn on Olive Street for their education. Parents were outraged that their students were sent away, and viewed the education that their children would receive at Olive Street as inferior to that of Lemon Grove Grammar School students. Parents formed the Neighborhood Association of Lemon Grove to fight the injustice. Many parents made a difficult choice: if their children could not attend Lemon Grove Grammar, they would not attend any school. This caused much unrest within the community, and resistance led to the deportation of some families back to Mexico, including the children who were American citizens.

The deportations incited further outrage among the Neighborhood Association. The Mexican consulate was contacted, and though the consulate could offer no direct intervention, it did offer the use of an attorney. Roberto Alvarez filed suit against the Lemon Grove School Board in 1931 in the landmark case of *Roberto Alvarez v. The Lemon Grove School Board*.

The ruling was in favor of Roberto Alvarez and the Mexican-American students: the courts found that the separation was a violation of the students' rights as U.S. citizens. According to the courts, Mexican students were considered Caucasian according to the laws that legally segregated African-American and Native-American students into Americanization schools. Therefore, the Mexican-American students could not be denied socialization with Anglo-American students at the Lemon Grove Grammar School. The School Board was ordered to immediately let the Mexican-American students return to the Lemon Grove School. This case paved the way for future cases based on segregation of students like *Brown v. Board of Education*.

A teacher in a rural school in Wisconsin in September 1939. By 1937 at least one year of college-level study was required in order to obtain a teaching position.

African Americans were not the only targets for separation, Mexican Americans in the Southwest and Native Americans in various parts of the country were also considered entirely too different to assimilate. Mexican schools in California used no entrance testing, but were created as vocational schools because of the belief that this was the potential of the population. In fact, two-thirds of Mexican-American students were classified as slow learners or mentally challenged because of language barriers and placed into vocational programs.

Highly subjective intelligence tests were used to determine IQ levels and a student's educational track. In addition to subjective IQ tests, students were subjected to culturally biased standardized tests to determine their scholastic aptitude. The Scholastic Aptitude Test was initially administered in 1926, but grew in popularity and was widely used in the 1930s and 1940s. Students began to face career tracking and schools evolved from being thought of as education for knowledge's sake to being considered stepping stones for future employment. Even the military implemented the use of testing to determine the best placement for soldiers during World War II. Soldiers who were deemed to have performed at lower levels were sent to more dangerous combat positions, and those who were deemed to have performed at higher levels were given assignments further from direct combat.

Though the dividing line was clear between assimilation and separation, there were two liberal reformers who rebelled against the notion that cultures had to completely segregate themselves. John Dewey and Jane Addams believed that a blending of cultures and a sharing of perspectives would be beneficial both to educational institutions and to the larger American society. They wanted a more moderate approach to blending foreign-born populations into a cohesive society that was not deprived of a rich cultural heritage. This moderate view, pluralism, asserted that all students would learn the common culture, but other cultures were celebrated, rather than eradicated.

TEACHER PREPARATION

By the early 1930s a focus on teacher qualification became clear, and a renewed interest in teacher quality was kindled. Though 25 percent of teachers in the late 1920s did not have higher than a high school diploma, by 1937 at least one year of college-level study was required in order to obtain a teaching position. In 1940 more changes to the certification of teachers arrived with the development of the National Teacher Examination by the Cooperative Testing Service, which was designed to ensure a minimum level of content and pedagogical knowledge for new licensees. This was partially due to a comparative study of student academic performance, and a teacher surplus that occurred during the Great Depression. Interest in teacher certification grew and mechanisms to select more qualified faculty were established. Theoretically, only the most highly qualified candidates would receive teaching positions. Compounding the issues of academic performance of students and the teacher surplus was the perception that teacher preparation programs at Normal Colleges were not academically stringent enough to promote only the most qualified candidates, placing substandard faculty in classrooms.

Since the growing population was entering schools in record numbers, divisions had been made between elementary level, junior high, and high school facilities. Teachers in almost half of the states, 21, were being issued junior high level certificates and just over half the states, 36, were issuing high school certifications. All states were issuing elementary certificates by 1930. Prior to applying for a license to teach, an educator did not have to possess a formal degree from a college, but was required to have taken courses in pedagogy, educational history,

A Girl Scout handbook from 1934.

The G.I. Bill

In 1944, Congress passed the controversial Servicemen's Readjustment Act in order to repay 16 million returning veterans for their service. The G.I. Bill allotted veterans up to $500 each for tuition, books, student fees, and training costs, and provided veterans with a small monthly living allowance. In the past, only rich Americans had been able to afford to attend colleges and universities. Don Balfour, a former corporal who had already enrolled at George Washington University in the nation's capital, became the first veteran to qualify for educational funding under the new bill. In the fall of 1945, General Omar Bradley announced that 119,641 applications for admission to American colleges had been filed, and 22,007 veterans were attending institutions of higher learning. Some 104,602 applications for vocational training had been submitted, and 16,102 veterans were currently receiving such training. By 1951, 7.8 million American veterans had attended college or received vocational, business, or agricultural training through the G.I. Bill.

When signing the bill on June 22, 1944, President Franklin Roosevelt acknowledged that American veterans had "been compelled to make greater economic sacrifice and every other kind of sacrifice than the rest of us, and are entitled to definite action to help take care of their special problems." American artist Norman Rockwell depicted the typical academic G.I. as Willie Gillis, who appeared on the cover of the *Saturday Evening Post* on October 5, 1946. Gillis was sprawled in the window of his college dorm smoking a pipe and studying. Rockwell's deft brush strokes revealed that Gillis was more mature and more self-assured than the pre-war college student. While some veterans entered the college life of partying and booze with enthusiasm, others remained aloof. Hazing became a contentious subject on some campuses when veterans refused to participate in fraternity traditions.

and legal issues in education. It would not be until 1950 that the majority of states, 37 in all, would begin requiring teachers to possess a four-year degree from a college or university prior to obtaining a teaching license.

SCHOOL STRUCTURE AND CURRICULUM

Students were held to a high standard, which included both curricular and behavioral goals. Within the structure of formal, traditional education, students were expected to memorize and recite their lessons rather than explore options and seek solutions that were meaningful. The teacher-centered approach assisted the teacher in holding students accountable for their knowledge, and was more easily demonstrated in testing situations. John Dewey's child-centered approach focused on learning by doing and investigating the world. Students exercised their bodies and their minds, which led to a curriculum that focused on educating the whole student, rather than just the mind.

Schools began to adopt a work-study-play curricular focus. Progressive schools also included programs on hygiene, health education, and services in order to better meet the needs of students and as an attempt to address social problems. Alternatively private schools of the era were predominantly religious, with the vast majority of students enrolled in Roman Catholic schools.

As a result of a more student-centered approach to the curriculum within public schools, and as a result of the expanding need for more specialized teachers, students began to change classes and investigate vocations in addition to the standard curriculum within the school day. Teachers who were more specialized in a single field were able to serve as experts to the increasing numbers of students who were attending schools and entering secondary schools.

By the 1930s, all states required compulsory attendance until age 16. Enrollment began increasing in the late 1920s, and grew further in the early 1930s, when children stayed in school in order to leave scarce jobs open for adults during the Great Depression. As a result, many school systems were adopting a middle or junior high school level of study for students. By 1945, 45 percent of all students were graduating high school.

The Bishop McDevitt Catholic high school was built in 1930 in Harrisburg, Pennsylvania. In the 1930s, school enrollment increased because of new state and federal laws and the lack of jobs.

Schools of the era were organized into elementary, grades one through six, junior high, grades seven through nine, and high school, grades 10 through 12. This made the population of each school more manageable, and overcrowding was less of a concern. This grouping remained dominant for three decades.

As schools themselves began to expand, their governance structures also became more complex. Local boards of education began to give some of their authority to superintendents, who delegated to increasing numbers of administrative personnel. Teachers began to feel that their voices were not being heard and increasingly found it a struggle to make their opinions known.

CONCLUSION

The federal government became increasingly involved in public education as a result of both the Depression and World War II. State and local governmental agencies remained in control of education, but the federal government began to intervene more. One example of this intervention was the creation of the G.I. Bill in 1944 that helped veterans returning from World War II go to college. This helped lead to a growing level of college education in the population, and schools benefitted as well from the infusion of money and larger enrollments. But even more dramatic changes in education after this period would be related to the ongoing tension over whether schools should work toward assimilation or continued segregation of minority populations. Federal government intervention in the desegregation of schools in the years to follow would soon eclipse its involvement in the 1930s and 1940s.

CARLISE WOMACK-WYNNE

Further Readings

Brinkley, Alan. *The Unfinished Nation: A Concise History of the American People*. New York: McGraw Hill, 2004.
Department of Veterans Affairs. "GI-Bill History." Available online: http://www.gibill.va.gov/GI_Bill_Info/history.htm. Accessed October 2008.
Jeynes, William H. *American Educational History: School, Society, and the Common Good*. Thousand Oaks, CA: SAGE, 2007.
Kirk, Samuel, et al. *Educating Exceptional Children*. New York: Houghton Mifflin, 2006.
Living History Farm. "The G.I. Bill." Available online: http://www.living historyfarm.org/farminginthe40s/life_20.html. Accessed October 2008.
Lucas, Christopher J. *Teacher Education in America: Reform Agendas for the Twenty-First Century*. New York: Martin's Press, 1999.

Martin, David J. and Kimberly S. Loomis. *Building Teachers: A Constructivist Approach to Introducing Education*. Belmont, CA: Thompson Wadsworth, 2007.

Mcelvaine, R. S. *The Great Depression: America 1929–1941*. New York: Random House, 1993.

Nelson, Jack L., et al. *Critical Issues in Education: Dialogues and Dialectics*. New York: McGraw Hill, 2004.

Newman, J. *America's Teachers*. Boston, MA: Pearson, 2006.

Rothbard, M.N. *America's Great Depression*. Auburn, AL: Ludwig von Mises Institute, 2000.

Ryan, Kevin and James M. Cooper. *Those Who Can, Teach*. New York: Houghton Mifflin, 2003.

Sadker, D.M., et al. *Teachers, Schools, and Society*. New York: McGraw Hill, 2008.

Shlaes, A. *The Forgotten Man: A New History of the Great Depression*. New York: Harper Collins, 2007.

Singer, Dorothy G. and Tracey A. Revenson. *A Piaget Primer: How a Child Thinks*. New York: Penguin, 2006.

Smiley, G. *Rethinking the Great Depression*. Chicago, IL: Ivan Dee, 2002.

Spring, Joel. *The American School, 1642–1996*. White Plains, NY: Longman, 1997.

Suarez-Orozco, Marcelo and Mariela Paez, eds. *Latinos Remaking America*. Berkeley, CA: University of California Press, 2002.

Chapter 9

Science and Technology

*"Concern for man and his fate must always form the
chief interest of all technical endeavors."*
—Albert Einstein

BY 1929 AMERICAN science and technology had reached a new level of competence. Americans had won the Nobel Prize in physics in 1923 and 1927, signaling that American science was fully mature. Whereas in an earlier era American scientists had looked to Europe for leadership, by the late 1920s they generated their own ideas and pursued their own research. They conducted research in a variety of settings: universities, foundations, and government agencies. They founded organizations to foster the diffusion of research findings, especially through peer-reviewed journals. The American Association for the Advancement of Science, for example, was a generic organization that admitted scientists of every discipline and published the journal *Science*, which welcomed papers in all branches of science. The specialization of science in the 20th century also led scientists to form organizations that limited their membership to the practitioners of a single discipline, such as the American Society of Agronomy, the American Association of Economic Entomologists, and the American Phytopathological Society, all of which published their own specialized journals.

Not only did scientists conduct research at universities, they trained the next generation of scientists on campus. Choosing a faculty member as a mentor, the scientist-in-training developed a program of original research in graduate school. Graduate school marked the transition from student

119

to professional scientist. In addition to communicating among themselves through peer-review research, scientists sought to communicate among a wide audience. A holdover from the 19th century, the public lecture aimed to kindle an interest in science among laymen. The Cooperative Extension Service of the land-grant colleges may have been the largest scientific effort in America to reach a wide audience, in this case farmers. Americans also learned about science through newspaper and radio journalism. The Scopes Trial of 1925 demonstrated that science could make headlines nationwide, while highlighting the uneasy relationship American science had with religion.

BASIC AND APPLIED SCIENCE
By 1929 American science had coalesced into two types: basic and applied. Basic science aimed to advance knowledge irrespective of its utility. The determination of the speed of light had no utility (at the time) and so was basic science. On the other hand, the breeding of a variety of corn resistant to the European corn borer was applied research. By its nature, applied research aimed to advance useful knowledge. Several historians have noted the applied character of much of American science.

In this context American scientists were eager to couple science and technology. This line of reasoning placed basic science at one end of a continuum, and technology at the other end. The funding of basic science yielded technology at the other end of the pipeline, emphasized scientists. Science and technology do not, however, work this way. Basic science yields knowledge, not technology. The link is closer between applied science, engineering, and technology.

Several universities sought in the 1930s and 1940s to further applied science with the aim of advancing technology. The Case Institute of Technology, the California Institute of Technology, and the Massachusetts Institute of Technology were the most notable of the universities that linked applied science, engineering, and technology. The North Carolina Agricultural and Technical College aimed to advance the agricultural sciences and technology. The agricultural sciences were the applied sciences par excellence in America. The link between the agricultural sciences and technology was evident in the tractor, which transformed agriculture much as the automobile transformed transportation.

The success of American technology lay, as Henry Ford understood, in the coupling of the technique of mass production with the purchasing power of mass consumerism. By 1929 American technology was not only state of the art; it underpinned the economy. Several technologies were standard in the home: the telephone, vacuum cleaner, electric clock, radio, electric iron, and clothes washer. To judge by the automobile and the airplane alone, American technology was the envy of the world by 1929.

ASTRONOMY

The pursuit of astronomy in the United States made clear that not all American science was applied. Astronomy aimed to describe the cosmos; it did not seek useful knowledge. More than several other branches of science, astronomy depended on large budgets and sophisticated apparatuses. Even in 1929 the observatory, with its telescope, cost millions of dollars to build and thousands more to maintain. At one of these, the Lowell Observatory, astronomer Clyde Tombaugh discovered on February 18, 1930, the ninth and final planet of the solar system. Following the tradition of naming planets after the gods of classical mythology, the staff at the Lowell Observatory voted to name the planet Pluto, after the god of the underworld, and in keeping with the suggestion of an English girl. The first two letters of Pluto stand for Percival Lowell, the American astronomer who had predicted its existence in 1906. Recent controversy has undermined Pluto's status, as the International Astronomical Union now classifies Pluto as merely a dwarf planet, not a full planet.

Another important discovery of the early 1930s was made by the American radio engineer Karl Jansky while he was working at Bell Laboratories. While tracking down the source of some unidentified interference, he gradually determined that the origin of the radio waves he was picking up with an apparatus he had constructed was not the sun, as he had first thought, and which would have corresponded with earlier theories about potential radio waves emanating from celestial bodies, but instead was coming from outside the solar system from a source in the Milky Way. Bell soon took Janksy off the project, but his work was published in 1933 and received some attention, and other researchers picked it up again in later years, eventually carving out a new field of radio astronomy.

In 1938 astronomer Seth Nicholson at Mount Wilson Observatory discovered Jupiter's 10th and 11th moons. The 10th, Lysithea, and the 11th, Carme, are named after two lovers of Jupiter, the greatest of the gods. That year Walter Adam and Theodore Dunham, Jr., also at Mount Wilson Observatory, discovered that Venus's atmosphere is

An astro compass from the 1940s used for navigating by the stars.

This astronomy-themed ceiling was designed for the Forum Building in the Harrisburg, Pennsylvania, state capitol complex in 1931.

carbon dioxide. This discovery clarified why Venus is so hot. A greenhouse gas, carbon dioxide traps heat from sunlight in the form of infrared radiation, raising the temperature of the atmosphere. In 1939 Cornell University physicist Hans Bethe determined that the sun produces light and heat by fusion, the binding together of two elements to form one heavier element. The heavier element weighs slightly less than the sum of the weights of the two lighter elements. This fraction of mass converts to energy in accord with Albert Einstein's famous equation $E=mc^2$. Because the speed of light squared is 90 million billion meters per second squared, a tiny amount of mass yields enormous energy. Fusion heats the surface of the sun to 10,000 degrees Fahrenheit.

In the 1940s Walter Baade at the Mount Wilson and Mount Palomar Observatories divided stars into two categories. The first, which he called population I, were young stars whose luminosity tended toward blue in the visible spectrum. The second, which he called population II, were old stars with a luminosity that tended toward red. Stars, in effect, are color-coded. In dying, population II stars exploded, scattering matter that coalesced into new stars. New stars formed in areas of interstellar dust, the detritus of dead stars. The arms of spiral galaxies contain young stars. In the center of spiral galaxies are old stars. The center is bereft of interstellar dust, and long ago ceased to support the formation of new stars.

In 1940 George Washington University astronomer George Gamow advanced the Big Bang Theory. Astronomer Edwin Hubble had proposed that the universe was expanding, raising the question of what caused this expansion. Gamow theorized that the universe had begun as a massive, dense point of matter in the form of neutrons, protons, and electrons. All the matter in the universe had been compressed under tremendous pressure into a single minute ball. Heat and pressure overcame the forces of attraction, and the ball of matter exploded in all directions. This sudden expansion formed the universe. The current expansion of the universe is the aftermath of the original explosion. The Big Bang Theory gradually won out over other theories in the postwar era. Along with new techniques developed during the 1930s and 1940s, the theory underpinned astronomical research that continued for the rest of the 20th century.

THE AGRICULTURAL SCIENCES

The development of hybrid corn applied Austrian monk Gregor Mendel's hybridization of pea varieties to the science of crop breeding. The first step in making a hybrid was to reduce a variety of corn to a series of homozygous lines by inbreeding the variety. The homozygous lines were analogous to the pea varieties that Mendel used. The homozygous lines appeared to hold no promise. They had scrawny ears with little seeds, and sometimes were vulnerable to insects and diseases. But by crossbreeding these inbreds, the breeder got corn plants with hybrid vigor, just as Mendel had hybridized pea varieties. Hybrid corn yielded more than traditional varieties of corn and was more resistant to insects and diseases. Despite these advantages hybrid corn made slow progress at first. Farmers were accustomed to buying a variety of corn and saving seed from it to plant year after year. Hybrid corn did not work this way. Hybrids yielded well only in the first year, requiring farmers to buy new seed every year. The drought of the 1930s, however, underscored the value of hybrids. Whereas traditional varieties withered and died, hybrids stood erect on their thick stalks and survived the drought. Success brought farmers to hybrid corn. Sales grew steadily in the 1930s and early 1940s so that by 1943 farmers in the Corn Belt planted hybrids on 90 percent of acreage.

Another beneficiary of the drought of the 1930s was soil science. Hugh Bennett, a leading scientist and spokesman for soil science, worried that soil erosion might diminish the land's capacity to produce food. A member of the U.S. Department of Agriculture (USDA) Bureau of Soils, Bennett dreamed of a larger agency that would seek to conserve soil and thereby the land's productivity.

The dust storms of the 1930s, vivid proof that erosion cost farmers their topsoil, prompted action. In 1933 Congress gave Bennett his agency, creating the Soil Erosion Service with a budget of $5 million. Congress placed the Soil Erosion Service in the Department of the Interior, however, an odd choice given that the soil erosion experiment stations were in the USDA. Bennett thought the USDA the natural home of the Soil Erosion Service. In 1935 Congress replaced the Soil Erosion Service with the Soil Conservation Service and placed it in the USDA. By 1939 the Soil Conservation Service had its scientists working to preserve soil on 88 million acres.

The development of new insecticides was a third achievement of the agricultural sciences. In 1939 Swiss chemical company J. R. Geigy discovered that dichlorodiphenyltrichloroethane (DDT) had the properties of an insecticide. But DDT was a new type of insecticide. It did not matter whether an insect ingested DDT as was necessary with the older generation of insecticides. Merely by contacing DDT an insect was poisoned. Moreover DDT remained potent for weeks and even months, requiring farmers to apply DDT less often than they had applied the previous generation of insecticides. The USDA acquired a sample of DDT in 1942. In turn the USDA gave samples of DDT to the agricultural colleges and experiment stations. Eager to impress farmers, agricultural scientists sprayed DDT throughout barns. Farmers toured these barns, amazed not to see any insects. Farmers distributed DDT by airplane and by tractor sprayers.

In the days of DDT popularity some scientists and farmers jettisoned other methods of insect control. The Nebraska Agricultural Experiment Station called on farmers to practice monoculture and thereby to abandon crop rotation, a traditional means of controlling the western corn rootworm. Instead scientists urged farmers to kill the rootworm with DDT. The success of DDT led scientists to seek other insecticides and between 1945 and 1953 agricultural chemists developed more than 20 new insecticides.

The era of DDT was short-lived. In 1944 two entomologists discovered that because DDT killed all types of insects, it killed the predators of mites. Its natural enemy dead, the population of mites increased rapidly in apple orchards. Around the same time scientists discovered that some insects were resistant to DDT. This phenomenon caught farmers off guard, but it was predictable given the mech-

Community-run refrigerators, part of cooperative rural electrification projects in the 1940s, helped reduce spoilage of meats and farm products.

anism of natural selection. An insect that, by the luck of the genetic draw, metabolizes DDT rather than is poisoned by it will survive to leave offspring, whereas insects that cannot metabolize DDT die without leaving offspring. In only a few generations the population of resistant insects will become very large. If DDT was no longer effective farmers would need to substitute other insecticides. Consequently farmers found themselves spraying more insecticides more frequently. The goal of an insect-free farm cost farmers money and time. Scientists could not develop new insecticides fast enough to keep pace with changes in insect populations.

ADVANCES IN BIOLOGY

By the 1930s and 1940s the biological sciences had benefitted from an increase in biology education in high schools and other institutions. Advances were made in biochemistry as a number of crucial techniques were developed. Molecular biology became a recognized field in the late 1930s, and in 1943 Oswald Avery, working at the Rockefeller Institute for Medical Research, determined that deoxyribonucleic acid (DNA) carried genetic information in cells, rather than proteins, paving the way for the next generation of discoveries about DNA in the 1950s.

Meanwhile, evolutionary biologists in the United States made important strides as well by focusing on the spread of genes through a population as a way of measuring the rate of evolution. In 1937 evolutionary biologist Ernst Mayr at the American Museum of Natural History concentrated his research on tiny populations of organisms. Given enough time, a mutation will occur in a population of organisms. If the mutation helps an organism survive and mate, the mutation will spread to offspring. The progeny, having the mutation, will likewise thrive and multiply. Mayr understood that an advantageous mutation would spread rapidly through a tiny population. This population of organisms, its genome enhanced by the mutation, may spread beyond its niche, displacing organisms that did not have the mutation. By spreading to other niches, the once-small population will grow large. Evolution need not be the gradual process Darwin had supposed. It can be rapid, as it was for the small population of organisms with an advantageous mutation. Once a population grows large, Mayr understood, the rate of evolution slows, as a mutation, no matter how advantageous, is unlikely to spread through the entire population. Evolution does not therefore proceed at a uniform rate.

A founder of population genetics, Sewall Wright pursued research similar to that of Mayr. Collaborating with evolutionary biologist Theodosius Dobrzhansky, Wright published five papers between 1941 and 1947 on genetic variability within a species of fruit fly. Wright used mathematical equations to describe gene frequencies, demonstrating the value of mathematical models in studying variations among organisms. Wright maintained that natural selection was only one of several mechanisms of evolution. Studying tiny pop-

Homo erectus

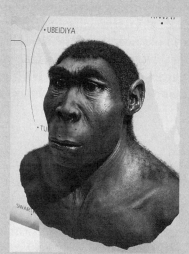

A model of Homo erectus, a hominid that populated Asia for more than one million years.

In 1927 the Rockefeller Foundation began funding the excavation of *Homo erectus* remains in Zhoukoudianzhen, a town near Peking (Bejing), China. From 1934 to 1941, University of Chicago anatomist Franz Weidenreich took charge of the expedition and under his leadership paleoanthropologists discovered the remains of 40 individuals. The number of skull fragments allowed anatomists to reconstruct the first *Homo erectus* skull and to estimate the size of its brain at 1,000 cubic centimeters, more than double the 450 cubic centimeters of the chimpanzee brain and only 350 cubic centimeters shy of the modern human brain.

Other than Neanderthal Man, *Homo erectus* was the earliest hominid found. *Homo erectus* evolved in Africa roughly 1.8 million years ago, probably from *Homo ergaster*. *Homo erectus* did not remain in Africa, as had all previous species of hominid, but was the first to migrate to new lands. The discoverer of Asia, *Homo erectus* settled large areas of the continent. The inhabitant of tropical regions, *Homo erectus*, as is true of modern humans, was adapted to warm weather. Its stout bones supported large muscles, suggesting that *Homo erectus* may have been larger and stronger than modern humans.

The presence of stone implements was the long awaited evidence that *Homo erectus* made tools, and the presence of hearths the first evidence that it used fire. The remains of animal bones suggested that *Homo erectus* hunted and therefore must have had a social structure and the foresight to organize and plan hunts. Some paleoanthropologists suggest that *Homo erectus* was a scavenger, rather than a hunter, but this is the minority position. Perhaps *Homo erectus* hunted when game was plentiful and scavenged when it was not. Paleoanthropologists may never know whether *Homo erectus* had language. Surely individuals had some way of signaling their intentions to one another. *Homo erectus* survived more than one million years in Asia. By comparison, modern humans have been on Earth only about 100,000 years.

The excavation, so promising at the outset, ended in disaster. Weidenrich and his colleagues left China in 1941 as war escalated between China and Japan. Weidenrich intended to resume work after the war ended but he never got the opportunity. The remains of Peking Man were lost or destroyed during the war. All that remains are the plaster casts of the fossils.

ulations as Mayr had, Wright posited that the random fluctuation of genes might cause tiny populations to evolve.

Along with several evolutionary biologists from Britain, Mayr and Wright were architects of the Modern Synthesis, which unified the study of genetics with the study of whole organisms and plants. Natural selection, the primary mechanism of evolution, operates on the whole organism, rather than on a single gene or a group of genes. The whole organism is an assortment of genes, and a population of organisms is a larger aggregate of genes. The frequency of genes in a population changes over time, and it is this change that biologists call evolution.

The biological sciences reached a new level of sophistication and specialization in this era, and researchers established several new areas of study that would become more prominent in the years that followed.

COMPUTERS

In the 1930s and 1940s American scientists and engineers made advances in the design and operation of computers. In winter 1937 Iowa State College physicist John Atanasoff worked out the design of a computer capable of simultaneously solving 29 equations. Searching for the money to build this computer, he petitioned both the college's agronomy department, which wanted a machine that would quickly calculate the solution to problems, and the Research Corporation of New York City. With more than $5,000 in grants, Atanasoff and graduate student Clifford Berry built their computer, the Atanasoff-Berry Computer or ABC, in the basement of the physics building. Building and testing a prototype first, they completed the full-scale computer in 1942. In the era before miniaturization computers were large. The ABC was no exception. Weighing more than 700 pounds, it had 280 vacuum tubes and was the size of a desk. In performing calculations the ABC used a binary code and electricity, as do contemporary computers, rather than wheels or switches that had to be operated by hand.

In June 1941 University of Pennsylvania physicist John Mauchly met John Atanasoff and examined the ABC, then under construction. Controversy clouds the question of whether Mauchly borrowed from the ABC in making the Electrical Numerical Integrator and Computer (ENIAC). Mauchly maintained he did not, but a court decided otherwise in 1973. On June 5, 1943, the U.S. Army's Ballistics Research Laboratory contracted the Moore School of Electrical Engineering at the University of Pennsylvania to build a computer capable of calculating artillery tables. With help from several faculty and students, John Mauchly and colleague J. Presper Eckert designed the ENIAC, completing it on February 14, 1946. Larger than the ABC, the ENIAC weighed 27 tons and had more than 17,000 vacuum tubes. The ENIAC could solve 5,000 addition and subtraction problems, nearly 400 multiplication problems, or 35 division problems or square roots per second.

John Vincent Atanasoff

Born in Hamilton, New York, on October 4, 1903, John Atanasoff grew up in Brewster, Florida. Early in childhood he displayed aptitude in mathematics. By age nine he could operate a slide rule. He completed high school in only two years. At the University of Florida he studied electrical engineering, graduating in 1925 with a B.S. and maintaining a perfect 4.0 average. Turning his attention to mathematics, Atanasoff entered Iowa State College for graduate study. Only one year after receiving his Bachelor's degree, Atanasoff earned an M.S. Changing schools again, in 1930 he received a Ph.D. in theoretical physics from the University of Wisconsin. Atanasoff returned to Iowa State, this time as an assistant professor of physics and mathematics. While at Iowa State, Atanasoff worked with a graduate student named Clifford Berry from 1939 to 1942 to build the Atanasoff-Berry computer, which would eventually be recognized as the world's first electronic-digital computer.

As did many scientists and engineers, Atanasoff pursued government research during World War II, and was to build a computer for the navy, but this part of his work was never funded. After the controversy over who would be recognized as the original inventor of the first electronic-digital computer (the ENIAC built by John Mauchly and J. Presper Eckert was the first to be patented), Atanasoff was finally acknowledged as such by a federal court in 1973. President George H.W. Bush awarded Atanasoff the National Medal of Technology on November 13, 1990. Atanasoff died in Maryland on June 15, 1995.

A model of the original Atanasoff-Berry computer, which used binary code and electricity, on display at Iowa State University.

The ENIAC computer, which was completed in February 1946 and weighed 27 tons, was originally built for a 1943 military contract made while the war was still in progress.

Harvard University physicist Howard Aiken designed the Mark I computer and assigned International Business Machines (IBM) the job of building it. IBM completed its work in February 1944 and delivered it to Harvard that August. At five tons the Mark I weighed in between the ABC and the ENIAC. The Mark I could store 72 numbers in its memory with each number up to 23 digits long. Slower than the ENIAC, the Mark I could solve three addition or subtraction problems per second. The Mark I could multiply two numbers in six seconds. It could divide two numbers in 15 seconds, and could plot a logarithm or trigonometric function in a minute. Aiken upgraded the computer, designing the Mark II in 1948 and the Mark III in 1949. The U.S. Navy purchased both computers, assigning them to the naval base at Dahlgren, Virginia. While the computers created in these years look far different from modern computers, the work done during this era laid an important foundation for computer science in the pivotal years of the 1950s and 1960s.

SCIENCE AND TECHNOLOGY DURING WORLD WAR II

Government agencies mobilized Americans in a variety of ways to fight World War II. Scientists and engineers were no exception, as the U.S. Army and Navy counted on their expertise in designing sophisticated weapons. President Franklin D. Roosevelt and engineer Vannevar Bush both approached World War II from their perspective of World War I. Both men believed that science and engineering could make a greater contribution to the war effort than they had in World War I. Bush believed that science and technology would best serve the nation by working independently of political machinations. Bush found allies in MIT president Karl Compton, Harvard president James B. Conant, and National Academy of Sciences president Frank Jewitt. With these men Bush formed the National Defense Research Committee in 1940 with the aim of overseeing the war work of scientists and engineers. Roosevelt put the committee under his control, making sure that developments in science and technology won his approval to go from planning to implementation. In 1941 Roosevelt established the Office of Scientific Research and Development, an agency that oversaw the work of Bush's National Defense Research Committee.

Perhaps the most momentous research that Roosevelt approved was the effort to build an atomic bomb. In 1934 Italian physicist Enrico Fermi bombarded uranium atoms with neutrons. Four years later German physicists Otto Hahn and Fritz Straussmann split uranium atoms by bombarding them with neutrons. The uranium atoms released energy in accord with Einstein's equation $E=mc^2$. Fermi, coming to the United States in 1938, and Hungarian-American physicist Leo Szilard both worried that Germany might build a uranium bomb. The United States, they concluded, must beat Germany in the race to build an atomic bomb; otherwise the Nazis would have the world's deadliest weapon. Fermi and Szilard urged Einstein to write a letter to Roosevelt, alerting him to the possibility that the Nazis might develop nuclear weapons. Whether Szilard or Einstein wrote the letter is a matter for debate, but the missive, written in 1939, carried Einstein's signature. The letter did not bring dramatic results. A few scientists working out of an office in Manhattan gave the project its name. Only with the Japanese attack on Pearl Harbor did Roosevelt give the Manhattan Project staff and money.

Under the oversight of the army, the Manhattan Project established a plutonium (like uranium, plutonium is fission-

This Norden bomb sight, an early analog computer that improved the accuracy of high-altitude bombing, was top secret during the war.

Einstein's Letter to Roosevelt

The 1930s witnessed a number of scientists coming to America seeking refuge from Nazi Germany. Many of these refugees grew increasingly apprehensive that Germany would develop a nuclear bomb in order to bring the war to a speedy conclusion. Albert Einstein was impressed upon in 1939 to write a letter to convince President Roosevelt of the necessity of a nuclear program. The letter, dated August 2, excerpted below, convinced President Roosevelt to establish a research committee within a month.

Some recent work by E. Fermi and L. Szilard, which has been communicated to me in manuscript, leads me to expect that Albert Einstein receiving his certificate of American citizenship on October 1, 1940.

the element uranium may be turned into a new and important source of energy in the immediate future. Certain aspects of the situation which has arisen seem to call for watchfulness and, if necessary, quick action on the part of the administration. I believe, therefore, that it is my duty to bring to your attention the following facts and recommendations.

In the course of the last four months it has been made probable—through the work of Joliot in France as well as Fermi and Szilard in America—that it may become possible to set up a nuclear chain reaction in a large mass of uranium, by which vast amounts of power and large quantities of new radium-like elements would be generated. Now it appears almost certain that this could be achieved in the immediate future.

This new phenomenon would also lead to the construction of bombs, and it is conceivable—though much less certain—that extremely powerful bombs of a new type may thus be constructed. A single bomb of this type, carried by boat and exploded in a port, might very well destroy the whole port together with some of the surrounding territory. However, such bombs might very well prove to be too heavy for transportation by air...

I understand that Germany has actually stopped the sale of uranium from the Czechoslovakian mines which she has taken over. That she should have taken such early action might perhaps be understood on the ground that the son of the German undersecretary of state, Von Weizsacker, is attached to the Kaiser-Wilhelm-Institut in Berlin, where some of the American work on uranium is now being repeated.

The atomic bomb's mushroom cloud over Nagasaki, Japan, on August 9, 1945.

able) reactor in Hanford, Washington, a gas-diffusion plant in Oak Ridge, Tennessee, and headquarters in Los Alamos, New Mexico, under the leadership of University of California physicist J. Robert Oppenheimer. At an underground laboratory in Chicago in 1942, Fermi controlled the first chain reaction of uranium atoms undergoing fission. Now all Fermi and the other physicists and engineers needed was enough uranium and plutonium to build three bombs. By July 1945 they had the bombs. Not sure that they would work, the team of physicists and engineers detonated one on July 16, 1945, at Alamogordo, New Mexico. The test succeeded and Oppenheimer described the light generated by the blast as "brighter than a thousand suns." Roosevelt's death left the decision whether to use the remaining two bombs to his successor, President Harry S Truman. With Germany defeated, Japan was the lone combatant. On August 6, 1945, a uranium bomb destroyed the Japanese city of Hiroshima. Three days later Nagasaki suffered the same fate. Japan surrendered August 10. Science and technology, many believed, had won the war.

SCIENCE, TECHNOLOGY, AND THE FEDERAL GOVERNMENT

The end of World War II did not signal an end to federal patronage of science and technology. Scientific and technological achievements during the war reinforced the importance of science and technology and forged a consensus that the federal government should continue to fund them in peacetime. At issue was the nature of science that government should fund. West Virginia Senator Harley Kilgore, perhaps gauging the mood of the public, asserted that Americans would gain more from the funding of applied science rather than basic research. In a democratic society everyone should derive value from scientific research. Science that benefited only specialists was elitist and undemocratic. The building of a new radio telescope, for example, benefited only radio astronomers and astrophysicists whereas the development of a new vaccine had the potential to benefit all Americans. Radio astronomy was basic science, which should be supported by the community of astronomers, not by the federal government. The new vaccine, however, merited government support because it promised to protect the masses from disease. The derivation of practical results for all citizens was the criterion by which government should judge science. The federal government should allocate resources to branches of science that democratized their results to benefit all. Kilgore, and Democrats in Congress like him, wanted to create a government agency that would advise the House and Senate on what areas of science to support. The creation of the National Science Foundation in 1950 would be the new agency Kilgore had sought. Not everyone shared Kilgore's enthusiasm. Some scientists, Vannevar Bush among them, were wary about growing government involvement in science policy. Politicians did not have the specialized training in science to be competent judges of the merits of science. Any agency that Congress would create should have scientists and not policymakers at the helm. Moreover, Bush, believing that practical results came from basic science, urged Congress to fund theoretical research.

CONCLUSION

In all their manifestations, U.S. science and technology emerged from the war with unprecedented prestige. One poll taken shortly after Japan's surrender suggested that Americans esteemed physicists more highly than people in any other profession. Thanks to their performance in the war, science and technology were in the mainstream of American culture. Increased government support in the 1950s and 1960s would only increase their visibility and influence.

CHRISTOPHER CUMO

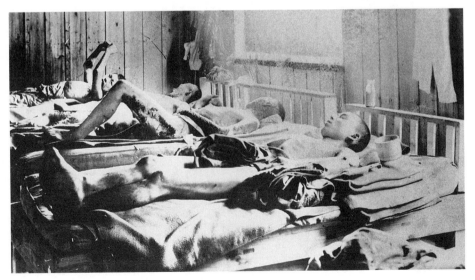

This photograph of survivors of the atomic bombing in Japan in 1945 only begins to suggest the human toll of the two atomic bombs dropped by the United States.

Further Readings

Cumo, Christopher. *Science and Technology in 20th Century American Life*. Westport, CT: Greenwood Press, 2007.

Grodzins, Morton and Eugene Rabinowitch, eds. *The Atomic Age Scientists in National and World Affairs*. New York: Basic Books, 1963.

Helms, Douglas. "Natural Resources Conservation Service Brief History." Available online: www.nrcs.usda.gov/about/history/articles/briefhistory.html. Accessed October 2007.

Jungk, Robert. *Brighter Than a Thousand Suns: The Story of the Men Who Made the Bomb*. New York: Grove Press, 1958.

Kevles, Daniel. *The Physicists: The History of a Scientific Community in Modern America*. Cambridge, MA: Harvard University Press, 1987.

Kleinman, Daniel Lee. *Politics on the Endless Frontier: Postwar Research Policy in the United States*. Durham, NC: Duke University Press, 1995.

Mayr, Ernst. *The Growth of Biological Thought: Diversity, Evolution, and Inheritance*. Cambridge, MA: Harvard University Press, 1982.

Perkins, John H. *Insects, Experts, and the Insecticide Crisis: The Quest for New Pest Management Strategies*. New York: Plenum Press, 1982.

Spencer, Donald D. *The Timetable of Computers: A Chronology of the Most Important People and Events in the History of Computers*. Ormand Beach, FL: Camelot Publishing Company, 1999.

Sprague, George F. and John W. Dudley, eds. *Corn and Corn Improvement*. Madison, WI: American Society of Agronomy, 1988.

Van Oosterzee, Penny. *Dragon Bones: The Story of Peking Man*. Cambridge, MA: Perseus Publishers, 2000.

Chapter 10

Entertainment and Sports

"We're in the money, the skies are sunny;
old man depression, you are through, you done us wrong!"
—Al Dubin

DURING THE 1920s the amount Americans spent on movies, dances, and other entertainments and sports tripled compared to the last decade. However, the stock market crash of 1929 marked a great change in the United States in both entertainment and sports. In the Great Depression, movie attendance declined as families struggled to meet even basic needs, and widespread unemployment ended the carefree extravagance associated with the Roaring Twenties. However, government programs arose to employ writers, musicians, photographers, and artists, and some created lasting works. World War II changed American culture yet again, bringing with it a profusion of new movies, big bands, and celebrities that greatly influenced American culture.

RADIO OF THE 1930s

Radio had been developing since 1887, when Heinrich Hertz proved radio waves could carry signals at the speed of light. By 1895 Guglielmo Marconi put this knowledge to practical use. By 1901 Marconi had transmitted radio messages across the Atlantic Ocean. In 1910 Lee DeForest broadcast from a lab, and in 1920 KDKA of Pittsburgh created America's first radio broadcast. By 1927 500 stations were broadcasting, and the Federal Radio Act (1927) established the Federal Radio Commission as part of the U.S. Department of

Commerce. By 1929 America's most popular radio show was *Amos 'n Andy*. Radio's influence spread further in the 1930s as electricity became increasingly accessible for American homes. In 1920 only 34.7 percent of American homes had electricity; by 1930 67.9 percent used electricity. Urban homes reflected a sharper rise, increasing from 47.4 percent of homes in 1920 to 84.8 percent in 1930. Frequency modulation (FM) was also developed in the late 1930s and provided signals that were less subject to interference.

During the Great Depression, radio was the principal means of media communications. In 1931 the Metropolitan Opera of New York began to broadcast its operatic performances. On Christmas day of that year they presented *Hansel and Gretel* by Engelbert Humperdinck. On February 26, 1934, the Federal Radio Act was superseded by the Communications Act that established the Federal Communications Commission to regulate the entire telecommunications industry, replacing the Federal Radio Commission.

Politicians used radio to great effect during the 1930s. It was crucial to Franklin D. Roosevelt's presidency from 1933 to 1945. He had even used radio during his governorship of New York. On March 12, 1933, Roosevelt presented his first Fireside Chat, as he explained his administration's response to the banking crisis, intended as an intimate and informal conversation with the people, not a speech. The term *Fireside Chat* was coined by Harry Butcher of CBS, preceding the president's second radio address of May 7, 1933. It was in this chat that Roosevelt presented the New Deal. In 1933 about half of all American families owned a radio, and 30 percent of these were tuned into this first Fireside Chat. Radio also did not expose Roosevelt to the risk of revealing that he used a wheelchair, as a public speech would.

By 1938 52.5 percent of radio airtime was devoted to music (mostly big bands), 9.1 percent to drama, and 9.8 percent to news and sports. Even before Pearl Harbor there were several broadcasts about European affairs. On four successive Sundays, September 7, 14, 21, and 28, 1941, the National Broadcasting Company presented the series *These Four Men*, radio docudramas that chronicled the lives of Winston Churchill, Joseph Stalin, Adolf Hitler, and Franklin D. Roosevelt.

By the end of the war news accounted for 20 percent of all radio broadcasts.

Woody Guthrie

Woody Guthrie may be the best-known composer and singer of folk songs in American
history. As the Dust Bowl forced thousands
to move west from the Great Plains in search
of employment in the early 1930s, Guthrie
was moved by the refugees' plight to com-
pose several songs, including "So Long (It's
Been Good To Know Yuh)," excerpted below:

What a long time since I've been home,
And I got to be drifting along.

The sweethearts, they sat in the dark
*   and they sparked,*
They hugged and they kissed in that
*   dusty old dark,*
They sighed and they cried and they
*   hugged and they kissed,*
But instead of marriage they talked like this: Honey,

Woody Guthrie in 1943. The sign on his guitar reads "this machine kills fascists."

So long, it's been good to know yuh . . .

I went to your family and asked them for you,
They all said take her, oh, take her, please do!
She can't cook or sew and she won't scrub your floor,
So I put on my hat and tiptoed out the door, saying:

So long, it's been good to know yuh . . .

My telephone rang and it jumped off the wall,
That was the preacher a-making a call,
He said, we're waiting to tie the knot,
You're getting married, believe it or not!

So long, it's been good to know yuh . . .

The church it was jammed, the church it was packed,
The pews were crowded from the front to the back,
A thousand friends waited to kiss my new bride,
But I was so anxious I rushed her outside, told them:

So long . . .

Shirley Temple

The Prime Minister of Canada speaking with Shirley Temple in 1944.

The entertainer that Americans most closely identify with the Depression years was a blonde moppet with corkscrew curls named Shirley Temple (1928–) who began her career in 1931 at the age of three. Between that time and 1949, Temple starred in 59 films, including *Bright Eyes* (1934), *Stand Up and Cheer* (1934), *Curly Top* (1935), *Dimples* (1936), *Heidi* (1937), *Little Miss Broadway* (1938), *Rebecca of Sunnybrook Farm* (1938), *The Little Princess* (1939), and *The Bachelor and the Bobby-Soxer* (1947). Americans also spent millions of dollars purchasing everything from dolls to hats that bore Temple's image. Little girls around the country sported corkscrew curls. Between 1936 and 1937, Temple was the number one box office draw in American movie theaters.

Shirley Temple was born in Santa Monica, California. A first marriage in 1945 to John Agar produced a daughter, Linda Susan, in 1948. The marriage ended in divorce the following year, but a second marriage was more successful. Shirley Temple married Charles Black on December 16, 1950. After 55 years of marriage, Charles Black died on August 4, 2005, survived by Shirley and two children, Charles (1952) and Lori (1954).

A staunch Republican, Shirley Temple Black served as the U.S. representative to the United Nations in 1969. She was appointed as the American ambassador to Ghana in 1974 and as ambassador to Czechoslovakia in 1989. She has been a strong presence in the fight against breast cancer since she was diagnosed with the disease in 1972. She won a special Juvenile Academy Award in 1935, and was awarded a Lifetime Achievement Award by the Screen Actors Guild in 2006.

MOVIES OF THE 1930s

Weekly theater attendance in 1930 was 90 million, but dropped to 60 million a week in 1932 and 1933. It eventually climbed back to 80 million by 1940. John Ford directed movies that portrayed the national culture in *Along the Mohawk* (1939) and *Young Mr. Lincoln* (1939). Rouben Mamoulian created a version of *Doctor Jekyll and Mr. Hyde* (1932). Other movies of similar scope were James Whale's *Frankenstein* (1931), starring Boris Karloff, and *The Invisible Man* (1933), which featured Claude Rains.

New technology and techniques opened new vistas in filmmaking. In 1932 three-color Technicolor paved the way for filmmakers to create "A" movies of higher visual quality. Audiences could choose from lavish musicals, biopics like *Catherine the Great* (1934), literary adaptations like *Vanity Fair* (1932), and light fare like the Bing Crosby–Bob Hope *Road* movies. Most films were shot in black-and-white, but two of the most popular films of all time were shot in color: *Gone with the Wind* and *The Wizard of Oz*, both of which came out in 1939. That particular year produced a crop of great movies beyond these two, including *Mr. Smith Goes to Washington, Dark Victory, Goodbye Mr. Chips, Young Mr. Lincoln,* and *The Women.* Until the 1960s, *Gone With the Wind* still ranked as Hollywood's highest-grossing movie at the box office. Full-length color animated features were also coming to the forefront: among them the Walt Disney classics *Fantasia, Bambi,* and *Pinocchio.*

Hollywood was organized around five major studios that dominated the field: 20th Century Fox, MGM, Paramount, Warner Brothers, and RKO. Each studio had a "stable" of stars. For example, MGM had about 60 major performers under contract, including Spencer Tracy, Katherine Hepburn, Jimmy Stewart, Judy Garland, Jean Harlow, and Clark Gable. Stars were relentlessly promoted in magazines and newsreels, always showing them in the best, most glamorous light, covering up alcoholism, drug use, homosexuality, failed marriages, abuse, and emotional problems that plagued more than a few of the biggest names.

THE NEW DEAL AND THE WPA

To reverse increasing unemployment, president Franklin D. Roosevelt (1882–1945) initiated the New Deal, comprised of the Works Progress Administration (WPA), Federal Project Number One, and other emergency measures. Federal Project Number One, a part of the new deal program Works Progress Administration, was also known as Federal One or the Federal Arts Projects. It consisted of four major programs, the Federal Music Project, the Federal Art Project, the Federal Theatre Project, and the Federal Writers Project.

Prohibition, through the Eighteenth Amendment (1919), had lowered employment for live music at night clubs and

A poster for an early WPA Federal Theatre Project production of a musical revue.

bars, and these businesses were forced to close their doors. Other factors leading to the mass unemployment of musicians included new technologies. The radio, like the phonograph, while allowing greater dissemination of the music, reduced live performances. Sound recording for films led to the demise of silent movies, and approximately 20 percent of American Federation of Musicians members were theater players. Nationwide, unemployment of musicians was above 60 percent, but in New York City it was nearly 80 percent in 1933.

In 1935, Nikolai Sokoloff, conductor of the Cleveland Symphony Orchestra, was appointed the first national director of the Federal Music Project (FMP), serving until 1939. The FMP made music accessible to more people by producing and issuing transcription discs, analog recordings 16 inches in diameter. Conducting the Los Angeles Federal Symphony, the New York Civic Orchestra, and the Federal Symphony Orchestra, Sokoloff recorded works in the standard repertoire, including music of Felix Mendelssohn, Carl Maria von Weber, Johannes Brahms, and Peter Ilich Tchaikovsky. Other conductors and ensembles performed and recorded music of American composers, including Charles Wakefield Cadman (1881–1946), John Philip Sousa (1854–1932), Edward MacDowell (1860–1908), Howard Hanson (1896–1981), Irving Berlin (1888–1989), Vincent Youmans (1898–1946), and Victor Herbert (1859–1924), plus spirituals and folk songs of Stephen Collins Foster (1826–64). Sokoloff and the FMP also sponsored radio broadcasts and music education sessions, including new works by George Anthiel, William Schuman, and Elliot Carter.

A Brunswick phonograph from the late 1920s or early 1930s.

The Resettlement Administration, an agency that relocated farmers to areas with more fertile soil and to planned communities for greater productivity, produced composer Virgil Thomson's *The Plow That Broke the Plains* (1936), a motion picture that depicted the economic history of the prairies. Seth Bingham's folk cantata *The Wilderness Stone* (1936) fused Native Americana and literature. *Gettysburg* (1938), an opera by Morris Hutchins Ruger and Arthur Robinson, produced by the Los Angeles Music Project, commemorated the 75th anniversary of the Gettysburg Address.

The FMP also preserved American folk music, ranging from Creole ballads of Louisiana, bayou songs of the Mississippi Delta, and Spanish songs of the Southwest, to African-American spirituals in North Carolina, and Appalachian folk music. The Oklahoma Music Project recorded Native-American music, including songs of the Cheyenne, Kiowa, Apache, Pawnee, and Osage tribes. In 1936 the FMP employed 15,000 musicians from 30 different orchestras.

The Public Works of Art Project (PWAP) ran from December 1933 to June 1934, led by Edward Bruce and Forbes Watson. Its purpose was to create murals and art for nonfederal buildings. This experimental relief program would cease in 1934. President Roosevelt appointed Holger Cahill (1893–1960), director of the Museum of Modern Art in New York, as the director of the Federal Art Project in 1935. By 1936, the FAP had employed 3,500 artists. The project launched careers of regionalist painter Stuart Davis, and abstractionists Jackson Pollock and Willem De Kooning. By 1938 the FAP had produced more than 42,000 easel paintings. FAP artists painted over 1,100 murals on public buildings, many influenced by the styles of Mexican painters Diego Rivera (1886–1957) and José Clemente Orozco (1883–1949).

Hallie Flanagan (1890–1969), previously with the Vassar College Experimental Theatre, directed the Federal Theatre Project. Over 30 million people attended FTP productions. Some, such as Arthur Sullivan's *The Pirates of Penzance* at the Savoy Theatre, were intertwined with work of the FMP, which provided musicians, and the FAP, which provided the poster for the musical. Two plays of the FTP attracted controversy: T.S. Eliot's *Murder in the Cathedral* and Sinclair Lewis's antifascist *It Can't Happen Here*.

MUSIC OF THE 1930s

Classical music drew from the folk elements of society. One of these was the ballet *Billy the Kid* (1938), with music by Aaron Copland, choreography by Eugene Loring, and performed by Lincoln Kirstein's Ballet Caravan. In the opera *Porgy and Bess* (1935), George Gershwin combined jazz with folk tales. Classical music followed some experimental paths in the 1930s. *Density 21.5* (1935), by Edgard Varèse, was to be performed on a platinum flute, because platinum is 21.5 times the density of water. Virgil Thomson's opera *Four Saints in Three Acts* (1934) defied the conventional opera. Its libretto by Gertrude Stein depicted the lives of four 16th-century Spanish saints. The music sounds postmodern, as a precursor to minimalism of the later 20th century. Its premiere in 1934, presented by the Friends and Enemies of Modern Music at the Wadsworth Atheneum, Hartford, Connecticut, featured an all-black cast.

Henry Cowell published *New Music*, a quarterly magazine, beginning in 1927. Its contemporary and often avant-garde music included the dissonant harmonies of Charles Ives, Carl Ruggles, and Milton Babbitt; Varese's *Ionisation* (1931) for 13 percussionists; new timbral explorations by John Cage in his *Amores* (1943) for piano and percussion; and humor of Nicolas Slonimsky in his *Studies in Black and White* (1929) for piano. Jazz and swing music

Dancing the Jitterbug in a club on a Saturday night in November 1939 outside of Clarksdale, Mississippi. Only a few years earlier, Prohibition had forced many night clubs and bars to close.

became increasingly popular in the 1930s, exemplified by Guy Lombardo, and clarinetists Benny Goodman and Artie Shaw. Duke Ellington and Count Basie, both jazz pianists, led their respective orchestras in several performances during this decade.

WORLD'S FAIRS
World's Fairs allowed many people to view futuristic technologies. "The Century of Progress" in Chicago (1933–34) attracted 22.5 million visitors in 1933, and an additional 16.5 million the next year. Visitors were able to view and partake of carnival-like rides, and movies derived from 64 millimeter film. The "California Pacific International Exposition" in San Diego (1935–36) featured a replica of the Globe Theater, where Shakespeare plays were performed.

The New York World's Fair (1939–40) coincided with the 150th anniversary of the inauguration of George Washington as the first president of the United States. The fair's theme, "The World of Tomorrow," was exemplified by two major structures. The Trylon was a triangular tower 610 feet high. The Perisphere, a globe 180 feet in diameter, contained the city of the future, "Democracity." The futurama displayed innovations by corporations. RCA (Radio Corporation of America) introduced television and transmitted the first broadcast of a president on television. The fair had 25.8 million visitors in its first year. In January 1940 the Soviet pavilion was dismantled due to the Soviet Union's entry into World War II. It was converted into an outdoor amphitheater, where musical and theatrical programs were staged. After the fair closed, the steel from the Trylon and Perisphere was sold for scrap and used in the war effort.

A promotional poster for the New York World's Fair of 1939 featuring the Trylon and Perisphere.

WARTIME MUSIC
During World War II radio proved to be an essential tool for entertainment, as well as for keeping up with news of the war. Ninety percent of American homes owned at least one radio, and the average family listened to the radio for three to four hours a day.

Eighty-six percent of those surveyed by *Fortune* magazine in 1939 insisted they could not live without radio in their lives. By 1945, 91 percent of the American population claimed that radio was a necessity. Audiences were vastly entertained by radio and film stars such as Judy Garland, Carmen Miranda, Gene Kelley, Alice Faye, Frank Sinatra, and Danny Kay.

When Germany invaded Poland on September 1, 1939, the Swing Era was in full gear in the United States. Big bands played in glittering night spots where Americans danced the night away. Support for the English, who were bearing the brunt of the war in Europe, was strong in America, and one of the most popular songs of the era was "(There'll be Blue Birds Over) the White Cliffs of Dover." With words (Nat Barton) and music (Walter Kent) by two Americans, the song seemed to sum up the spirit of the war and the fight for democracy:

> *There'll be blue birds over*
> *The white cliffs of Dover*
> *Tomorrow*
> *Just you wait and see*
>
> *There'll be love and laughter*
> *And peace ever after*
> *Tomorrow*
> *When the world is free*

WPA Controversies

Federal Project Number One, a part of the New Deal Works Progress Administration, was rooted in earlier Roosevelt administration programs—the Federal Emergency Relief Administration and the Civil Works Administration. New York's Wicks Act (1931), supported by then Governor Franklin D. Roosevelt, became a model for the WPA. New attacks on the perceived liberal agenda of Federal One Projects came from the newly formed House Committee on Un-American Activities. Martin Dies (R-Texas) was the committee chairman.

The Federal Music Progam managed to escape most of these attacks, as the music could be purely instrumental, without reference to political views. Sinclair Lewis and John C. Moffitt produced the antifascist drama *It Can't Happen Here* (1936), performed around the country by the FTP in 17 cities, including Birmingham, Tampa, and Miami. However, officials in Louisiana blocked its performance in New Orleans, only one year after the assassination of Huey Long. Marc Blitzstein's opera, *The Cradle Will Rock*, was closed down by the government the day it was scheduled to open in New York, on June 16, 1937. The cast sang in another theatre from positions in the audience as the composer played the piano from the stage. *Lysistrata* (1936), originally written 2,000 years earlier by Aristophanes, received a critical review from local WPA officials in Seattle, who declared it too "risqué" for their audiences, and locked the doors after one night.

While not as controversial as the Federal Theatre Project, the Federal Art Project had to contend with censorship. Victor Arnautoff's "City Life," in San Francisco, drew charges of being communist. In his 12-foot mural, "A Social History of the State of Indiana," Thomas Hart Benton touched on several aspects of that state's history: agriculture, labor, industry, and even the Ku Klux Klan. Nudity in Frank Mechau's mural on the Post Office in Washington, D.C., "Dangers of the Mail" (1937), drew criticism even from his hometown newspaper, the Colorado Springs *Sunday Gazette and Telegraph*.

One of the more controversial WPA Federal Theatre Project productions.

After Japan attacked Pearl Harbor on December 7, 1941, Americans were immediately plunged into war, and patriotism became the order of the day. Popular songs such as "We'll Knock the Japs Right into the Laps of the Nazis," "You're a Sap, Mr. Jap," and "They Started Something (but We're Gonna Finish It" showed that Americans were eager to seek revenge for Pearl Harbor. Other songs, including "For the Flag, For the Home, and For the Family" and "Goodbye, Mama (I'm off to Yokohama)," spoke of leaving loved ones behind to risk their lives in battle. Romance continued to be an important theme during the war, and both new and old songs were employed to express regret over being separated from loved ones. Two of the most popular love songs of the period were "Don't Sit under the Apple Tree (with Anyone Else but Me)" and "I'm Dreaming Tonight of My Blue Eyes." Americans were encouraged to join the war effort in numbers such as "Dig Down Deep." Certain songs, including Dennis Morgan's "You Can Always Tell a Yank," presented a clear message about the purpose of the war:

Singer Bing Crosby promoting a scrap rubber drive for the war effort in June 1942.

You can always tell a Yank
By the way he drives a tank
To defend a thing called democracy
And save the world from tyranny

When Bing Crosby's "White Christmas" was released in 1942, the nostalgic tune became the best selling song of all time. Male musicians joined the military, and all-girl bands were formed to entertain a nation at war. Women's roles in the war effort were extolled in songs such as "Rosie the Riveter" who worked "all day long—whether rain or shine" on the assembly line while "making history working for victory."

WARTIME HOLLYWOOD

Although movies continued to be an important element of wartime entertainment, 80 percent said they could live without movies if necessary. Hollywood had to redefine itself during the war. Cartoon characters such as Donald Duck and Mickey Mouse were allowed to appear free of charge in military films. A number of filmmakers were engaged in "war propaganda." Even before Pearl Harbor, films such as *Blockade, Escape,* and *Mortal Storm* took up the banner

A Real League of Their Own

Women famously served in American industry during World War II, but the war provided them expanded roles even beyond the workplace. Women found themselves the de facto heads of families, home bookkeepers and managers, "handymen" and mechanics. They also got a chance to play in professional sports.

Baseball had long been considered America's sport, but the induction of millions of men into the military services threatened to deplete team rosters. Professional team owners were certain baseball would not survive the war. They then started the All-American Girls' Professional Baseball League, which eventually became the subject of the popular 1992 movie *A League of Their Own*, starring Tom Hanks and Geena Davis.

One player, Wilma Briggs, born in 1930, commented that, "Had it not been for the war, I never would have played professional baseball...Phil Wrigley of the Chicago Cubs was certain that all the men would be drafted, and the major league ballparks would be empty. That's the reason he started the [All-American League]." The league outlasted the war, continuing until 1954. Wilma joined it in 1948 after graduating from high school, and saw it as an empowering experience: "I think because I went out there and played ball—I met a lot of people from all over the United States, Canada, and Cuba, which I never would have done ... I think it gave me the courage years later to say, 'I think I'll go to college.'"

of anti-fascism. By 1940, 36 movies dealing with military themes had been released. Films such as *I Married a Nazi, Sergeant York*, and *British Intelligence* sent a clear message that it was America's war, as well as Europe's.

One of the most admired films of all times was released in 1942 as "unofficial war propaganda." *Casablanca*, starring Humphrey Bogart and Ingrid Bergman, told a tale of soul mates separated by war, but also painted a clear portrait of the "right" and "wrong" sides of World War II. Films such as *Yankee Doodle Dandy* (1942), starring James Cagney, firmly established the reputation of Warner Brothers as socially and politically conscious. The premiere of the film was turned into a war bonds sale. Other premieres donated proceeds directly to military emergency funds.

Many homesick soldiers used "pin-up girls" such as actresses Betty Grable and Rita Hayworth to boost morale in foreign lands. English-born comedian Bob Hope began a decades-long career of entertaining American troops abroad. Hollywood's glamour girls were involved in fighting the war in their own way, traveling around the world to entertain the troops, volunteering for civil defense and United Services Organization (USO) work, and promoting the sale of war bonds. Actress Carole Lombard was killed in a plane crash on a war bond tour and was replaced by Dorothy Lamour. Studio heads turned their studio and script rooms over to the military at intervals and produced and directed training films that included *The Battle of China, Why We Fight,* and *Notes on Jungle Warfare.*

Actors by the score put their careers on hold to join the military. When he joined the Army Air Force in 1941, perennially popular actor Jimmy Stewart became the first American actor to join the military. Clark Gable, the male lead in *Gone with the Wind,* made a meteoric rise from private to major, using both a camera and a machine gun at different points in his military career. William Wyler, the director of *Mrs. Miniver,* a film about a British family during the early years of the war, became a colonel in the Air Force. Frank Capra, who is best known for his post–World War II film, *It's a Wonderful Life,* produced the *Why We Fight* training films before joining the military and seeing action in three separate combat theaters. Actor Robert Montgomery served as a volunteer ambulance driver in France before becoming a lieutenant commander in the Navy and seeing action in the Atlantic, Pacific, and Mediterranean. Actor Tyrone Power was a Marine pilot; Henry Fonda served in the Navy; and Victor Mature enlisted in the Coast Guard.

Newsreels and documentaries played an integral role in bringing the war to life for Americans. In 1937, when the Japanese sank the *USS Panay* in Chinese waters, a photographer was on hand to film recovery of survivors. Newsreels also showed the eight-month German Blitz that left much of Britain in ruins and allowed American audiences to see the pain on Prime Minister Winston Churchill's face as he toured the ruins. Photographers were also there for the victories, including the Allied invasion of Normandy on June 6, 1944, which was depicted in great detail.

POSTWAR PROGRESS

By 1945 unemployment in the United States was at 2 percent, and after the war consumers had more money to spend on everything, including entertainment. Box office receipts rebounded nicely after the war; 1946 was one of the highest-grossing years in movie history. As 1950 approached, social-consciousness films like *The Best Years of Our Lives* (chronicling the lives of returned veterans), *The Lost Weekend* (a drama about alcoholism), and *Gentlemen's Agreement* (condemning anti-Semitism) came into vogue. The golden age of musicals was also on the horizon, when Frederick Lowe and Alan Jay Lerner produced *Brigadoon* (1947), Richard Rodgers and Oscar Hammerstein created *South Pacific* (1949), and Frank Loesser composed *Guys and Dolls* (1949).

In the world of theater there was Tennessee Williams's *A Streetcar Named Desire* (1947) and Arthur Miller's *Death of a Salesman* (1949), the saga of

Ebbets Field in Brooklyn, New York, with a large crowd on the opening day of the 1920 World Series. The August 26, 1939, game at Ebbets Field was the first televised baseball game.

a traveling salesman who is ruined by his own ego and competition. Virgil Thomson's opera *The Mother of Us All* (1947) depicted the life of American suffragist Susan B. Anthony and featured a libretto by the writer Gertrude Stein.

BASEBALL AS AMERICA'S SPORT

Baseball changed through the 1930s. At Cincinnati's Crosley Field, the first night game was played on May 24, 1935. President Roosevelt flipped the switch to begin this era of sports in America. Other teams followed, and on June 15, 1938, at Ebbets Field in Brooklyn, Johnny Vander Meer (1914–97) of the Cincinnati Reds pitched the first nighttime no-hitter against the Dodgers. This was also the first night game played at Ebbets Field. The first night game at Yankee Stadium was May 25, 1946. Ebbets Field in Brooklyn was also the site of the first televised game, played on August 26, 1939, between the Cincinnati Reds and the Brooklyn Dodgers. This game was not viewed widely however, as only 400 televisions existed in the United States at the time.

The first radio broadcast of a professional game occurred on August 5, 1921, by KDKA in Pittsburgh, though it was not until the late 1930s that more games were broadcast. The Yankees, Giants, and Dodgers blacked out these broadcasts until 1939. Legendary announcers, each with his own unique approach and sound, included Red Barber, who began announcing for the Cincinnati Reds in 1933, and Harry Caray, who announced for the Chicago Cubs.

In postwar baseball, Jackie Robinson (1919–72), an African American, broke the color barrier in major league baseball, playing for the Brooklyn Dodgers on April 15, 1947. After being named Rookie of the Year in 1947, he went on to lead the National League in batting average and stolen bases in 1949, and was named the league's Most Valuable Player that year.

CONCLUSION

In the 1930s and 1940s, radio personalities and traditional musicians thrived in the last days before widespread television or rock 'n' roll. An era that began with the shock of the stock market crash, and then the further traumas of Pearl Harbor and World War II, ended in America's rising power on the world stage, both economically and politically. After the war Americans would have more money to spend on entertainment than ever before. In some ways, the years that introduced such landmark achievements as *Gone With the Wind* and *Casablanca* now mark a sharp divide before the rise of a new American generation.

RALPH HARTSOCK
ELIZABETH R. PURDY

Further Readings

Ashby, LeRoy. *With Amusement for All: A History of American Popular Culture since 1830.* Lexington, KY: University of Kentucky Press, 2006.

Bindas, Kenneth J. *All This Music Belongs to the Nation: The WPA's Federal Music Project and American Society.* Knoxville, TN: University of Tennessee Press, 1995.

Craig, Douglas B. *Fireside Politics: Radio and Political Culture in the United States, 1920–1940.* Baltimore, MD: Johns Hopkins University Press, 2000.

Douglas, Susan J. *Listening In: Radio and the American Imagination, from Amos 'n' Andy and Edward R. Murrow to Wolfman Jack and Howard Stern.* New York: Times Books, 1999.

Editors of Look. *Movie Lot to Beachhead: The Motion Picture Goes to War and Prepares for the Future.* New York: Arno Press, 1980.

Fowke, Edith and Joe Glazer, eds. *Songs of Work and Freedom.* New York: Roosevelt University, 1960.

Harris, Jonathan. *Federal Art and National Culture.* New York: Cambridge University Press, 1995.

Harrison, Helen A. *Dawn of a New Day: The New York World's Fair, 1939/40.* New York: New York University Press, 1980.

Horten, Gerd. *Radio Goes to War: The Cultural Politics of Propaganda During World War II.* Berkeley, CA: University of California Press, 2002.

Jones, John Bush. *The Songs That Fought the War: Popular Music and the Home Front, 1939–1945*. Waltham, MA: Brandeis University Press, 2006.

Miller, Edward D. *Emergency Broadcasting and 1930s American Radio*. Philadelphia, PA: Temple University Press, 2003.

Silvia, Tony. *Baseball Over the Air*. Jefferson, NC: McFarland, 2007.

Tyler, Ben. "A Farm Girl Plays Professional Baseball." In *What Did You do in the War, Grandma?* Available online: http://www.stg.brown.edu/projects/WWII_Women/tocCS.html. Accessed April 2008.

Woll, Allen L. *The Hollywood Musical Goes to War*. Chicago, IL: Nelson-Hall, 1983.

Young, William H., and Nancy K. Young. *Music of the World War II Era*. Westport, CT: Greenwood Press, 2008.

Chapter 11

Crime and Violence

"If we are to keep democracy, there must be a commandment:
Thou shalt not ration justice."
—Learned Hand

FROM 1919 TO 1933, Prohibition had the unintended effect of increasing organized crime in America, as manufacturing, importing, and selling illegal alcohol provided a financial windfall for gangs of criminals in the cities. The money was used to expand the influence of organized crime into gambling, prostitution, narcotics, and some legitimate businesses. Murder increased during Prohibition; the national rate rose from 6.5 homicides per 100,000 people in 1918 to above 8 for most of the 1920s. The murder rate spiked to 9.7 in 1933, the last year of Prohibition, and then began a long decline until the 1970s. In cities, robbery and theft were also commonplace, and prostitution was conducted more openly than before. To compound matters, corruption in law enforcement was a problem. To counter this surge in crime, the professionalization of police forces begun earlier in the 20th century continued in the 1930s. The most famous law enforcement organization to be officially established during this time was the Federal Bureau of Investigation under the leadership of J. Edgar Hoover.

The Federal Bureau of Investigation, commonly called the FBI, did not get that official designation until July 1, 1935. However, it traces its origins back to July 26, 1909, when the attorney general at that time ordered the formation of a group of special agents to report to Chief Examiner Stanley W. Finch, in the Justice Department. In March 1909, this force was named the Bureau of Investigation (BOI). The passage of the Mann Act in 1910 (also called the White Slavery Act), gave the BOI significantly more jurisdiction over interstate crime. Even so, the agency had very few powers.

When Franklin Roosevelt took the oath of office in March 1933, the mood in the country was bleak. In his inaugural speech, he tried to reassure a worried populace with his now famous line: "Let me assert my firm belief that the only thing we have to fear is fear itself." Roosevelt paused, then said, "This nation asks for action, and action now." He went on, "We must move as a trained and loyal army, willing to sacrifice for the good of a common discipline . . . I shall ask Congress for the one remaining instrument to meet the crisis—broad executive power to wage war against the emergency, as great as the power that would be given me if, in fact, invaded by a foreign foe."

One part of the country's emergency was domestic crime, and Roosevelt would fight this internal war through the man who would become his FBI Director, J. Edgar Hoover. Known for wielding power over both powerful politicians and ordinary Americans, Hoover began his career young and rapidly acquired power. He both hunted violent criminals who were wreaking havoc in the streets, and persecuted others by backing Senator Joseph McCarthy's anti-Communist campaign and by keeping tabs on civil rights leaders. His legacy is problematic, but at the time of his rise the country was in need of a check on rampant mafia violence, Ku Klux Klan activities, bank robberies, illegal gambling, and even spying. He achieved this by professionalizing American law enforcement like never before.

Several of Hoover's most famous targets, including the Rosenbergs (Ethel and Julius), Alger Hiss, and even Martin Luther King, Jr., were accused of having Communist ties. Alger Hiss, and later the Rosenbergs, were tried and convicted of spying for the Soviet Union. Hiss received 10 years in prison, but the Rosenbergs were sentenced to die for their crime of passing on critical information about the atomic bomb, which allowed the Soviets to develop their own bomb years ahead of schedule. They were both executed in 1953. Soviet records have shown that they were indeed engaged in espionage for the Soviet Union.

DECLINE OF THE KU KLUX KLAN

The rise and fall of the second "Invisible Empire" (KKK) began after World War I and lasted until the end of World War II. The incarnation of the Klan that peaked in the 1920s especially targeted the growing numbers of Roman Catholics who had immigrated to the United States in the early years of the 20th century. KKK organizers stirred up hatred in speeches in rural gathering places. As Ralph McGill puts it in his book *The South and the Southerner*, they shouted, "the Pope was coming to America; the Catholic conspiracy was to destroy us all; only the KKK and one hundred percent Americanism could save us." African Americans and the foreign-born in general were also considered enemies, but the Roman Catholic Church and the Pope were the new focus.

J. Edgar Hoover in December 1924, around the time he was made director of the Bureau of Investigation, the predecessor to the FBI. He was 29 years old.

A politically savvy advertiser named E.Y. Clarke got involved in the Klan and started working state political machines to wrangle jobs for Klan members. The atmosphere of the times was primed for the spread and infiltration of the Klan in society. As McGill puts it, "Isolationism, America for Americans, was in the air. The hysteria about the 'Reds', the Depression, the explosion on Wall Street, the rural discontent, unemployment, the strikes, the race riots in Eastern cities, all of these created a perfect climate and soil for Klan development." Clarke rose quickly in the Klan, and later claimed that the Klan had had members working in as many as 47 state governments, including in some of the highest positions, such as congressmen, governors, and judges.

However, the Great Depression weakened the underlying system of money and influence, and the Klan had already been in decline because of a lack of public support after the scandalous conviction of the prominent Indiana Klan leader D.C. Stephenson for rape and murder in 1925. Klan membership declined dramatically, though the organization was not entirely eradicated.

As World War II engulfed Europe, McGill, who was both the author of *The South and the Southerner* and the publisher of the *Atlanta Constitution*, became convinced that some of the Klan leaders were trying to initiate some sort of association with Fritz Kuhn's German-American Bund groups in the East. Both raged against Roosevelt and were irrationally anti-Semitic, but he was unable to prove the Klan's connection with Nazism until after the war

Julius and Ethel Rosenberg after they were convicted of spying for the Soviets during World War II. They were executed in the summer of 1953 when Julius was 35 and Ethel was 37 years old.

when McGill had the opportunity to visit Kuhn in Nuremberg, West Germany. Kuhn was asked then if the Ku Klux Klan had ever approached him. "Oh yes," he said. "We had two meetings about it. The Southern Klans did not want it to be known so the negotiations were between representatives in New Jersey and Michigan, but it was understood that the Southerners were in. We all approved what Hitler was doing. Had Roosevelt not brought us into the war, we would have got together against the Jews and the Negroes."

MAYHEM IN THE MIDWEST

Between 1920 and 1929, the Travelers Insurance Company reported that property crimes, from bank robberies to drugstore stick-ups, jumped from 17 to 965 in Saginaw, Michigan. In fact, the years between 1925 and 1932 (the year Roosevelt was elected President), became known as the golden age of bank robbers. The spread of bank robberies was, in part, the result of technology outstripping the legal system. Faster, more powerful weapons, especially the 800-rounds-per-minute Thompson Submachine Gun, introduced after World War I, allowed the *yeggs* (a press term for bank robbers) to outgun all but the best-armed urban policemen. But perhaps the greatest impetus was the automobile, especially new models with reliable, powerful V-8 engines. While the county sheriff was still hand-cranking his old Model A, a modern *yegg* could speed away untouched. Bank robberies were so frequent between Texas and Minnesota that the area became known as the "crime corridor." The federal government was of no help since bank robbery was not yet a federal crime. In addition, coordination between police was spotty; only a few states had introduced statewide police, and they seldom possessed the resources to break a major case. A single bank robbery could change a dirt farmer's life. At a time when the average household income in states like Oklahoma and Missouri hovered below $500 a year, bank robbers could make off with $10,000 for a morning's work.

The man credited with introducing a new level of professionalism to bank robbery was Herman K. Lamm, a German immigrant known to the underworld as the Baron. Born in 1880, Lamm was a quasimythic figure who began his criminal career with the Hole-in-the-Wall gang. In 1917, while in a Utah prison, Lamm pioneered the casing of banks, the observance of bank guards, alarms, and tellers. A bank was known as a *jug* and an expert caser of banks was known as a *jugmarker*. Each member of a gang was assigned a role in the robbery: the lookout, the get-away driver, the lobby man, and the vault man.

JOHN DILLINGER

A letter written to an Indiana newspaper in 1934, quoted in the book *Our Times: An Illustrated History of the 20th Century*, captured the essence of Dillinger as "A Dashing Desperado": "Dillinger did not rob poor people. He robbed those who became rich by robbing the poor, I am for Johnny." John Dillinger was born in Indianapolis, Indiana, in 1902. In 1920, he moved to Mooresville, Indiana, where he committed his first robbery (a grocery store) in 1923. Sent to prison, he was paroled in 1933, and soon thereafter began a string of violent bank robberies. Dillinger and his gang stole many thousands of dollars, including $75,000 taken in a single robbery in Greencastle, Indiana. Dillinger was held responsible for 16 killings. By late 1933, the FBI had declared him Public Enemy Number One.

After his parole in 1933, he promptly robbed five banks, cutting a dashing profile with his natty clothes, jaunty humor, and agile leaps over bank turnstiles. One example of his impudence occurred when, low on cash, he decided to rob a Muncie, Indiana, roadhouse, the Bide-a-Wee Tavern. A few minutes after midnight, Dillinger and a partner walked in, guns drawn, handkerchiefs over their faces, and within minutes, backed out of the bar with $70. On the way out, Dillinger encountered a couple coming in. With a grin, he crudely pinched the woman's bottom; when her male friend objected, Dillinger slugged him.

The Scottsboro Boys

As a result of the Depression, thousands of Americans illegally hopped freight trains in search of work. In March 1931, on a train crossing into Alabama, a group of white youths brawled with a group of African Americans. Forced off the train, the whites filed a complaint at the next station. Sheriff's deputies searched the train, rounding up nine black youths, aged 13 to 20, and two white women. Possibly fearing prosecution for vagrancy or prostitution, the women claimed that the blacks had raped them. Accusers and accused were taken to the county seat. The ensuing case was one of the most controversial of the century.

The "Scottsboro Boys" went to trial the following month. Despite contradictions between the alleged victim's stories and the doctor's testimony that no rape had occurred, the all-white jury convicted a pair of defendants on the first day (while outside the courthouse, 10,000 spectators cheered the verdict and a brass band played). The rest were judged guilty soon afterward; all but the 13-year-old were sentenced to the electric chair. Although the 13-year-old was too young to be executed, seven jurors insisted that he be given the chair anyway. The judge then declared his case a mistrial.

Amid a storm of international protest, the case was appealed, and in 1932, the U.S. Supreme Court, citing the defendants' inadequate legal counsel, overturned the convictions. One of the nine was then convicted again in a trial marred by the prosecution's blatant anti-Semitic attacks on the defense attorney, Sam Leibowitz. A 1935 Supreme Court ruling overturned the new conviction, ruling that the state had systematically excluded blacks from juries. Despite the landmark ruling (and a recantation from one of the accusers) the Scottsboro Boys were tried again and again, while the NAACP and the Communist Party battled publicly over who would represent them. Under rising political pressure, the state dropped charges against the five youngest defendants in 1937, and later paroled all but one. The last, Clarence Norris, was paroled in 1946, and pardoned by Alabama's governor in 1976.

Caught in September 1933, "Gentleman" Johnny was sprung by some former prison mates whose escape he had engineered. Dillinger's gang staged hold-ups from Florida to Arizona—where he was again captured. This time, he threatened jail guards with a wooden pistol, then drove off in the sheriff's car. After Dillinger repeatedly eluded the FBI—once escaping from his Wisconsin hideout with new gang member, "Baby-face" Nelson while panicky FBI agents fired on bystanders—FBI agents surrounded the tavern a little after midnight. In the dark, the agents saw three men leave the tavern and get into a pickup truck. When they refused to stop, the agents fired into the truck, kill-

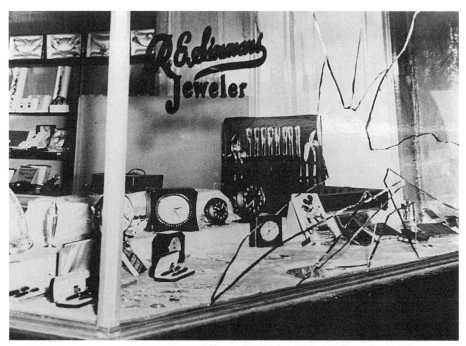

After Prohibition led to a rise in organized crime, police departments grew more professional in the 20th century. This police photograph of a break-in at a jewelry store in York, Pennsylvania, was taken in 1949.

ing all three men. They turned out to be members of the local Civilian Conservation Corps (CCC) out for a drink. In the meantime, Dillinger escaped out the back door of the tavern.

Two months later, a Romanian-born brothel madam named Anna Sage, who was about to be deported, offered to help capture Dillinger. FBI agents led by Melvin Purvis ambushed him as he and the "Lady in Red" left Chicago's Biograph Theatre on the evening of July 22, 1934. Both Purvis and Hoover emerged from the operation as national heroes. Over the next year, G-men (as his agents had become popularly known) would kill or capture all of the famous fugitives.

If Dillinger had known mobster Lucky Luciano, he might have stayed away from Chicago. Chicago, in the 1920s and 1930s, was "Scarface" Al Capone's town; Al Capone was the symbol of the "lawless decade." All through the 1920s Capone's name frightened ordinary citizens. Chicago got the name Mobtown, and was so violent that even Lucky Luciano called it "a real goddamn crazy place. Nobody's safe in the street!"

THE ST. VALENTINE'S DAY MASSACRE
By 1929, the twenties gang wars in Chicago had left Al "Scarface" Capone, who ruled a $50 million dollar empire, at the top of the heap. Only one

Safecrackers in Chicago in the 1930s used this tool to push pintles out of safe hinges.

organization challenged his control of the city's underworld: George "Bugs" Moran's Northside Gang. Capone chose Valentine's Day to put a bloody end to the rivalry. The scheme relied on killers masquerading as cops. Although most policemen took mob payoffs, they routinely raided gangs for appearance's sake. On February 14, a Cadillac disguised as a police car pulled up in front of the garage that served as Moran's headquarters. Four men got out—two dressed as patrolmen, two as plain-clothes detectives. Inside the garage, the phony plain-clothed men lined up six gangsters (and a visitor, a local optometrist, Reinhardt Schwimmer) against a wall. Suddenly, they opened fire with submachine guns; the other two assassins used shotguns to finish off anyone still alive. With his prestige as a mobster ruined, Moran left the rackets.

Bugs Moran escaped the massacre by chance; arriving late, he'd seen the "police raid" and decided to wait it out at a local coffee shop. Pressed for a comment by a reporter after the massacre, he shouted: "Only Capone kills like that!" Public outrage against Capone was enormous, and President Hoover gave orders to have Capone "jailed at any cost." Two-and-a-half years later, "Scarface" was a federal prisoner, convicted, improbably, of the quiet crime of tax evasion, thanks to a 28-year-old Justice Department agent named Elliot Ness.

FRANK COSTELLO AND GAMBLING

Meanwhile, back in New York, Frank Costello was well into the slot machine business. Slot machines had made him wealthy and, as a result, made him a political power. The Depression had dried up private sources of campaign funds, forcing politicians to go to the man who had cash—Costello. However, with the election of a new mayor, Fiorello La Guardia, the slot machine business suffered a setback. Determined to run crooks and racketeers out of New York City, La Guardia began by raiding slot machine palaces and dumping them into the East River.

Costello then took his slots to New Orleans—some say at the invitation of a person more colorful than La Guardia—Huey P. Long, the governor of Louisiana. There are many legends surrounding the relationship between Louisiana's governor and Costello. One claims that Long, while spending his weekends in New York, had become involved with a woman. Some underworld characters attempted to blackmail the "Kingfish" and he went to Costello for help. Frank

The "Real" Bonnie and Clyde

Unlike the cinematic creation, neither Bonnie nor Clyde were rebels or philosophers. Vain and insecure, Clyde Barrow was a preening Dallas burglar who, a friend claimed, had been repeatedly raped in prison and would do anything to avoid going back. Bonnie Parker, on the other hand, was a bored waitress who viewed Clyde as a ticket out of her humdrum existence. Contemporaries disdained them; one called them "just a couple of cheap filling station and car thieves."

Both came from Dallas. Both the Barrow family, subsistence farmers from south of the city, and Bonnie's mother, a West Texas widow, had joined the flood of rural families moving into Southwestern cities in the early 1920s. The Barrows were so poor they lived for a time beneath a viaduct. Dropping out of

Clyde Barrow and Bonnie Parker posing with a 1932 Ford V-8 Sedan.

school at age 16, Clyde became a teenage burglar, joining his older brother, Ivan, known as Buck, sneaking into stores at night. According to Clyde's sister Nell, their first arrests came after they stole a flock of turkeys from an East Texas farm; stopped by police in a truck loaded with stolen poultry, Buck drew a few days in jail and Clyde was released.

Clyde met Bonnie in January 1930. She was a fan of detective and movie magazines, and her diary entries reveal a young woman looking to break out of a dull life of waitressing and babysitting. Soon after, they "partied" up and down the "crime corridor" between Texas and Minnesota, holding up gas stations and small banks. In the process, 12 murders were committed. On May 23, 1934, near Gibsland, Louisiana, the couple met their end when they were ambushed and shot by five sheriff's deputies and a Texas Ranger. Perhaps because they died young in a hail of gunfire, the legend that grew up around them became far more glamorous than the reality of their hard lives.

supposedly called in the blackmailers and ordered them to lay off. In return, Long invited Frank to bring his slot machines to Louisiana. Unfortunately, almost as soon as Frank's machines were being set up around New Orleans, the Kingfish was assassinated on September 8, 1935. The new mayor of New Orleans, Robert S. Maestri, promptly announced that Costello's slot machines would not be permitted to operate in his city.

When Mayor La Guardia ran Frank Costello's slot machine business out of New York City, Costello moved his operations to Louisiana. These adults and children crowded around slot machines in Pilottown, Louisiana, in September 1938.

Two days later, Mayor Maestri made an unexplained trip to Hot Springs, Arkansas, where a friend of Costello's, Owney Madden, held sway. The mayor vacationed there for two weeks and when he returned, he found all of Costello's machines in their old locations and, more surprising, he did not object. What happened in Hot Springs is unknown. By 1945, there were more than 8,000 slot machines in New Orleans, and in Jefferson and St. Bernard Parishes.

DUTCH SCHULTZ AND THE NEW YORK MAFIA

Dutch Schultz, or the Dutchman, was a Bronx-born criminal whose real name was Arthur Flegenheimer. He exemplified the flagrant violence and opportunism of Prohibition-era organized crime, and ended up living only a few years past the repeal of the law. Schultz had run many operations related to illegal alcohol during Prohibition, but found his options limited afterward. A trial for income tax evasion, in which he was acquitted, had also taken him away from his domain for a long period in 1933. In an attempt to renew his influence and increase revenues, he turned to a new scheme to shake down New York restaurants and wielded control over the unionized waiters in the Hotel and Restaurant International Alliance. According to Rick Cowan and Douglas Century in their book *Takedown: The Fall of the Last Mafia Empire*, Schultz's attorney, Richard Davis, recounted that Dutch soon murdered Jules Martin, his own right-hand man in the restaurant operation, with a single shot to the mouth because he thought he had stolen $70,000 from the association. Davis recalled that "the Dutchman did that murder just as casually as if he were picking up his teeth."

Dutch was under increasing pressure from New York's determined Chief Assistant U.S. Attorney Thomas Dewey, and feared he would eventually be caught and imprisoned. Dewey was indicting many underworld figures. The Dutchman therefore came up with a bold plan to kill Dewey and shared it with others. He began by posting a lookout across from Dewey's apartment on Fifth Avenue, and watching his movements. This plan would be Dutch's undoing.

A police "all-tube" radio from the 1940s.

On October 23, 1935, Schultz was going over his accounts with three associates at the Palace Chop House and Tavern on East Street in Newark, which was otherwise empty. The Dutchman got up and went to the bathroom just before two men entered the tavern and shot all three of his associates using a .38 and a sawed-off shotgun. Dutch was shot in the bathroom and then staggered out; he later died of his wounds. The other members of the New York mafia had decided that Dutch's planned assassination of Dewey would bring too much attention from the government, so the reckless Dutch, so rooted in Prohibition-era ways, had to go.

LUCKY LUCIANO AND WORLD WAR II

When the Japanese bombed Pearl Harbor on December 7, 1941, they indirectly brought peace and prosperity to the underworld. New opportunities opened up on every side. Stolen ration cards and black market products such as sugar, meat, and gas were in great demand. The underworld rivalries were settled at sit-downs. In late 1942, something unexpected happened: The U.S. Navy needed Lucky Luciano's help. Lucky was in prison at the time. In 1942, Naval Intelligence was concerned about the possibility of sabotage and espionage along the sprawling New York waterfront. The French liner *Normandie*, converted to a troop ship, had burned and sunk under mysterious circumstances at her Manhattan pier. German submarines seemed to have been supplied with accurate information about ship sailing dates of convoys bound for England. Naval Intelligence suggested that the underworld could

The influential mobster Charles "Lucky" Luciano in 1936.

help. Underworld figures were contacted and reluctantly agreed to aid the Navy but not without Luciano's approval.

Luciano, who was in a prison near the Canadian border nicknamed "Siberia" due to extreme cold weather, agreed to help if the government would move him to a more pleasant location. They did and Luciano cooperated in return. As a result, there was no sabotage at the Port of New York for the remainder of the war. In addition, when American forces invaded Sicily in the summer of 1943, an American combat plane dropped a packet containing a yellow flag with the letter "L" at a pre-arranged location in Sicily. This "L" flag was passed along to the head of the Sicilian Mafia, Don Calogero Vizzini.

When American troops landed, they found the countryside crowded with Sicilians ready to help the troops oppose the hated Italian dictator, Mussolini. The American military was so impressed with the assistance of these "patriots" that they supplied them with arms, and turned over the machinery of government to Don Vizzini.

In January 1946, Dewey, the governor of New York, announced that Lucky Luciano would be freed and deported to Italy as a reward for his service to the military intelligence during World War II. However, deportation to Italy did not keep Luciano from influencing the crime scene in the United States.

THE SPREAD OF THE MAFIA
By the late 1940s, the American mafia had gained more power than anyone realized. The American public was largely ignorant of how entrenched they had become, and even the FBI continued to ignore the extent of their operations. Meanwhile, the mafia continued to organize and attempt to extend their control over multiple sources of income. In December 1946, a group of mafia leaders, often called the National Crime Syndicate, met in Havana, Cuba at the Hotel Nacional. At the meeting, these leaders decided to eliminate Las Vegas mafia figure Benjamin "Bugsy" Siegal after losing several million dollars on the syndicate-owned casino, The Flamingo Hotel. On June 20, 1947, Siegel was shot by an unidentified gunman in Beverly Hills. Their collective response to their problem and organized meetings represented a new level of large-scale control of their operations. However, law enforcement was not yet ready to counter this development, and their leadership would consolidate further. By the end of the decade, one man, Frank Costello, the "Boss of all Bosses," was firmly in control of the National Crime Syndicate.

CONCLUSION

The crime wave inspired by Prohibition, and the flourishing of organized crime in those years, meant that the country faced more than just economic despair during the Great Depression. It faced a brutal enemy within the country itself, though not a new one. J. Edgar Hoover's crackdowns were warranted in some cases, though he often went too far. In spite of the growing professionalization of the police and FBI, the influence of organized crime was here to stay and would rise and fall in the decades that followed. Trade in illegal alcohol during Prohibition was easily replaced with more narcotics, prostitution, and gambling. Another theme of crime in this era, as in years before, was racially-motivated violence, which would also draw widespread attention and action by both government and ordinary citizens in the postwar era and beyond.

FRANK R. DURR

Further Readings

Burrough, Bryan. *Public Enemies: America's Greatest Crime Wave and the Birth of the FBI, 1933–34*. New York: Penguin Press, 2004.

Cowan, Rick and Douglas Century. *Takedown: The Fall of the Last Mafia Empire*. New York: Berkley Books, 2002.

Dodds, John W. *Everyday Life in Twentieth Century America*. New York: Putnam's, 1973.

Federal Bureau of Investigation. Available online: http://www.fbi.gov/fbi-history.htm. Accessed April 2008.

Glennon, Lorraine, ed. *Our Times: The Illustrated History of the 20th Century*. Atlanta, GA: Turner Publishing Inc, 1995.

Lerner, Michael A. *Dry Manhattan: Prohibition in New York City*. Cambridge, MA: Harvard University Press, 2007.

McGill, Ralph. *The South and The Southerner*. Boston, MA: Little Brown & Company, 1965.

Shlaes, A. *The Forgotten Man: A New History of the Great Depression*. New York: Harper Collins, 2007.

Stein, R. Conrad. *The Home Front During World War II in American History*. Berkeley Heights, NJ: Enslow, 2003.

Susman, Warren I. *Culture as History: The Transformation of American Society in the Twentieth Century*. New York: Pantheon Books, 1984.

Wiebe, Robert. *The Search for Order*. New York: Hill and Wang, 1966.

Wolf, George and Joseph DiMona. *Frank Costello*. New York: William Morrow & Company, 1974.

Chapter 12

Labor and Employment

*"But while they prate of economic laws,
men and women are starving."*
—President Franklin Roosevelt

GREAT CHANGES TOOK place in the American workplace from 1929 to 1949, as the United States struggled to cope with the Great Depression and World War II. The prosperity of the 1920s ended with the stock market crash in October 1929. The vast profits made by stock market speculators and corporations were based on credit, margin purchases, and an unregulated business arena that enabled bankers, owners, and even acting New York Stock Exchange President Richard Whitney to commit financial frauds and embezzlement on grand scales. The collapse of these fortunes and the bankruptcy of companies ranging from banks to barber shops had a significant impact on American labor. As bankrupt stock speculators scrambled to raise cash, they began to liquidate assets by canceling orders to industry and laying off workers, often permanently. As the factories shut down, banks often followed, and depositors lost their life savings in the collapse.

Organized labor in 1929 was still as weak as it had been in previous decades. The new auto industry was completely unorganized. The once-mighty Western Federation of Miners had collapsed. William Green, president of the American Federation of Labor (AFL), had to cope with his small craft unions' declining numbers and divisions within the federation, particularly with John L. Lewis, head of the United Mine Workers. AFL membership slumped from 5.1 million in 1920 to 3.4 million in 1929. When an Ohio rubber plant's workers tried to unionize through the AFL, the organizer sent to the factory divided the workers into 19 separate craft unions far too weak to take on the bosses.

When the stock market crash hit, AFL unions crumbled with the economy. With the exception of railroaders, industrial workers were completely unorganized. Coal mine company guards manned machine guns at the entrances to their pits, and kept miners in company towns. Most mineworkers were still powerless and poor.

Children still labored in factories, mines, and sweatshops across the nation. The average steelworker's clothes caught fire once a week, and steel barons, facing 20,000 workers maimed each year by industrial accidents, found it cheaper to simply hire new workers than invest in safety devices. When workers tried to organize, they found that the local police, prosecutors, and judges were happy to cooperate with the bosses and their security forces.

Henry Ford in particular was ruthless in keeping his 90,000 employees under his thumb. To do so, he relied on Harry Herbert Bennett. Bennett, head of personnel on the company's organization chart, commanded 3,000 hand-picked guards. Ford proclaimed himself a generous employer, with eight-hour days and $5-a-day wages, but left out the fact that the $5 pay only went to workers who were aged 22 or more, and could demonstrate to the company's spies that they were living "a clean, sober, and industrious life." The base rate for most of the Ford workers sweating on the assembly lines was $2.34 a day,

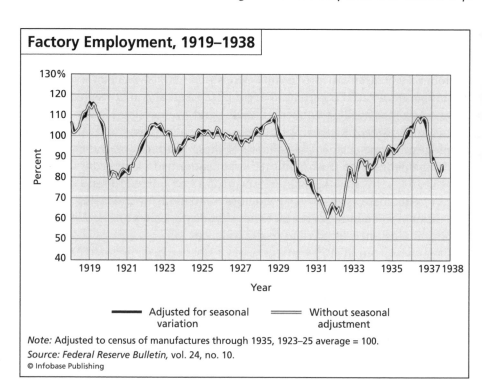

Factory Employment, 1919–1938

Legend:
— Adjusted for seasonal variation
= Without seasonal adjustment

Note: Adjusted to census of manufactures through 1935, 1923–25 average = 100.
Source: Federal Reserve Bulletin, vol. 24, no. 10.
© Infobase Publishing

with 15-minute lunch breaks. More importantly, Ford sub-contracted much of his work to other companies that paid as little as 12½ cents an hour.

While Ford enjoyed one of the best industrial safety records, all the first-aid stations, buzzers, alarms, locks, shields, and signs could not prevent the stock market crash. Within months factories, mines, shipyards, businesses, and banks were closing, leaving thousands and then millions of workers jobless. That led to disaster for millions of working families, as unemployment insurance, food stamps, Section Eight housing, and Social Security were not yet implemented. By the middle of 1930, unemployment had surged from 1.5 million to at least 3.2 million, and those Americans were ragged and desperate.

THE DESPAIR OF JOBLESSNESS

With no jobs to be found in their hometowns, millions of Americans of both sexes hit the rails, riding as hobos on freight cars out of the industrial cities, desperately seeking work. They did not find much, but instead ran into fore-closed farmers and dispossessed sharecroppers going in the opposite direction. Both groups met the same fate: no jobs, serious wounds in rail accidents, ferocious railroad guards, and harsh treatment by the government. In 1932, the Southern Pacific Railroad tossed 683,000 people from their freight cars, while the Missouri Pacific removed 387,313 nomads, 335 of which had become casualties to exposure and violence. Those who could not or dared not ride the rails found themselves sleeping in rat-infested and lice-ridden flophouses, paying 10 cents a night for a urine-stained mattress, or subsisting in parks and empty lots in shelters that rapidly became vast shantytowns known as Hoovervilles after President Herbert Hoover, blamed by many for letting the country slide into depression.

With despair and starvation stalking the land, radical solutions were sought. The Communist Party (down to less than 10,000 in 1929) tried to gain power through displaced workers. The highlight of Communist efforts to organize labor in this period came on March 6, 1930, when the Communist International in Moscow declared "International Day for Struggle Against World-wide Unemployment," and ordered mass marches across the world, including America's major cities. Nearly one million people marched in demonstrations across the United States, with 35,000 in New York's Union Square. Most went off peacefully, but Seattle and Washington police used tear gas to disperse the marchers, and New York Police Commissioner Grover Whalen had his mounted police charge into the crowd to break up the show.

The Trade Union Unity League (TUUL) did not give up, though, trying again in California with migrant cannery and farm workers in 1931 and 1932, but these strikes only engendered an official backlash that called for deporting the mostly Mexican workers back across the border. The Communists also tried reaching out to blacks, but with little success. For all their rhetoric of worker equality, Red leadership would not admit blacks, while the rank and

Ben Shahn photographed this man outside a Hooverville shack in Circleville, Ohio, in summer 1938. He was a former farmer who had traveled west for work, but had been unemployed for at least four years.

file retained traditional bigotry over Marxist rhetoric, and blacks themselves did not trust the Communists. The Reds still tried to unionize sharecroppers in Alabama, but with little success.

UNREST IN DETROIT

By 1932, America was in desperate straits, with between 15 and 17 million men unemployed, and 34 million Americans without any income at all. With vast pools of job-seekers, bosses cut wages. That February, Henry Ford cut his legendary $5-a-week pay to $4 a week, making him a logical target for the Communist TUUL and the Detroit Unemployed Council. On the frigid morning of March 7, 1932, some 3,000 men and women walked the few hundred yards from Detroit to Ford's River Rouge plant employment office in neighboring Dearborn to stage a hunger strike. Dearborn police met the marchers at the city border and told them to turn back. The marchers refused. The police fired tear gas, then attacked with billy clubs. However, the police misjudged the wind, and were hit by their own gas. The police retreated, pursued by angry marchers hurling rocks.

The Detroit authorities reacted with vigor, arresting 60 of the marchers, then hundreds of Communists and "suspected Communists," charging the whole lot with "criminal syndicalism." The incident battered Ford's image, but was the high point of Communist involvement in union activities during the Depression. In November, the voters elected President Franklin D. Roosevelt by a landslide over Herbert Hoover, and Roosevelt brought new energy to the White House.

FEDERAL PROJECTS

Already Senator George Norris and Congressman Fiorello La Guardia had pushed through a federal law that barred federal courts from using injunctions to ban strikes, boycotts, and picketing. Now President Roosevelt both mobilized and empowered labor. He mobilized it first with the Works Progress Administration (WPA), the Civil Works Administration (CWA), and the Public Works Administration (PWA), three organizations that launched 30,000 New Deal projects, ranging from the massive Boulder Dam to sewers, culverts, swimming pools, and post offices across the nation.

Another federal effort that changed laboring life was the legendary Civilian Conservation Corps, which enlisted young unemployed men aged 17 to 27 to work in forests, parks, and federal public lands. Working for the National Park Service, they built roads, campgrounds, bridges, and recreation facilities, and for the Army Corps of Engineers built flood control projects in West Virginia, Vermont, and Tennessee. In return the young men escaped the grinding poverty, ignorance, and crowding of urban America. More than 100,000 of them gained basic literacy.

But while these projects changed the landscape of America and provided the nation with the infrastructure it would need for World War II and the 1950s boom, it did not change the status of unions in private industry. That began on June 16, 1933, when Roosevelt signed the National Industrial Recovery Act. Section 7(a) legitimized collective bargaining, and created a National Labor Board (with John L. Lewis as its chairman) to negotiate disputes. By midsummer, nine million workers and one million employers were covered by the codes of the new National Recovery Administration (NRA),

A recruiting poster for the Civilian Conservation Corps designed by a WPA artist.

which included $12-a-week pay for 40 hour work-weeks, but of the nation's 10 largest industries, only textiles had signed up, and only after six weeks of furious campaigning. Even so, Section 7(a) proved critical. Long-moribund unions sent recruiters and organizers across the nation, shoving fliers at workers that read, "The President says that you must join the union." The workers responded. In Akron, home of Goodyear and Firestone, workers snapped up the fliers and between 1933 and 1934, AFL membership jumped seven-fold.

This burst of union organization frightened the major employers. *Iron Age*, the magazine of the iron industry, warned of "collective bludgeoning," while the *Commercial and Financial Chronicle* speculated on 10 million AFL members becoming a class "within the State, more powerful than the State itself."

UNION ORGANIZING AND STRIKES

Yet despite the propaganda and fears of the employers, the Communists were out of the picture, replaced by legally empowered union organizers who sought to revise the existing system and gain a portion of the profits, not overthrow it. Even so, the strikes often turned bloody. The AFL organized a strike on the Electric Auto-Lite Company of Toledo in December 1933, demanding a 22 percent hourly wage hike. The result was National Guardsmen, violence, two strikers dead, hundreds injured—but the threat of a city-wide general strike ensured the union got its raise in May 1934. In Minneapolis, the General Drivers and Helpers Union, a subsidiary of the Teamsters, took four months to win its raises and unionize trucking in the Twin Cities, battling armed deputies. Even so, four people died and hundreds were wounded in the violence.

After a San Francisco General Strike, the United Textile Workers (UTW) were next, an AFL affiliate based on the eastern seaboard, dating back to 1901. Taking advantage of Section 7(a), their membership leaped from 20,000 in 1930 to 300,000 in May 1934, when the NRA caved in to industry pressure, permitting corresponding 25 percent cuts in working hours and pay. By August, textile workers were earning a mere $11.50 a week, while enduring accelerated production schedules. On Labor Day, September 3, the UTW went out on strike, closing textile mills from South Carolina to Massachusetts.

In one of America's largest and most violent strikes, the workers walked out of plants and drove to the next mill to demand the workers there join them. Once they did so, a larger group went to the next plant and so on. Pickets and police clashed in Massachusetts, Georgia, Rhode Island, and both Carolinas, with dead and wounded on both sides. National Guardsmen were called out in New England and Georgia Governor Eugene Talmadge declared statewide martial law, hauling off strikers to internment camps. Roosevelt created a three-man board of inquiry for the industry, which came up with a ponderous proposal to study the situation further, but granted nothing concrete to the workers. Nevertheless, FDR pressured the union, and it called off the strike, which broke the union's strength, and it remained weak for decades.

California farmworkers were angry, too, particularly the 200,000 migrant farm laborers in the state, whose exhausting and limited jobs were challenged by the "Okies" driving in from the Dust Bowl region of the Great Plains. The Cannery and Agricultural Workers Industrial Union struck the state's cotton industry on October 4, 1933, and the 24-day job action resulted in three strikers being shot, hundreds on both sides injured, and a 25 percent wage hike for the union.

Section 7(a) was clearly not enough to empower labor, and it would take more to do so, particularly when the Supreme Court tossed out the National Recovery Act as unconstitutional in 1935. That drive came from New York Senator Robert F. Wagner, who drafted the Labor Disputes Act in 1933, which became the Wagner National Labor Relations Act of 1935. This made the National Labor Relations Board a supreme court for labor. The board would have the power to order representation elections, define and prohibit unfair labor practices like company unions, and the power to enforce decisions. Wagner believed correctly that the act was the only way management-labor relations and disputes could be conducted in a civilized manner, based

Police officers armed with billy clubs hustling a bloodied sit-down striker away from a Yale and Towne Manufacturing plant in Detroit, Michigan, in 1937.

A master baker at work in the 1940s. During the war, industry operated around the clock, wages rose 70 percent, and nine million unemployed workers found jobs.

on equality at the table. Passing comfortably in the House and Senate, the bill reached FDR's desk on July 5, 1935, and he signed it. But the most dramatic gain for American labor in the 1930s would come not from the Wagner Act, but from an internal dispute that led to the creation of the Congress of Industrial Organizations (CIO), leading to the unionization of millions of industrial workers.

JOHN L. LEWIS
John L. Lewis was the son of a blacklisted Welsh miner, and had labored in Midwest mines since the age of 15. He had carried out the bodies of miners killed in disasters, and become active in the United Mine Workers (UMW), then part of the AFL. He became president of the UMW in 1920 at age 40, along the way bullying the Illinois State Legislature into passing workers' compensation and safety laws in the wake of mine disasters.

By 1933, Lewis was chafing at the AFL's refusal to expand beyond its narrow trade unions. The AFL steel union, for example, mustered only 5,000 dues-paying members. Unionized auto workers fell from 100,000 in 1934 to 10,000 by the winter of 1935. These workers all labored for massive corporations in appalling conditions. The auto, steel, and coal industries were among 2,500

American employers that employed strikebreaking companies. The largest of these were Pearl Bergoff Services and the legendary Pinkerton National Detective Agency. The latter earned about $2 million between 1933 and 1936, for its standing army of armed men who could move at short notice into struck jobs to open the gates for strikebreakers. Both agencies also sent undercover agents into the plants to spy and inform on union activities.

There was also no shortage of strikebreaking workers: at a time when millions were unemployed, many people were willing to cross picket lines to feed their starving families. Some large corporations, like Ford, cynically exploited racial divisions by bringing in black workers as strikebreakers, knowing that these men, often holding menial jobs in the best of times and often helpless in the face of white racism, would meekly obey orders. The automakers also hoped that the white union men would become infuriated by black strikebreakers, and create violence that could break the strike, or simply surrender to regain their jobs.

In 1934, the United Mine Workers (UMW) began flexing its muscles, taking 70,000 Pennsylvania miners out on strike. The bosses responded with violence: Frick mine guards shot union workers as they came out of the pits. All through 1935, the UMW, and its new cousin, the United Auto Workers (UAW), struggled. That year 32 strikers and their sympathizers were killed, and National Guardsmen were called out to break strikes in six states.

Lewis formed the CIO, and with it, the Steel Workers Organization Committee (SWOC), with fellow miner Philip Murray. The CIO was soon joined by David Dubinsky's International Ladies' Garment Workers' Union (ILGWU) and the Reuther brothers and their brand-new United Auto Workers. The CIO got down to business on February 17, 1936, striking the Goodyear Tire & Rubber Company's Akron plant. Rubber workers camped out in 58 shanties and tents along an 11-mile perimeter around the factory, demanding better hours and wages. For four weeks, the strikers held fast, despite fierce winter wind. The cops threatened to open the factory gates, but when they found thousands of strikers massed at the gate, the police backed off. Goodyear created a Law and Order League and threatened to attack the picket line. The strikers leased a local radio station and broadcasted all night long, which forestalled the planned vigilante action. On March 22, Goodyear recognized the union. By July 1937, so did all of Akron's other rubber companies.

THE U.S. STEEL AGREEMENT

The next target was the auto industry, one of the most powerful in the nation, and after the United Auto Workers gained recognition there, the CIO took on the most powerful corporation in America, U.S. Steel, known as "Big Steel." Despite the Great Depression, U.S. Steel had earned $35.2 million in 1934, selling a quarter-million tons of goods ranging from ammonia to cement. Yet

The Memorial Day Massacre

While U.S. Steel, or "Big Steel," consented to a contract with its workers in early 1937, several smaller steel companies known collectively as "Little Steel" did not make a similar deal. On May 27, 1937, John L. Lewis took 70,000 men out of 27 Little Steel plants, including the companies Republic Steel, Youngstown Sheet and Tube, and Inland Steel. The Little Steel plants deployed company police and put hired guns in local police uniforms, and put strikebreakers to work inside the mills, keeping them fed by parcel post and airdrops. The steel companies also got the cooperation of local newspapers in "back-to-work" campaigns. Tom M. Girdler, head of Republic Steel, paid informers $25 a week, while fulminating against union leaders for interfering "in a man's private affairs." He also claimed the union men were Communists (they were not) and that no law compelled him to bargain with unions (the Wagner Act did). The steel companies spent $4 million (including $141,000 on munitions) to break the strike.

The strike went on anyway. Violence resulted on Memorial Day, outside Republic Steel's South Chicago plant. Thousands of strikers and their families massed on a flat prairie near the factory to march and demonstrate. Between the plain and the mill, the marchers found hundreds of Chicago police there because an "anonymous source" had told authorities the marchers were planning to march into the mill and seize it. About 250 yards from the mill a force of police attacked workers' wives with nightsticks and gas guns. Workers retaliated with taunts and soda bottles, so the police hit back with tear gas. Once the gas broke up the march, the police opened fire on the fleeing mob with their revolvers, and pursued the marchers through the gas and smoke, shooting people in the back and lying on the ground, all caught on newsreel cameras. Ten lay dead and more than 90 wounded in the "Memorial Day Massacre," but that was not the only outrage in the Little Steel strikes. Other strikes followed with violent results as well.

Senator La Follette investigated the Memorial Day Massacre, and his committee determined that: "The force employed by the police was far in excess of that which the occasion required. Its use must be ascribed either to gross inefficiency in the performance of the police duty, or a deliberate attempt to intimidate the strikers." La Follette's investigation changed the public perception of the massacre. In 1945, Republic paid $350,000 to settle suits against the company over the Memorial Day Massacre. National Labor Relations Board proceedings reinstated 7,000 workers with back-pay awards coming to $2 million. Bethlehem Steel held out until after Pearl Harbor, but by then that case went to the new War Labor Board, which granted the steelworkers a 5½-cent-an-hour wage hike, a closed shop (union membership would be required as a condition of employment), and dues checkoff (automatic payroll deduction for union dues).

the average steelworker took home only $369 a year to support a family of six. When steelworkers watched Charlie Chaplin pantomiming an assembly-line worker's five-minute break in the movie *Modern Times*, they didn't laugh—Chaplin's parody of moving his food and drink like his machine was too close to their own miserable existence. Worse, there seemed no way to change it. Decades of labor battles with U.S. Steel had ended in massacres like the 1892 Homestead strike and company victories.

This time, John Lewis tried a different tactic. On January 9, 1937, while his UAW workers were in the third week of their sit-down strike against the equally powerful General Motors Corporation in Michigan, Lewis met U.S. Steel CEO and board chairman Myron Charles Taylor at Washington's fashionable Mayflower Hotel, while having lunch, and the two chatted for 20 minutes. The next day, Taylor invited Lewis to his hotel for another conversation.

Lewis brought information to show that the SWOC had unionized enough workers to cripple it just as big orders would start piling up. Lewis suggested that five decades of violence between U.S. Steel management and labor should end with a union contract. Amazingly, Taylor consented. Eight weeks later, he initialed a contract that agreed to an eight-hour $5 day and a 40-hour week, with paid vacation, seniority rights, and grievance procedures.

UNION EXPANSION

The U.S. Steel settlement was a major step in union history. It was followed by SWOC signing agreements with 90 companies, including all of U.S. Steel's subsidiaries and key independents, and began modern corporate welfarism, the idea that businesses—and their unions—had to provide employees with health, retirement, and other benefits as part of their employment. These, on top of new federal programs like Social Security and unemployment compensation, would help lift American workers out of the serfdom they had endured for decades.

The CIO had won its biggest battle, and as 1937 rolled on, it signed 30,000 company contracts and grew to over three million members. Organized labor expanded on a vast scale, but the CIO's battles went on. Having defeated Big Steel, Lewis now took on "Little Steel," the nickname for the five major steel companies

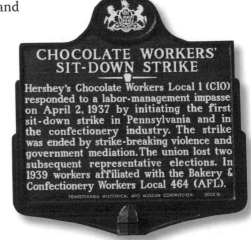

CHOCOLATE WORKERS' SIT-DOWN STRIKE

Hershey's Chocolate Workers Local 1 (CIO) responded to a labor-management impasse on April 2, 1937 by initiating the first sit-down strike in Pennsylvania and in the confectionery industry. The strike was ended by strike-breaking violence and government mediation. The union lost two subsequent representative elections. In 1939 workers affiliated with the Bakery & Confectionery Workers Local 464 (AFL).

PENNSYLVANIA HISTORICAL AND MUSEUM COMMISSION   2005 ©

A strike by Hershey's chocolate workers in 1937 was a failure for the CIO.

that ranked below U.S. Steel: Republic, National, Inland, Bethlehem, and Youngstown Sheet and Tube. Republic's Tom M. Girdler was their leader, and he said he would quit his $130,000 a year job as company president and resume hoeing potatoes before sitting down with the CIO.

1937 was the most savage year in the century for labor, but of the 3,720 strikes that year, 82 percent were won by workers, and December ended with eight million American workers in unions. In 1938, some long-standing labor grievances were addressed in the Fair Labor Standards Act, also known as the Wages and Hours Bill. This law established minimum wages for the first time, later upgraded to adjust for inflation. The law also required "time and a half" pay for overtime work in most jobs, and outlawed most child labor. With these gains in hand, by 1941 American unions had 15 million members as the nation's industry surged with orders for the defense push.

Despite that, labor still struggled. There were nine million unemployed in 1940, and three million still jobless in 1941. About 50 percent of the nation's automobile manufacturing capacity remained idle. Labor continued to fight management. Making matters worse were Communist agitators, still trying to infiltrate unions. After Hitler and Stalin signed their cynical Non-Aggression Pact of 1939, Germany and the Soviet Union were nominal allies, and American Communists were instructed to oppose the defense push. War was coming, and unions had to act. Philip Murray called for the creation of industry councils for each major industry, with equal numbers of labor and management and a government official as chairman, to coordinate production, train workers, and promote labor peace.

It proved illusory: Lewis still ran the United Mine Workers, and he wanted to unionize the mines owned by the major steel companies. FDR created the National Defense Mediation Board in March 1941, and after a two-day mine shutdown in late October, the board voted 9-2 to reject the UMW demands. Furious, Lewis took his miners out of the Pennsylvania pits on November 15. It looked like the old days again: 11 picketers were shot at the Frick plant in Edenborn, Pennsylvania, and Lewis was criticized for blocking the defense effort. He accepted a White House proposal for a three-man board to arbitrate the situation: U.S. Conciliation Service Director John Steelman, U.S. Steel President Benjamin Fairless, and himself. The trio voted 2-1 in favor of the UMW, on December 7, 1941.

WARTIME EMPLOYMENT

With the U.S. at war, the nation's young men, the core of its industrial base, went overseas to fight, creating massive worker shortages. These were filled almost overnight by women, teenagers avoiding school, Mexican migrants in Texas and California, black sharecroppers leaving their fields to work in shipyards in Mobile, Alabama, and destitute "Okies" in California at Lockheed and North American Aviation plants, and even midgets, whose small

"I've found the job where I fit best!"

FIND YOUR WAR JOB
In Industry–Agriculture–Business

This 1943 government poster urged women to try new kinds of work. By the end of the war, 14 million women were industrial workers, with two million of them in defense plants.

size made them perfect for work in small areas like aircraft cockpits. These jobs and changes resulted in more upheaval for American workers. Wartime industry operated round the clock, with workers hot-bunking in cheap hotels, boardinghouses, and apartments. Wages shot up 70 percent during the war. The "Okies" became affluent. Nine million unemployed workers found jobs.

Across the nation, factories changed from peacetime pursuits to war. Civilian automobile production was ended in 1942 (only 139 cars were produced during the war), and Ford's factory churned out more military equipment than all of Italy. General Motors and its 19,000 subcontractors alone supplied 10 percent of the U.S. war production, hiring three-quarters of a million workers to do so. Henry Kaiser revolutionized shipbuilding by creating his Liberty Ships in pre-fabricated sections. Workers became bosses overnight.

In 1940, 90 percent of women were in just 10 employment categories: whites worked in teaching, nursing, social work, and civil service, mostly Depression-proof occupations. Black and Latina women were domestic servants. With millions of men in uniform, government and industry advertised for women to take up all kinds of jobs, and by the end of World War II, more than 19 million women were working, 14 million of them as industrial workers, 2 million of them in defense plants. By the war's end, black and

The Full Employment Bill of 1945

Early in 1945, as the end of World War II was drawing near, President Roosevelt took up the issue of full employment with the Full Employment Bill of 1945. The bill permitted the federal government to use its investments and expenditures in order to provide jobs to everyone. Excerpted below is testimony to a Senate committee provided by Secretary of Commerce (and former vice-president) Henry Wallace in support of the bill.

In the President's message to Congress last year and this year he set forth eight self-evident economic truths as representing a second Bill of Rights under which a new basis of security and prosperity can be established for all—regardless of station, race, or creed.

America led the world in establishing political democracy. It must lead the world once more in strengthening and extending political democracy by firmly establishing economic democracy. Let us not forget the painful lessons of the rise of Fascism. Let us remember that political democracy is at best insecure and unstable without economic democracy. Fascism thrives on domestic insecurity, as well as on lack of or divided resistance to external aggression. Fascism is not only an enemy from without, it is also potentially an enemy from within...

Let us therefore affirm this economic bill of rights—and keep affirming it—until it is as familiar and real to us as our political bill of rights.

The economic bill of rights as embodied in the President's message to Congress last January is:

The right to a useful and remunerative job in the industries or shops or farms or mines of the nation;

The right to earn enough to provide adequate food and clothing and recreation;

The right of every farmer to raise and sell his products at a return which will give him and his family a decent living;

The right of every businessman, large and small, to trade in an atmosphere of freedom from unfair competition and domination by monopolies at home or abroad;

The right of every family to a decent home;

The right to adequate medical care and the opportunity to achieve and enjoy good health;

The right to adequate protection from the economic fears of old age, sickness, accident, and unemployment;

The right to a good education.

female workers were stronger and empowered. Trained in wartime trades, they rose up from the ranks of unskilled labor, and strengthened by their experience, were no longer in a mood to put up with or submit to pre-war social norms. However, taking advantage of these gains came sooner for the black worker than the female worker.

WARTIME LABOR DISPUTES

In 1941, A. Philip Randolph, leader of the Brotherhood of Pullman Car porters, organized a march on Washington to protest the exclusion of black workers from defense industries. FDR responded on June 25, 1941, issuing an executive order creating a Committee on Fair Employment Practices (FEPC) to investigate complaints of discrimination. It also ordered that defense production contracts be administered without discrimination, required no-discrimination clauses in all contracts, and no discrimination in training programs for workers.

In three years, the FEPC handled 8,000 complaints and held 30 public hearings. While its work ended with the war, the gains black workers made were valuable and important: many blacks escaped the serfdom of sharecropping through higher-paying jobs and training programs in wartime defense industry, gained valuable business or industrial skills, and were able to move off their farms and into Northern cities where there were greater opportunities. Many of these workers gained union cards, which helped put an end to race-based strikebreaking by employers.

Battles between management and labor continued during the war, but with far less violence and acrimony. The Wagner Act meant that strikes were settled by federal mediators instead of bayonets. The government's cost-plus pricing of war contracts that assured company profits, wage and price controls, and labor shortages gave bargaining power to unions in negotiations. Intransigent bosses could no longer use strikebreakers and private cops to break up unions. Nor could they count on support from friendly judges and politicians.

Even so, strikes still took place, with 13.5 million man-days lost in 1943, but one year of work gained for every hour lost, as union-boss battles once fought in streets, coal mining towns, and factory yards were now simply part of the War Labor Board's 17,000-case backlog solved in hearing rooms by arbitrators. The problems of inflation were temporarily solved when FDR issued a "hold-the-line" order on wages and prices.

Nevertheless, coal miners and coal operators continued to spar, and strikes rippled through the coalfields in March and April 1943. Roosevelt seized the nation's coal mines in response on May 1, putting Secretary of the Interior Harold Ickes in charge of the mines. Despite this, Lewis kept pulling his miners out of the pits for sporadic strikes, which irritated many Americans, particularly G.I.s overseas—many of them conscripts who were peacetime union men—who saw the miners as unpatriotic.

The Smith-Connally Act was passed over FDR's veto in the summer of 1943, and that empowered the president to seize struck facilities, fine or jail strikers at a defense plant in the government's possession, and impose a 30-day cooling-off period following a strike notice. Lewis was blamed for this "vicious anti-labor bill." More strikes followed, and FDR had to seize the mines again in October, authorizing Ickes to negotiate directly with the mine union.

After negotiations that gained miners a $1.50 wage increase, Lewis ordered the miners back into the pits on November 3. A month later, the government vetoed an eight-cent-an-hour raise to railroad workers, and they voted by 98 percent to go on strike. Roosevelt had the army seize the railroads, and a settlement in January gave a four- to 10-cent increase.

THE END OF THE WAR

The trade unions emerged from war greatly strengthened. Union membership soared from 10.5 million at Pearl Harbor to 14.75 million on V-J Day. The CIO's unions were well-entrenched in even their most bitter enemies' plants, and the AFL was also more powerful. Average real weekly earnings had jumped from $24 a week in 1939 to $36.72 in 1944.

The end of the war also put defense plants out of business and brought returning G.I.s home to compete for jobs. Employers feared the return of

Workers in a frozen juice concentrate factory in 1946. By 1949, the labor situation had changed dramatically compared to 1929, and former defense factories successfully moved to producing consumer products.

the Great Depression, and unions feared the return of open shops and labor wars. President Truman pleaded for a continuance of the no-strike pledge during the war-to-peace transition, but labor ignored his request. The last four months of 1945 saw 28.4 million man-days lost to strikes, and 4.5 million workers on picket lines in 1946, costing 113 million man-days of labor. Coal, auto, steel, electric, maritime, and railroad industries slammed to a halt.

Nevertheless, the strikes of 1946 saw little or no violence. New Deal-era reforms like unemployment insurance, wartime savings, and the G.I. Bill, made life easier for picketing workers. Wartime profits enabled management to withstand strike losses. Legal reforms meant that unions were recognized bargaining agents, and the Wagner Act made union-busting illegal. Federal and state government agencies acted as mediators instead of employer muscle.

Strikes still rolled on, though. In November 1945, Walter Reuther took 200,000 General Motors workers out of the corporation's 96 plants nationwide. At issue was Reuther's demand that GM open its books to prove or disprove the United Auto Workers' contention that the corporation could grant a 30-percent raise without hiking car prices. The Truman administration supported Reuther, and GM stormed out of the hearings, only offering a 19½-cent-per-hour hike. The union was out for 113 days, which wore out the auto workers, and they had to settle for an 18½-cents-an-hour raise.

The January 1946 steel strike took 750,000 men out of the plants, but Philip Murray was only concerned with wages, not prices. The White House allowed U.S. Steel to raise its prices $5 a ton, and Benjamin Fairless quickly settled with Philip Murray after 30 days, at Truman's suggested 18½-cents-an-hour increase.

Coal miners were also intransigent: as soon as the steel strike was over in April 1946, 400,000 soft-coal miners in 21 states left their pits. With the miners out, the railroad workers threatened to strike in May, imperiling the coal-dependent economy. Truman seized the railroads, and gave the union five days to accept federal arbitration awards. The union refused. Truman asked his attorney general if he could draft all the railroad workers, regardless of age, into the Army. The attorney general said such a move was unconstitutional. Truman responded, "We'll draft them first and think about the law later."

Truman went to Capitol Hill to ask Congress to grant him authority to draft the striking rail workers, but soon after arriving he got word that the strike had been settled. The coal strike still rolled on, though, imperiling 62 percent of the nation's electricity and 55 percent of its industrial power. Truman put his Secretary of Interior, Julius A. Krug, in charge of the mines, and declared that a union strike against the government was illegal. Krug then granted nearly all of the UMW's demands, but Lewis repudiated the contract in October over a trivial point on vacation pay, and demanded full re-negotiation of the entire contract. The miners went out of the pits in No-

The Taft-Hartley Labor-Management Act

A major defeat for unions came in 1947 with the passage—over Truman's veto—of the Taft-Hartley Labor-Management Act, a conservative backlash to the strikes of 1946. This law prohibited closed shops, gave the National Labor Relations Board and the federal judiciary the power to again impose strike-ending injunctions, approved "right-to-work" laws, and ended jurisdictional strikes and secondary boycotts. It also called for 60-day "cooling-off" periods after strike votes.

Labor saw the law as coercive against unions, but the bill was more powerful than Taft originally intended, and the injunctions and fines could also be used against intransigent employers. The law also barred employers from forming "company unions," which would ironically help baseball players organize two decades later. Large unions were not hurt by the act but small ones were.

vember, and in 10 days, cities faced electrical cuts, factories shutdowns, and railroads immobility.

On Thursday, November 21, Judge T. Alan Goldsborough cited Lewis for contempt of court. Six days later, the judge hit Lewis and the UMW with a $3.5 million fine, the greatest in labor history, staggering Lewis. As he rose to argue the point, his lawyers dragged him back to his seat—a judge who tossed out $3.5 million fines was not a judge to be debated with. The UMW appealed to the Supreme Court, which cut the fine down to $700,000 on the proviso that the union purge itself of the contempt charge in a reasonable time. A stunned Lewis called off the strike on the terms originally agreed with Krug, and tottered off the podium. He remained in control of the UMW, but his autocratic behavior and bullying manner were no longer as powerful.

CONCLUSION

By 1949, the entire picture of labor in America had changed dramatically from its 1929 condition. Factories that been idle during the 1930s produced B-17 bombers and Sherman tanks during the war and then seamlessly switched over to producing cars and refrigerators, ensuring high employment and prosperity. Unlike the 1920s, this prosperity extended to management and labor alike, with unionized workers the norm in major and minor industries. In many industries and states, management accepted the concepts of federally-mediated or arbitrated collective bargaining with fairly-elected unions representing their workers. The violence, bloodshed, and union-busting of the past were eliminated, as was much of the radicalism of many previous unions. Twelve-hour days, company spies, and child labor were eliminated. Seniority rights, grievance procedures, and pension plans became accepted as standard procedures.

Unions, now recognized as legitimate organizations, added to their spheres of interest by creating job training and education programs for members and youth. Unions in dangerous professions became heavily involved with health issues: black lung for coal miners, asbestos for shipyard workers, and later, mental stress for postal workers. The United Federation of Teachers created career development programs for its members, and Walter Reuther created interracial bowling leagues for the United Auto Workers.

Most importantly, American workers moved into a better way of life, escaping the near-slavery of the previous decades and centuries. No longer just cogs in an assembly line, they could enjoy the fruits of their work, safer working conditions, and better lives for themselves and their children.

DAVID H. LIPPMAN

Further Readings

Brooks, Thomas W. *Toil and Trouble: A History of American Labor*. New York: Delacorte Press, 1964.

Dodds, John W. *Life in Twentieth Century America*. New York: Putnam's, 1973.

Glennon, Lorraine, ed. *Our Times: The Illustrated History of the 20th Century*. Atlanta, GA: Turner Publishing Inc, 1995.

Kennedy, David M. *Freedom from Fear: The American People in Depression and War, 1929–1945*. New York: Oxford University Press, 1999.

Manchester, William. *The Glory and the Dream: A Narrative History of America, 1932–1972*. Boston, MA: Little, Brown, and Company, 1972.

Phillips, Cabell. *From the Crash to the Blitz, 1929–1939: The New York Times Chronicle of American Life*. New York: MacMillan, 1969.

Shlaes, A. *The Forgotten Man: A New History of the Great Depression*. New York: Harper Collins, 2007.

Stein, R. Conrad. *The Home Front During World War II in American History*. Berkeley Heights, NJ: Enslow, 2003.

Susman, Warren I. *Culture as History: The Transformation of American Society in the Twentieth Century*. New York: Pantheon Books, 1984.

Watkins, T.H. *The Great Depression*. Boston, MA: Little, Brown, and Company, 1993.

Wiebe, Robert. *The Search for Order*. New York: Hill and Wang, 1966.

Chapter 13

Military and Wars

"For this comrade is dead, dead in the war,
a young man out of millions yet to live."
—Karl Shapiro

BEFORE WORLD WAR I the Americans had attempted to keep themselves isolated from the rest of the world. While American manpower tipped the war in favor of the Allies, Americans retreated into isolationism after the war. Even though President Woodrow Wilson advocated the League of Nations, through which member nations could mediate disputes before they boiled over into another war, Americans opposed U.S. membership for fear of possible military obligations. Furthermore, in 1924 the United States and 61 other countries signed the Kellogg-Briand Pact, a remarkably naïve agreement that outlawed war as an instrument of foreign policy. Such a pact was futile since enforcement would likely lead to war.

During the 1930s, all of the future Axis Powers—Nazi Germany, Fascist Italy, and Imperial Japan—began territorial conquests. Between 1936 and 1939, Adolf Hitler's Germany conquered the Rhineland, Austria, and Czechoslovakia, and it attacked Poland, touching off World War II. Italy, a junior member in the fascist alliance, attacked primitive Ethiopia in an imperial land-grab in 1935. Japan, hoping to achieve imperial hegemony in the Pacific, invaded Manchuria in 1931. In 1937, it began systematic invasions in other parts of China.

Through it all, the United States did nothing. President Herbert Hoover's Secretary of State Henry Stimson issued the country's only response to Japan's

185

A B-25 Bomber painted with nose art typical of World War II. Congress approved the purchase of 5,500 planes even before entering the war.

Manchuria incursion; the Stimson Doctrine simply said that the United States would not recognize Japan's annexation of Manchuria. With no American reprisals coming, Japan would later feel free to do as it wished in the Pacific.

President Franklin D. Roosevelt, inaugurated in March 1933, was an internationalist, but public isolationism stymied much of his foreign policy instincts. When Italy invaded Ethiopia, largely using American oil to fuel its armor, Roosevelt urged American oil producers to begin a "moral embargo" against Italy. It never materialized.

Between 1935 and 1939, the U.S. Congress passed five neutrality acts designed to keep the United States from selling arms to belligerents and thus avoid war. By 1939, Congress had also implemented the policy of "Cash and Carry." If foreign nations wanted to buy American goods, they had to pay for them in cash (lest a war destroy their credit and deprive the U.S. of payment) and carry them home in their own ships. Americans did not want a repeat of World War I (or the War of 1812 for that matter) when U.S. attempts to carry on neutral trade across the Atlantic dragged it into war.

The high point of American isolationism came in 1937 when the House of Representatives nearly approved the Ludlow Amendment. The amendment would have mandated a general election and voter approval before the United States entered another war. Congressmen were so paralyzed by the thought of another war that they nearly gave away one of their basic constitutional privileges—that of declaring war.

Beginning in 1933, the United States did embark on some naval improvements, but they had more to do with Depression economics than war preparation. Roosevelt's New Deal included the National Industrial Recovery Act and the Public Works Administration (PWA), which gave money to industries in an attempt to kick-start the economy. Some of that money could be earmarked for naval construction, and Roosevelt signed an executive order to build two aircraft carriers, four cruisers, and 20 destroyers for $240 million.

Representative Carl Vinson, chair of the House Naval Affairs Committee, with FDR's backing, pushed two more spending packages to approval. A 1934 bill, the Vinson-Trammell Act, authorized 102 more ships. By 1939, the U.S. Navy was essentially even with Japan as far as carrier, battleship, cruiser, destroyer, and submarine numbers, but it had no significant bases west of Pearl Harbor. Roosevelt also called for $500 million to expand airpower by 10,000 planes. Congress approved 60 percent of that, which would build about 5,500 planes.

END OF ISOLATIONISM

American isolationism began to abate in 1940 after Germany overran France and began an aerial campaign to defeat England. September 1940 was a turning point for the United States. With Great Britain fighting Germany in both the skies over southern England and in the North Atlantic, British Prime Minister Winston Churchill asked Roosevelt if Great Britain could use some old American warships. The result was an executive order known as the Destroyers-Bases Deal, in which the United States transferred 50 destroyers to the Royal Navy in return for the rights to eight British naval bases in the Atlantic and Caribbean.

That same month, Congress approved the Selective Service and Training Act, which enacted the first peacetime draft in American history. Two months earlier, the army had already called the National Guard into active service. The two measures, combined with additional volunteers, boosted army manpower to almost 1.2 million men by mid-1941. Not only did this direct involvement of American men bring the real possibility of war home to Americans, it affected the economy as well. With the Great Depression still not over, it gave hundreds of thousands of men jobs and created job vacancies for others to fill. The Selective Service act did much to slash American unemployment.

Realizing that Great Britain could not fight the war alone indefinitely, Roosevelt proposed to Congress a method whereby the United States could bring its industrial might to bear on the Axis even while a nonbelligerent. He called the plan Lend-Lease. In it the United States would manufacture all types of materials of war—from canteens, helmets, and rifles to tanks, trucks, and aircraft—and either lend them or lease them to fellow Allies. Roosevelt said Lend-Lease would make the United

An American-made canteen and canvas cover from World War II.

December 7, 1941

For most Americans, December 7, 1941, became one of those "where-were-you-when-you-heard" days, comparable to September 11, 2001, for Americans of the early 21st century. In 1941, the population of the United States was reported at 134 million. Some 56 million Americans labored in the work force, and another 1.5 million were employed by the military. The median income was approximately $2,000 a year, and average take-home pay was around $40 per week. The Great Depression was winding down, and most Americans ate three meals a day and were reasonably well-housed. Despite these gains, 4 million Americans were still out of work. Regardless of the desire of President Franklin Roosevelt to add America's strength to that of the Allies fighting World War II, the nation was not at war. Talks with Japan were not going well, but hopes were high for eventual compromise.

American complacency came to an end early on the morning of December 7, 1941, when Japanese forces attacked the American fleet at the Pearl Harbor naval station in Hawaii. Some 2,280 died during the attack, and another 1,709 were wounded. All battleships were destroyed or damaged in the attack, and 11 other water vessels were destroyed. The Japanese destroyed a total of 188 aircraft, including 27 fighter planes. American towns, particularly those along the Pacific Coast, went into full alert. Patrols were dispatched as Americans waited for a Japanese attack on the mainland that never materialized.

Responding to Roosevelt's demand for action to revenge the unprovoked attack, Congress declared war on Japan on December 8. Germany and Italy responded by declaring war on the United States. "Remember Pearl Harbor" became a rallying cry for American males who rushed to enlistment offices and for American females who joined the war effort. They worked at jobs formerly filled by males serving at the front and in a myriad of volunteer positions that ranged from engaging in civilian defense and Red Cross activities to promoting war bonds and collecting scarce materials for military use.

States the "arsenal of democracy." Congress agreed and approved the plan in March 1941. The United States shipped $50 billion in Lend-Lease aid during the war; Great Britain received $31.6 billion of that, and the Soviet Union got some $11 billion worth.

In August 1941, Churchill and Roosevelt further cemented the Anglo-American alliance when they met on a British destroyer off the coast of Newfoundland. They affirmed a "Germany first" strategy, and issued the Atlantic Charter, which listed the war aims of both countries and their vision of a post-war world. The next month, hostilities flared between U.S. and German ships

The 31,800-ton USS West Virginia *burning in the attack on Pearl Harbor. The small boat in the foreground is rescuing a sailor, while at least two more men can be seen high in the burning ship's superstructure. Almost 2,400 people died in the attack.*

in the North Atlantic. Germans fired on the USS *Greer* (an attack Americans provoked); the USS *Kearny*, killing 11 sailors; and the USS *Reuben James*, killing 115 men. With no public mandate yet for official war, Roosevelt was content to wage undeclared war. And while Adolf Hitler's advisors argued that Americans had become aggressors and Germany should declare war on them, he was content to leave the United States alone while his troops attacked the Soviet Union, Germany's former ally.

PEARL HARBOR

It would remain for Japan to drag the United States into the war. Since 1937, Japan had been moving down the coast of China and into Indochina. Japan wanted to create the Greater East Asia Co-Prosperity Sphere, a glorified name for a Japanese empire. Chief among Japanese targets were the oilfields of the Dutch East Indies, for Japan had no oil reserves of its own. In fact, its aggression during the 1930s had been fueled by American oil. Now the U.S. State Department demanded that Japan cease its expansion and pull out of China, or the United States would cut off its supplies of scrap iron and oil.

Japan had no intention of doing either, and it entered negotiations with the United States knowing they would eventually break down. At the same time, Japan planned for war. The United States obviously would block any Japanese drive to the Dutch East Indies, for the Philippines (U.S. territory since 1898) sat squarely across the Japanese route south. Thus Japan wanted to knock the U.S. Pacific Fleet out of action long enough for Japan to seize the oilfields and establish a defensive perimeter throughout the central Pacific.

Admiral Isoroku Yamamoto designed a carrier-based, two-pronged offensive to hit the U.S. naval base at Pearl Harbor, Hawaii, and army bases in the Philippines. Japan unleashed the attacks on December 7, 1941. At Pearl Harbor, aerial attacks sank or disabled eight battleships, three cruisers, three destroyers, several support ships, and destroyed or damaged nearly 300 aircraft. Almost 2,400 people died and another 1,200 were injured. The attack demonstrated the importance of aircraft carriers in the coming war. As such, the victory at Pearl Harbor was hollow—it destroyed none of the American carriers, as all were out of port at the time. The United States declared war on Japan on December 8. On December 11, as a result of Germany's Tri-Partite Pact with Italy and Japan, Adolf Hitler declared war against the United States. Now the United States was fully involved in both theaters of war.

MOBILIZATION

The start of war meant that the United States had to quickly mobilize in two areas—military and civilian. The Selective Service was already in operation, and Pearl Harbor caused an initial rush of volunteerism. Congress required all men between ages 18 and 64 to register for the draft; optimum service ages were 18 to 44 (later 38). While the Selective Service registered 36 million men, it drafted only 10.1 million. Draft-aged men could get deferments for health impairments or employment in war industry or agriculture. During the war and its immediate aftermath, 16.3 million people served in branches of the American armed services—11.2 million in the army, 4.1 million in the navy, and the rest distributed among other units.

Women entered the military in large numbers as well. About 74,000 women served as military nurses, and some 330,000 of them served in army and navy auxiliary corps. Five percent of those saw service overseas, and 30 died during enemy attacks. Women also served as Women's Air Force Service Pilots (WASPs). These women, about 1,000 of them, trained as pilots, tested new aircraft, and ferried them to debarkation points where men took the planes on to combat zones. WASPs suffered wartime fatalities as well.

Industrial mobilization required much government intervention. First, it had to ensure that industry had enough raw materials. Second, it had to direct industry to meet military requirements. And third, it had to negotiate war contracts that ensured a good profit for manufacturers, but did not gouge the government. A series of government agencies starting with the War

Resources Board, followed by the Office of Production Management (OPM), the Supply Priorities and Allocation Board, and the War Production Board, accomplished all those things effectively. The agencies instructed manufacturers to set aside their typical output in favor of military goods. Thus, car builders began making Jeeps, 2½-ton trucks, and even some aircraft. Appliance manufacturers did the same. Even at that, new factories and shipyards had to be built.

Industrial and agricultural mobilization soaked up the unemployed of the Great Depression, some seven million of them, and added another seven million new employees to the workforce. Five million of those workers were women, many of whom had not worked out of the home before. Women filled jobs that had been traditionally held by men. They welded, fitted pipes, operated heavy machinery, and riveted (hence the enduring image of Rosie the Riveter). They made everything from helmets and parachutes to tanks, bombers, and aircraft carriers. A small baby boom came soon after American servicemen left for the war (they were called "bye-bye babies"), and the government made sure that working women had daycare for their children. In another new development, women found membership in labor unions.

A group of WAVES (Women Accepted for Volunteer Emergency Service) at work during the war. They were the U.S. Navy counterpart to the WACs (Women's Army Corps).

At left, a World War II breakfast K-ration set, including utensils and cookware. At right, a soldier wearing a "doughboy" helmet in 1942 (the year they were replaced by the U.S. M1 helmet) eating U.S. Army World War II dinner K-rations in the field from a similar set.

Women also saved money. With no new cars or appliances during the war years, and with rationing of everyday goods like sugar and flour, there was little to buy. Federal price controls also curtailed inflation, so women kept much of what they made. The military also encouraged husbands in service to send nearly half of their monthly $50 paycheck home to their wives. Thus people who had become accustomed to having little in the Depression found themselves with a nest egg at the close of World War II.

War industry also caused an internal migration in the United States. With most war industry in the north and army bases in the South, more than 15 million American civilians moved at least once during the war. An estimated one million African Americans moved out of the South to seek war-related jobs. They found some, but racism was still rampant in the United States, even as it fought a war against Nazi racism in Europe. Protesting the lack of jobs for blacks, labor leader A. Phillip Randolph threatened Roosevelt with an African-American march on Washington, D.C. Roosevelt avoided the demonstration by creating the Fair-Employment Practices Committee to oversee nondiscriminatory hiring.

American industrial mobilization worked stupendously. During the war, American workers turned out an estimated 200,000 aircraft (more than 96,000 in 1944 alone); 86,000 tanks and self-propelled artillery; 120,000 artillery pieces; 1,200 warships; 2,600 pre-fab Liberty ships, which workers could turn out in less than two months; and 2.4 million trucks and Jeeps. The equipment was not only for American servicemen, but supplied Lend-Lease partners as well.

Industrial mobilization did something else as well—it helped fund the war. The Revenue Act of 1942 extended an income tax to all American workers, not just a wealthy few. That raised the tax base from seven million to 42 million people, and the increase in personal and farm wages meant that 45 percent of the $318 billion in U.S. war costs came from "current revenues" rather than loans.

WARTIME ENTERTAINMENT AND THE HOME FRONT

American civilians on the home front also did much to mobilize their own morale and patriotism during the war. Millions of Americans, young and old, participated in scrap metal drives to collect metal for recycling to military uses. Because rubber was unavailable after Japanese occupation of rubber producing areas of the Pacific, Americans also collected old rubber tires. Also, to save rubber, the government instituted 35-mile-per-hour speed limits and rationed gas. Americans, with some griping, participated in the government rationing of everyday items like sugar and flour as well. They bought war bonds, which gave the government an influx of money with

A typical World War II soldier's foot locker with cigarettes, toiletries, and mementos from home. Scrap drives and rationing on the home front kept supplies flowing abroad.

promised repayment and interest after the war; the bonds also gave civilians personal ownership in the war. Thousands planted "victory gardens," which meant they grew many of their own vegetables to free up commercial farms to produce for the army and navy. In fact, victory gardens produced more than eight million tons of produce in 1943; that was more than half of the nation's total produce output.

The USO

Throughout World War II the Camp Shows branch of the United Service Organization (USO) sent entertainers from New York and Hollywood to entertain U.S. soldiers, sailors, and marines in every theater of operation. Excerpted below is a 1944 article written by John Desmond for the *New York Times* describing the experience of traveling with a USO show.

The stage is a rough board affair, supported by freshly hewn logs. On it a girl, dressed in a simple cotton dress like those you see on the boardwalk at Jones Beach on a summer afternoon, is singing. Behind her two other entertainers are sitting on camp stools and to the right an accordionist pumps his arms. His instrument pours out a volume of sound that somehow manages to approximate the tune of "Shoo-Shoo Baby."

The scene is in New Guinea. It is hot—115 degrees in back of the stage, 130 plus under the arc lights that are powered by a mobile Army generator standing nearby . . .

Now the accordion's tones swell to a crescendo for the closing phrases. The singer's last note is cut short by a roar that breaks across the jungle stillness. A thousand pairs of hands are clapping. Men are shouting and whistling. Out of the din an occasional shout comes clear, "How about some more, baby?" or "Let's have 'Take It Easy,'" or "Give us 'Don't Sweetheart me.'" The girl looks at the musician and nods. Then the roar suddenly ceases and the strains of another song float over the vast and almost unseen audience of United States servicemen.

The singer and the performers with her on New Guinea make up an overseas company of the Camp Shows branch of the United Service Organizations. At the present time, eighty such companies are out of the country, giving shows in bomb-damaged opera houses in Italy, in rickety Nissen huts in North Africa, in storage barns in Alaska and the Aleutians, in jungles, deserts, mountain hideouts—in fact, wherever American boys are stationed.

In the simplest terms, Camp Shows' job is to bring Hollywood and Broadway to the servicemen . . . camp shows have been given before audiences totaling 37,000,000 servicemen in the United States and an uncalculated number abroad.

The United States made thousands of Sherman tanks similar to this M4A1 model to supply the Allies under the Lend-Lease plan, and had shipped $50 billion in Lend-Lease aid by the end of the war.

The American entertainment industry also mobilized for war. Hollywood turned out patriotic fare, some lighthearted like *Stage-door Canteen* (1943) and *Four Jills in a Jeep* (1944), others more serious like *Bataan* (1943) and *Destination Tokyo* (1943) although they generally lacked historical accuracy. Hollywood also worked for the army. Popular director Frank Capra directed the now-classic series *Why We Fight* (seven episodes between 1942 and 1945 for which Disney animators did map illustrations), designed to remind Americans exactly why America was in the war. Others, like a young B-movie actor named Ronald Reagan, made training films for the army. Still other celebrities left Hollywood for the war itself. One was Jimmy Stewart, famous for such movies as *The Philadelphia Story* and *Mr. Smith Goes to Washington*. Joining the U.S. Army Air Force, he became a B-24 bomber pilot and flew a full rotation of missions over Europe.

WAR CHRONOLOGY
The United States adhered to the "Germany first" plan, but opportunities to strike Japan arose first. On April 18, 1942, Army Colonel James H. "Jimmy" Doolittle led 15 carrier-based B-25 bombers in a raid on Tokyo. The raid did only token damage, but struck a blow against Japan's morale. The raid proved the value of aircraft carriers in this war, and made Pearl Harbor a hollow victory for Japan.

In May 1942, the U.S. Navy under Admiral Chester Nimitz blocked a Japanese move toward Australia. The ensuing Battle of the Coral Sea on May 7 was the first naval battle in which aircraft did the fighting and combatant ships did not see each other. An American strategic victory there halted any further Japanese push to the south. Next, Japan tried to draw out American carriers by attacking a U.S. base at Midway Island, northwest of Hawaii. Nimitz sent Admiral Raymond Spruance there with a task force. The Battle of Midway began June 4, and it became the turning point in the Pacific War. Again an aerial duel, Midway cost the United States one carrier, but Japan lost four. The battle reversed the strategic situation in the Pacific, placing Japan on the defensive.

After Midway, the United States began a long campaign to wrest territory away from Japan. On August 7, 1942, backed by a naval task force, the 1st Marine Division landed on Guadalcanal in the Solomon Islands, touching off a six-month battle. Americans won the fight for the island and surrounding sea lanes in February 1943 after losing 615 planes, 25 ships, and about 7,500 men. They had killed 30,000 Japanese soldiers and destroyed 680 enemy aircraft and 24 ships. Late 1942 also saw American soldiers begin ground campaigns in the European theater of war with Operation Torch, the invasion of North Africa. Torch involved more than 500 ships from the United States and Great Britain, and more than 100,000 troops. They landed on the coasts of Morocco and Algeria on November 8, 1942.

Operation Torch was a turning point. It secured North Africa for the Allies and provided just enough of a diversion for Germany that the Soviet Red Army was able to launch a counterattack to lift the German siege of Stalingrad, which had been underway since 1941. Torch also provided the Allies with a launching point for an attack on Europe.

In July 1943, American and British troops invaded Sicily, forcing Germans from the island within six weeks. On September 3, Allied troops invaded Italy in a campaign that became one of the bitterest of the war. Even though the Allies captured Rome on June 4, 1944, fighting in Italy continued until war's end. At best, the Italian campaign drew German troops away from Soviet advances in eastern Europe and the invasion of France in June 1944. For that, the Allies had 312,000 total casualties in the long Italian campaign, with 31,886 of them killed. Of the dead, 19,475 were American. Germany had almost 435,000 casualties in Italy, with 48,000 of them dead.

D-DAY AND GERMAN DEFEAT

On June 6, 1944, almost 176,000 American, British, and Canadian troops invaded German-occupied France on the beaches of Normandy, about 100 miles south of England across the English Channel. Some 13,000 aircraft (including fighters, bombers, and transports), and more than 6,000 naval vessels (mostly landing craft, but including battleships and destroyers), supported

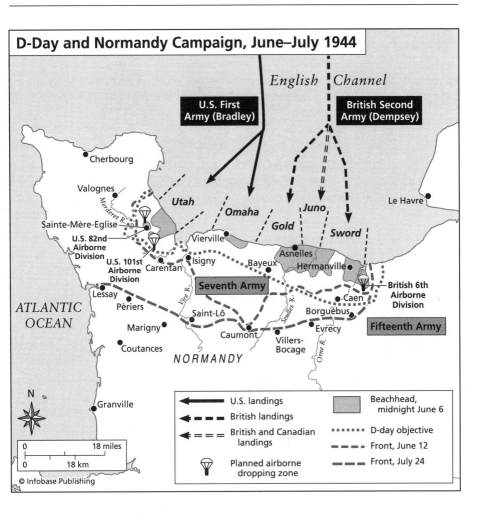

D-Day and Normandy Campaign, June–July 1944

English Channel

U.S. First Army (Bradley)

British Second Army (Dempsey)

Cherbourg

Valognes

Merderet R.

Utah

Omaha

Juno

Le Havre

Sainte-Mère-Eglise

U.S. 82nd Airborne Division

Vierville

Gold

Sword

U.S. 101st Airborne Division

Isigny

Carentan

Bayeux

Asnelles

Hermanville

Seventh Army

British 6th Airborne Division

Lessay

Vire R.

Caen

ATLANTIC OCEAN

Pèriers

Saint-Lô

Borguébus

Seulles R.

Marigny

Caumont

Evrecy

Fifteenth Army

Coutances

Villers-Bocage

Orne R.

NORMANDY

N

Granville

U.S. landings

British landings

British and Canadian landings

Planned airborne dropping zone

Beachhead, midnight June 6

D-day objective

Front, June 12

Front, July 24

0   18 miles

0   18 km

© Infobase Publishing

the landings. While Winston Churchill feared the loss of 50,000 men on D-Day, as planners called this landing, the Allies actually lost only 2,500 men.

D-Day was the beginning of the end of the war in Europe. After consolidating a foothold on the beaches, the Allies initiated a breakout in July with Operation Cobra. Led by General George Patton's 3rd Army and British Field Marshall Bernard Montgomery's 2nd Army, the Allies shoved beleaguered German troops aside, then began a sprint across northwestern France that culminated in the liberation of Paris on August 25.

By September, Allied Supreme Commander Dwight D. Eisenhower had sanctioned a broad-front advance into Germany that became a race between Patton's and Montgomery's armies and critically stretched Allied supply lines. In December 1944, correctly judging that the rapid Allied advance was straining their supply lines, Hitler ordered German troops to counterattack. They struck on a narrow front in Belgium. The resulting Battle of the Bulge halted

Soldiers helping the wounded on the beach during the D-Day invasion. The Allies lost 2,500 men, far fewer than anticipated.

"An Army of Liberation"

By the summer of 1944, Adolf Hitler had established what he considered an impregnable fortress along the coast of Europe. Hitler's Atlantic Wall stretched from Norway to the France–Spain border and contained 15,000 strong points, which were manned by 200,000 Axis troops.

Nevertheless, American and British leaders, who were convinced that Hitler's defenses could be breached, planned an invasion of the coast of Normandy in the spring of 1944. In May, the decision was made to postpone the attack for a month in order to give shipyards the opportunity to ready additional landing craft. General Dwight D. Eisenhower gave the order to proceed in the early hours of June 6, 1944 because he realized that "the inescapable consequences of postponement were almost too bitter to contemplate."

Within 15 minutes of sunrise, American and British troops arrived in Normandy. British and Canadian troops invaded on beaches code-named Gold, Juno, and Sword to the west of Le Havre, and further west, toward Cherbourg, the Americans landed on beaches code-named Utah and Omaha. An American journalist who arrived with the second wave of 2,000 paratroopers described the experience, "Out, out, out fast into the cool night air, out, out, out over France." As the RAF Spitfires flew overhead, an unidentified voice on the radio cried out, "For God's sake get those mortars quick. Dig them out, boys, they are right down our necks."

By late afternoon, the beaches had been secured. Leslie "Bill" Kirk, who landed with the 82nd U.S. Airborne Division, remembered rescuing a casualty who "had a nice clean hole in his leg and seemed happy about the whole thing." Throughout the night of June 6, Kirk recalls that "mortar fire came in hot and heavy." He bemoaned the fact that many paratroopers became disoriented and drowned when they landed in the water. When Allied forces reached French towns, residents were at first unsure whose forces were arriving, but were reassured that the new arrivals composed "an army of liberation."

the Allies only briefly, and it was Germany's last offensive effort. Between January and April 1945, the Allies moved unstoppably into Germany and toward Berlin. The Anglo-American offensive in northwest Europe had also allowed the Soviet Red Army to begin a major offensive against Germany from the east. Now, Germany was surrounded. By early May Berlin was finished, Hitler had killed himself, and Germany sued for peace.

THE PACIFIC THEATER AND THE END OF THE WAR

The American campaign in the Pacific proceeded at an equally determined pace. In 1943, land troops under General Douglas MacArthur "leapfrogged" (a method of advance that took critical positions, bypassing others to let them die for lack of supply) up the coast of New Guinea, securing that place and the nearby Admiralty Islands by February 1944. In the central Pacific, the navy and marines under Admiral Nimitz invaded critical islands using a similar leapfrog approach. Within 10 months he had traveled 4,500 miles.

In February 1945, 30,000 Marines landed on the island of Iwo Jima. Japanese soldiers considered Iwo Jima part of their home islands, and they defended it stubbornly. More than 5,000 Marines died in combat for the island; they killed more than 23,000 Japanese. Okinawa, at the southern end of the Japanese island chain, was the United States' next target. More than 150,000 troops began landing on April 1, 1945; the battle lasted until June 21. Americans suffered 49,000 total casualties; more than 100,000 Japanese soldiers died, along with a very large number of civilians, some of whom were trapped in caves in which they sought to hide. The fight for Okinawa saw Japan launch some 700 *kamikazes*—suicide planes—at American naval ships, damaging 13 of them.

Allied military chiefs worked on plans to invade Japan next, but scientists in the New Mexico desert successfully exploded an atomic bomb and changed their plans. Code-named Manhattan, the project to build an atomic bomb had proceeded throughout the war in top secret. Harry Truman, who became president upon the death of Roosevelt in April 1945, approved dropping two bombs on Japan. The first atomic strike was against Hiroshima on August 6; the second was against Nagasaki on August 9. Japan sued for peace the next day, and formally surrendered on September 2.

Of the 16 million Americans in uniform during the war, 405,399 of them died, almost 300,000 of them in combat. Compared to the eight million Axis troops who died, American losses were light. That stems largely from the fact that the war did not occur on American soil, and that Americans preferred to fight long-distance—telegraphing their punches with artillery and aircraft—as much as possible before engaging in close fighting.

THE POSTWAR PERIOD

The American economy, which experienced a boom during the war, stuttered briefly in 1946 as industry retooled to peacetime standards, then boomed

Red Ball Express

While it would take another two decades for the Civil Rights movement to see real fruition, the reputation that African Americans earned by serving in World War II did much to set the Civil Rights era in motion. More than 210,000 African Americans served in the European theater of war; of those, more than 93,000 were in the Quartermaster Corps—many of them in the legendary Red Ball Express.

Allied armies invaded German-occupied France on June 6, 1944. After spending several weeks consolidating a beachhead, American and British armored divisions broke out of the coastal area and began a speedy push across northwestern France. They liberated Paris in late August, and then pressed on toward Germany. They traveled so far so fast that they were in constant danger of running out of fuel and supplies.

Quartermasters and other provisioning units had to devise a way to keep the forward armies supplied and the advance moving. The Red Ball Express was the answer. It consisted of some 140 truck companies making continuous round trips along a route to the front marked with red balls. At its peak, the Red Ball Express was making a 400-mile trip to one front, 350 miles to another. An estimated 900 trucks were on the routes at any one time.

American racism was the reason so many African Americans, almost 75 percent of the whole system, were on the Red Ball Express. African Americans were first allowed to join American military service during the Civil War, but their initial assignments were often behind the lines, building fortifications or hauling supplies. Even though they eventually compiled an excellent fighting record and even saw combat with the army in the post–Civil War West and the Spanish-American War, administrative attitudes toward African Americans were hard to change. During World War II, they were often relegated to rear-echelon quartermaster and commissary duties, but they also gained access to other positions and attained higher ranks than ever before.

again in 1947. Americans' savings and their desire to purchase new goods for the first time since 1941 fueled the boom. A second, larger baby boom (this one *the* baby boom), also spurred consumerism. Americans, driving new cars, rushed to the suburbs. Suburban housing also boomed and the nature of American home life changed forever.

The G.I. Bill of Rights also did much to support the boom. In 1943, vowing to support the men and women who were fighting the war, Roosevelt introduced the G.I. Bill, calling for college tuition and subsidies, life insurance, medical care, rehabilitation benefits, pensions, and re-employment rights. The bill was later amended to include guaranteed home and farm loans and to create the Veterans Administration to oversee the reintegration of vets into society.

Newman C. Golden, a Tuskegee Airman from Cincinnati, Ohio, watches the sky outside a parachute shed in Ramitelli, Italy, in March 1945.

Congress passed the G.I. Bill unanimously in March 1944. An estimated seven million Americans took advantage of the bill's educational benefits, including some 250,000 African Americans. Another five million used readjustment allowances, and four million took advantage of home and farm loans.

African Americans had seen a slow shift toward desegregation in the military over the course of the war, and this accelerated in the postwar period. Even though Roosevelt had ordered that 10 percent of those drafted into the U.S. military be African Americans beginning in December 1942, most of these black servicemen were at first relegated to support roles in the army, and galley, steward, and laborer posts in the navy and Marine Corps. However, in the U.S. Army Air Corps, a group of black fighter pilots from the Tuskegee Institute, who became known as the Tuskegee Airmen, were stationed in southern

The Berlin Airlift

These scavengers picked through trash at a Berlin dump after the end of the war.

After the breakdown of the Four Powers agreement for the occupation of Germany in the beginning of the Cold War, Berlin became a bone of contention. The tiny island of West Berlin was isolated from the rest of West Germany by hundreds of miles of Soviet-held East Germany. In June of 1948 the Soviet military closed off the road, rail and water corridors that provided vital supplies to the city. Soviet dictator Joseph Stalin expected the Americans and British to solve the resulting humanitarian crisis by capitulating.

Instead he ignited a grim resolve in both nations to hold out at all possible cost. In order to supply the people of West Berlin, they launched the greatest humanitarian airlift of history. It required so many cargo planes that the only way to prevent midair collisions was a rigorous air-traffic control system. Every possible economy was used to increase the amount of useful food being brought into the city. Taking the time to debone meat before shipping enabled a one-third increase in edible protein. Because baked loaves are mostly air and water, only flour was transported and Berlin's bakeries were rebuilt to bake it into bread.

But the most heroic part of the airlift was keeping Berliners from freezing through the unusually cold winter that year. Every bit of coal had to be flown in, which meant allotments were so tiny they barely raised the ambient temperature of a room above freezing. But the beleaguered city persevered, whether by scavenging coal dust from under piles of coal sacks or by breaking up heirloom furniture for fuel.

On May 12, 1949, the Soviets finally lifted the blockade. However, the British and American air forces continued to airlift vital supplies until September 30 of that year in order to ensure that they would not be caught unawares again. Their heroism is memorialized in a modernistic span of concrete that rises into the air in a sweeping curve in the Platz der Luftbrücke—literally Airbridge Square—near Templehof, one of the airports vital to the airlift.

Europe, where they racked up an excellent record as bomber escorts. Before the war, the Marine Corps had not accepted blacks, but following Roosevelt's orders, it opened a segregated training area near Camp Lejeune in 1942 and deployed two African-American battalions to support operations in the Pacific. As the war progressed, more positions opened to African Americans in the navy, and the first African-American naval officers were commissioned in 1944. By the end of the war 900,000 African Americans had served in the army, and a decorated African-American officer, Benjamin O. Davis, Sr., was promoted to the rank of brigadier general after serving in the army for 42 years—the first African-American to achieve this rank.

In 1948, President Truman banned segregation and discrimination in the armed services, and he also commissioned an internal report on segregation and discrimination within the federal government. Truman's postwar actions and the contributions of African Americans during the war, both overseas in the military and on the home front in defense industries, helped set the stage for the coming Civil Rights movement.

RESPONSES TO COMMUNISM

Fresh from defeating fascism around the globe, Americans might have expected a sustained period of peace, but it was not to come. Soviet leader Josef Stalin, an ally during the war, quickly showed that the Soviet Union was not going to give up territory in eastern Europe that it had occupied racing into Germany. He also made it clear he would support revolutionary movements around the world that wanted to challenge capitalistic imperialism. When communists moved to take power in Greece in 1946, Truman announced his Truman Doctrine; the United States would do what was necessary to prevent the spread of communism worldwide. Under the Marshall Plan, the United States would also allocate billions of dollars to rebuild war-torn countries in an attempt to keep communism from taking root there. In 1947 and 1948, with Soviets trying to cut off supplies to Westerners in Berlin and force them out of East Germany, Truman committed U.S. and allied British air forces to continued resupply of the city in the Berlin Airlift. The determination of the allies forced Stalin to give up his plan.

The rise of "red fascism" prompted more response from the United States. First, Congress created a separate U.S. Air Force and expanded its role in defense of the country. It also approved the National Security Act of 1947, which established the National Security Council to help the president interface with the joint chiefs of staff. The next year, Congress voted to keep a limited draft in place lest the United States once again fall behind in war preparedness.

The next year, 1949, proved demoralizing for Americans who were growing tired of war and war worries. Using stolen American plans, the Soviet Union exploded its own atomic bomb, and, after a period of civil war, China became communist. Americans also shuddered as the United States and its allies created NATO—the North Atlantic Treaty Organization. Few failed to comprehend that NATO was the alliance that would fight World War III in Europe should it erupt.

CONCLUSION

World War II had ended American isolationism. One positive and lasting development after the end of the war was the founding of the United Nations, which took the place of the failed League of Nations. Established on October 24, 1945, by 51 member countries, the United Nations then chose the United States as the site of its headquarters, and construction began in 1949 in New York City. The period 1929 to 1949 had seen the United States mature into a global power, and its people rise to the challenge of world leadership.

R. STEVEN JONES

Further Readings

Ambrose, Stephen E. "The War on the Home Front." In *Americans at War*. Jackson, MS: University of Mississippi Press, 1997.

Botting, Douglas and Time-Life Books. *The Second Front*. Alexandria, VA: Time-Life Books, 1978.

Chambers, John Whiteclay, II, ed. *The Oxford Companion to American Military History*. New York: Oxford University Press, 1999.

Cochran, Thomas C. "The Second World War." In *The Great Depression and World War II*. Glenview, IL: Scott, Foresman, and Co., 1968.

Goralski, Robert. *World War II Almanac, 1931–1945: A Political and Military Record*. New York: Bonanza Books, 1984.

Leckie, Robert. *The Wars of America, Vol. II From 1900 to 1992*. New York: Harper Collins, 1992.

Miller, Marilyn. *D-Day*. Morristown, NJ: Silver Burdett, 1986.

Millett, Allan R. and Peter Maslowski. *For the Common Defense: A Military History of the United States of America*. New York: The Free Press, 1984.

Murray, Williamson and Allan R. Millett. *A War to be Won: Fighting the Second World War*. Cambridge, MA: Belknap Press of Harvard University, 2000.

Neillands, Robin H. and Roderick de Normann. *D-Day 1944: Voices from Normandy*. Cold Spring Harbor, NY: Cold Spring Press, 2004.

"Powers of Persuasion: Poster Art from World War II," Available online: http://www.archives.gov. Accessed April 2008.

Williams, Rudi. "African Americans Gain Fame as World War II Red Ball Express Drivers," U.S. Department of Defense. Available online: http://www.defenselink.mil. Accessed April 2008.

Wilt, Alan F. *The Atlantic Wall, 1941–1944: Hitler's Defenses for D-Day*. New York: Enigma, 2004.

Chapter 14

Population Trends and Migration

"To California or any place—every one a drum major leading a parade of hurts, marching with our bitterness."
—John Steinbeck

ANYONE FAMILIAR WITH John Steinbeck's *Grapes of Wrath* can summon the image of an impoverished family—the Joad family in the case of Steinbeck's novel—packing up its belongings and heading west in the midst of the Great Depression. Similarly, lyrics by folk musician Woody Guthrie have immortalized the plight of what Guthrie termed the "Dust Bowl Refugees," uprooted from their homes and forced to travel the "hot and dusty road that a million feet have trod." The photographs of Dorothea Lange (some of the most recognizable images from the Depression era in American history) also reinforce in the public mind the association between the Great Depression and migration. One of Lange's most poignant photographs, for example, "Migrant Mother," captures the sort of rootless poverty that plagued parts of the country during the Depression.

In truth, migration rates during the 1930s were considerably lower than in either of the surrounding decades. A 1944 report prepared by the federal Social Security Board estimated that population shifts in the United States due to migration were cut nearly in half during the Depression decade, as compared with the previous 10 years. As labor markets contracted, economic

205

opportunities everywhere became harder to find. Many Americans were understandably reluctant to leave home without any guarantee of finding employment elsewhere. It was not until the wartime boom of the following decade that migration rates would once again rise and ultimately reach unprecedented levels.

Though small in comparison with migrations before and after the Great Depression, internal migration played a significant role in the population shifts of the 1930s. Between 1930 and 1940, 21 states and the District of Columbia witnessed population increases totaling an estimated 2.6 million people. Leading the way in terms of population growth were the western mountain and Pacific states; California alone gained over one million residents during the 1930s. In addition, a considerable amount of intrastate migration occurred during the Depression, much of it in response to New Deal work programs. According to a 1940 survey, approximately 11 percent of the population had migrated since 1935, 60 percent of them having relocated within the same state. In a decade in which fertility rates reached a historic low and U.S. immigration and emigration essentially offset each other, the areas of the country that did gain in population did so largely as a result of internal migration.

An alternate view of Dorothea Lange's famous "Migrant Mother" that reveals the canvas tent in which the woman (right) was living with her seven children in Nipomo, California, in March 1936.

POPULATION TRENDS DURING THE GREAT DEPRESSION

The economic hardship of the Depression years took a toll on the demographics of that era. In the first half of the 1930s, the marriage rate fell by 22 percent as economic instability prompted many couples to postpone or cancel wedding plans. The fertility rate among married couples, which had been showing a protracted decline for several decades, dropped more precipitously with the onset of the Depression, decreasing by 15 percent between 1929 and 1933. By 1936, the national fertility rate reached a historic low of 2.1 children, which was considered the bare minimum necessary to replenish the population.

There was, of course, some regional variation with respect to the fertility rate; according to U.S. Census Bureau estimates for 1935–40, the total fertility rate was 1.8 in the Northeast, 2.2 in both the West and the Great Plains states, and 2.8 in the South. Variation was present within a given region as well, with higher birth rates among rural families than urban, among unskilled laborers than professionals, and among blacks than whites. Looking at the nation as a whole, however, the fertility rate reached the lowest level in American history up to that time. A lower rate would not be seen until the final decade of the 20th century.

Immigration to the United States also declined sharply during the Depression. Whereas 4.1 million immigrants had arrived between 1921 and 1930 (down from the prior decade's total of 5.7 million due to restrictive immigration legislation), a mere half a million legal immigrants entered the United States in the 1930s. At the same time, emigration from the United States was on the rise. For each year from 1931 to 1936, emigration from the United States outpaced immigration. Deportations and voluntary emigration, together with decreased immigration and a low fertility rate, helped to ensure the lowest 10-year population growth rate in U.S. history during the 1930s.

Despite the fact that the total U.S. population increased by only 7 percent during the 1930s (down from a rate of increase of 15–16 percent during the several decades prior), the populations of California, Nevada, New Mexico, and Florida all increased by more than 20 percent. Meanwhile, the Northeast and North Central regions experienced net losses in population, as depressed economic conditions spurred migration from large cities and industrial areas. This was particularly the case in the early years of the Depression, before business and industrial conditions began to show some improvement. The South, with the exception of Florida, also continued to lose population, albeit at a slower rate than during the 1920s.

THE TRANSIENT POPULATION

Even before the onset of the Great Depression, America had a long history of out-of-work transients traveling from town to town. Known as hobos, these wanderers tended to be unattached males in search of employment or adventure. The final years of the Hoover administration saw a significant increase in the number of unemployed transients, as hundreds of thousands took to the road or the rails in search of work, food, and shelter in the midst of the worsening economic crisis. Given the itinerant lifestyle of the transient population, an exact count was difficult to obtain. A one-day census of 765 cities conducted in March 1933 counted more than 201,000 transients. Officials estimated that during the Hoover administration between 400,000 and 2 million Americans traveled within or beyond their home states in search of economic opportunity.

Illegally hitching rides on freight trains, a practice that had declined throughout the 1920s, became commonplace once more in the early years of the Depression. By the winter of 1931–32, small towns along the route of the Southern Pacific Railroad in Texas, New Mexico, and Arizona reported an influx of 200 transients a day. Birmingham, Alabama, reported as many as 2,000 hobos arriving on the trains during a typical month in 1932. Railroad authorities frequently found themselves overwhelmed by the number of stowaways, as did the towns on the receiving end of what *Fortune* magazine called the "vast homeless horde."

According to data obtained in 1934–35, the majority of the transients came from urban areas and 80 percent of them were unmarried. Most were between the ages of 25 and 40, although the spectrum of the transients broadened during the Depression years to include both older and younger men than would typically migrate in search of employment. A study of transients in one state found that over 10 percent were 55 or older. At the other end of the spectrum, approximately 20 percent of the unemployed transients in 1934 were 19 years old or younger.

TRANSIENT WOMEN AND CHILDREN

Most women or girls who migrated during the Great Depression did so with their families. During the early 1930s, however, a number of unattached girls and young women hit the roads and rails as well, often disguised as males for safety. In 1934–35, approximately 3 percent of the unattached transients were females—a figure much higher than in the past. One study suggests that the number of female hobos increased at least tenfold during the early years of the Depression. These female transients were generally younger than their male counterparts, with a much higher proportion under the age of 20.

The increase in youth transience among both boys and girls was the subject of great national concern. In 1932, the National Children's Bureau estimated that 250,000 youngsters under the age of 21 had joined the ranks of the homeless transients riding freight trains or hitchhiking from town to town. Children as young as 14 could be found riding the boxcars, in part because so many schools had closed. By 1934 school terms had been drastically shortened in one out of four U.S. cities, and 5,000 schools had closed due to insufficient resources. While wanderlust or a sense of adventure no doubt impelled some of

In another well-known photograph by Dorothea Lange, two people walk along a road toward Los Angeles, California, in March 1937. California gained over a million residents in the 1930s.

the young migrants to leave home, most left in search of employment. Many of them had sought work for two or three years in their hometowns before departing in desperation. In a survey of 20,000 transients who passed through Buffalo, New York in 1935, 85 percent of the white youths and 98 percent of the African-American youths in the 15 to 24 age group reported that they were traveling to seek work.

RELIEF FOR TRANSIENTS

As the size of the transient population continued to grow, municipalities and private charitable organizations found themselves less and less able to cope with the mounting crisis of homelessness. With resources stretched to capacity in providing assistance for unemployed residents, many towns could offer indigent migrants only an evening meal and a night in the local jail before sending them out on the next train. Given residency requirements for relief

A dust storm fills the sky as it approaches Stratford, Texas, on April 18, 1935.

"This Withering Land of Misery"

Beginning in 1932 as prolonged drought continued, dust storms plagued the southern Great Plains. Within four years, 850 million tons of top soil had simply blown away. The "black blizzards" brought death and destruction as people suffocated or developed respiratory diseases such as "dust pneumonia," sinusitis, pharyngitis, laryngitis, and bronchitis. Cattle suffocated or went blind as farms were blanketed by black dust. One resident remembers that "It seemed as if it were the end of all life," while another resident described it as a "nightmare becoming life." Inside their homes, homemakers labored to protect their families from the pervasive dust, and sterilization became almost impossible for physicians, dentists, and hospitals.

Scores of families from Kansas, Colorado, New Mexico, Oklahoma, and Texas fled the region. The population of Broken Bow, Kansas, declined from 300 to three. At the age of 86, Isaac Osteen remembered the town of Richards, Colorado, which declined from a thriving small town to a deserted area with the "smell of death on it." During the dust storms, *Atlantic Monthly* published a series of letters from writer Caroline Henderson, who had married a farmer. Over time, both Henderson's letters and her township dwindled, causing her to declare that her beloved farm had become "just a place to stand on." Many families left because the health of their children was threatened. Hazel Shaw, who had lost one baby to the storms, relocated to save the life of a new baby.

The Roosevelt administration gave $35 grants for relocation, and 3.5 million people left the southern plains, taking only what they could pile into their Model Ts. Some 300,000 residents left Oklahoma, causing others to label all migrants from Dust Bowl states "Okies." A Kansas minister declared, "The land just blew away; we had to go somewhere." Around 40 percent of all migrants relocated to California's San Joaquin Valley where they found jobs picking grapes and cotton. Noted journalist Ernie Pyle described the Dust Bowl in the summer of 1936 as "this withering land of misery."

in most places, the itinerant nature of the transient population rendered the drifters ineligible for assistance. In fact, many states began strengthening settlement laws in order to increase residency requirements and thus keep newcomers off public relief.

A partial solution to the transient crisis became available in the summer of 1933 with the passage of the Federal Emergency Relief Act. According to this act, the federal government agreed to fund all expenses for the care of transients, defined as nonresidents who had been in a state for fewer than 12 months. In order to qualify for the federal funding, states were required to submit a transient relief plan for federal approval. Some states were slow to act, fearing that the provision of transient relief would only encourage the influx of more drifters. By autumn 1934, however, 340 transient bureaus had been established across the country in every state except Vermont, which declined to participate.

In addition to the urban transient bureaus—which provided transients with food, lodging, and medical care—states used federal funding to establish transient camps for longer-term care. Over 300 camps were established in rural areas across the country, each of them affiliated with one or more urban transient bureaus. In addition to providing for the transients' basic needs, the rural camps also afforded educational and employment opportunities to lodgers. Taken together, the transient bureaus and camps provided relief for over a million homeless wanderers.

The Federal Transient Service was abolished in 1935, when federal relief was reorganized under the Works Progress Administration and the Social Security program. During 28 months of operation, the Federal Transient division had spent more than $86 million caring for the nation's transient population and had caused the number of homeless persons on the road or living in shantytowns to decline sharply. The system of transient bureaus and camps had, however, catered primarily to single males. A separate problem was the rapidly expanding number of migrating families—like the fictional Joad family—who took to the road in search of work during the middle years of the depression decade.

THE DUST BOWL MIGRATION

While less substantial in both absolute and proportional terms than the westward migrations of the 1920s and 1940s, the migration of over a million Americans to California during the 1930s constituted the most important regional population shift of the Depression decade. Whereas the movement of hobos and transients to the nation's urban centers had largely tapered off by 1935, the so-called Dust Bowl migration was just beginning in earnest and would not peak until 1937–38. It is with this westward movement of American families that popular conceptions of Depression-era migration tend to be associated.

The term "Dust Bowl migration" is a misnomer as applied to the vast numbers of migrants who flocked to California during the mid-1930s. The area of

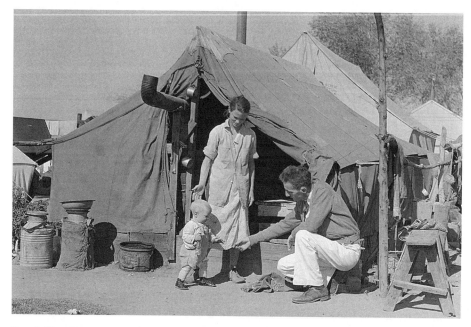

Tom Collins, the manager of the Farm Security Administration's Kern County migrant camp in California, checks on a small child from a drought refugee family in November 1936.

extreme wind erosion known as the Dust Bowl comprised 97 million acres in southeastern Colorado, northeastern New Mexico, western Kansas, and the Texas and Oklahoma panhandles. Certainly many farms in the immediate area were devastated by the spectacular dust storms that struck the southern Great Plains between 1933 and 1935. Fewer than 16,000 people from the Dust Bowl, however, migrated to California, comprising merely 6 percent of the total from the Southwestern states. Many of the Dust Bowl farmers displaced by drought and poor soil conditions headed instead to the nearest towns, where they sought employment through government work programs or in the expanding petroleum industry.

Far more prevalent among the westward migrants were families from the states of Oklahoma, Texas, Missouri, and Arkansas. Because Oklahomans comprised a plurality of the roughly 300,000 migrants from these states during the 1930s, Californians tended to refer to all migrants from the region as "Okies." Most of the migrants were young (60 percent of the adult "Okies" were under 35) and, on the whole, slightly better-educated than their cohorts who stayed behind. Males comprised just 53 percent of the migrants, a testimony to the preponderance of families in this particular migration as men usually made up a much larger percentage of migrants compared to women.

Although dislocated farmers were certainly among the approximately half a million people who left the southwestern states during the 1930s, not all

Repatriation of Mexicans

As the effects of the 1929 stock market crash made themselves felt, Mexican workers in the United States were among the first to lose their jobs. Since the early 20th century, Mexican labor had been in high demand on the railroads, in the mining companies, and particularly in the fields of large growers. Lax enforcement of immigration laws prior to the late 1920s had allowed thousands of Mexican nationals, many of them indigent, to enter the country illegally. With the onset of the Great Depression, however, President Herbert Hoover and his newly appointed Secretary of Labor, William N. Doak, were determined to root out and deport illegal immigrants. Mexicans comprised nearly half of all those deported during the 1930s.

Approximately 500,000 U.S. residents of Mexican descent (an estimated 60 percent of them U.S. citizens) left for Mexico between 1929 and 1935. Less than one-fifth of those who left were deported; most agreed to voluntary repatriation. The first wave of repatriates in the winter of 1929–30 were relatively affluent, and took with them automobiles and other material possessions that they had accumulated in the United States. Hoping to ease the burden on relief rolls, municipal welfare agencies urged unemployed Mexican immigrants to repatriate voluntarily as well. Municipalities and private relief organizations sponsored trains to transport the repatriates, often at reduced fares. With a Mexican population of approximately 175,000, Los Angeles offered the most ambitious repatriation scheme. Similar programs could also be found in other urban centers with significant Mexican populations.

Confronted with unemployment, poverty, and racial hostility, many Mexican families (including their American-born children) agreed to return to Mexico voluntarily. From February 1931 to early 1933 an estimated 50,000 to 75,000 Mexicans were repatriated from cities in California. In many cases the decision to return to Mexico was motivated by fear, particularly following a series of highly-publicized raids by the Department of Labor's Bureau of Immigration. One particularly sensational raid occurred on February 26, 1931, when immigration officials rounded up 400 men and women during a daytime raid on a popular square in Los Angeles. Although few arrests ultimately resulted, the raid was enough to frighten many Mexican immigrants into departing voluntarily. The decision to leave was also influenced by promises of land and assistance offered by the Mexican government.

By late 1933 the rate of Mexican repatriation had begun to wane. Most Mexican families who were disposed to leave had already done so. For those still considering repatriation, reports from those who had gone before revealed that conditions were no better in Mexico, and that the promises of help from the Mexican government were not to be trusted. New Deal programs also seemed to offer relief for those who remained. In the end, most Mexican Americans remained in the United States throughout the Depression, but the departure of nearly 500,000 left a bitter legacy for many.

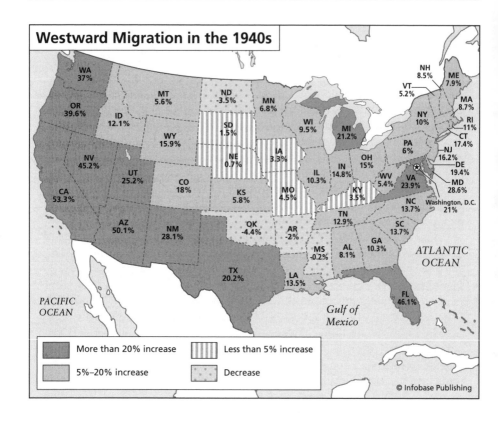

Westward Migration in the 1940s

WA	37%
OR	39.6%
ID	12.1%
MT	5.6%
ND	-3.5%
MN	6.8%
WY	15.9%
SD	1.5%
NV	45.2%
UT	25.2%
CO	18%
NE	0.7%
IA	3.3%
WI	9.5%
MI	21.2%
CA	53.3%
AZ	50.1%
NM	28.1%
KS	5.8%
MO	4.5%
IL	10.3%
IN	14.8%
OH	15%
KY	3.5%
WV	5.4%
VA	23.9%
TX	20.2%
OK	-4.4%
AR	-2%
LA	13.5%
MS	-0.2%
AL	8.1%
GA	10.3%
TN	12.9%
NC	13.7%
SC	13.7%
FL	46.1%
NH	8.5%
VT	5.2%
ME	7.9%
MA	8.7%
NY	10%
RI	11%
CT	17.4%
PA	6%
NJ	16.2%
DE	19.4%
MD	28.6%
Washington, D.C.	21%

Legend:
- More than 20% increase
- 5%–20% increase
- Less than 5% increase
- Decrease

PACIFIC OCEAN

ATLANTIC OCEAN

Gulf of Mexico

© Infobase Publishing

migrating families fit the destitute dirt-farmer image portrayed in Steinbeck's *Grapes of Wrath*. On the contrary, nearly one out of six migrants who made the trek to California was a professional, a proprietor, or a white-collar employee. Blue collar workers and small businessmen also featured prominently among the numbers who chose to migrate.

Several of the factors that contributed to the out-migration from the southwestern states had preceded the 1929 stock market crash, but were exacerbated by the worsening economic conditions of the 1930s, as well as a series of natural events. Declining international markets for wheat, corn, and cotton—together with mineral depletion, erosion, pests, and drought—made it increasingly difficult for small farmers to earn a living during the Depression years. Agricultural modernization also played a large part in forcing small farmers and tenants off the land, a situation that was unintentionally exacerbated by federal intervention in the form of the Agricultural Adjustment Act.

These factors alone do not fully account for the migration patterns, however. Small farmers and tenants east of the Mississippi suffered many of the same hardships as their "Okie" counterparts, but did not resort to migration in nearly the same numbers during the Depression years. Fewer than 30,000 whites migrated out of the southeastern states during the 1930s as compared

Japanese-American Internment

Not all migration during the war years was voluntary. In the spring of 1942, over 112,000 persons of Japanese descent—two-thirds of them American citizens—were removed from their Pacific Coast homes and detained in relocation centers in California, Utah, Idaho, Arizona, Wyoming, and Arkansas. The forced evacuation resulted in both physical dislocation and economic hardship for the thousands of first- and second-generation Japanese immigrants who became the victims of wartime hysteria.

In the aftermath of the December 7, 1941, bombing of Pearl Harbor, federal agents took more than 2,000 Japanese immigrants into custody for questioning. While the size and vital economic role of the Japanese community in Hawaii made wholesale evacuations there impracticable, the same was not true on the mainland, where approximately 130,000 *Issei* (first-generation Japanese immigrants) and *Nisei* (their American-born offspring) resided, most of them in Pacific Coast states. Despite their small number relative to the total population, Japanese-Americans were perceived as a threat to U.S. security. False reports of Japanese-American espionage and sabotage along the Pacific Coast circulated in early 1942.

In response to the rumors of Japanese-American disloyalty, General John L. DeWitt, head of the army's new Western Defense Command, requested permission to remove all *Issei* and *Nisei* from the Pacific Coast. On February 19, 1942, President Franklin D. Roosevelt signed Executive Order 9066 authorizing the removal of "any or all persons" from sensitive military zones. On March 2, DeWitt designated the western portions of Washington, Oregon, and California and the southern quarter of Arizona as a military zone and imposed a curfew on residents of Japanese descent. Authorities encouraged voluntary relocation, but by the end of March over 100,000 Japanese-Americans remained in the military zone.

Deeming voluntary relocation a failure, DeWitt ordered all remaining Japanese to report to makeshift assembly centers where they would be held until they could be transferred to one of 10 relocation camps established by the War Relocation Authority. Within weeks, over 100,000 Japanese were uprooted from their communities and livelihoods. Between June and October 1942, evacuees were transferred from assembly centers to inland relocation camps. It was not until December 17, 1944, however, that the War Department revoked its evacuation orders and evacuees were free to return home.

In 1944, the Supreme Court, in the case of *Korematsu v. U.S.*, upheld the constitutionality of Executive Order 9066. In a 6-3 decision, with a majority opinion written by Justice Hugo Black, the court held that the interest of national security outweighed the personal rights of a Japanese American, Fred Korematsu. Despite a minority opinion that claimed the decision was based on racism, the majority held that the case did not depend on race, but on protecting the nation in time of war.

to an outflow of roughly 500,000 from the southwestern region. The difference can be explained in large part by the personal ties that many "Okies" had to the Pacific Coast. Thanks to the 430,000 southwesterners who had preceded them to California by 1930, "Okies" could take advantage of a fully developed migration network to provide them with information and assistance as they contemplated making the move themselves.

WARTIME CHANGES

For every "Okie" who migrated to California between 1935 and 1940, twice as many came during World War II. Oklahoma alone sent 95,000 migrants to California during the war, with Texas and Missouri following close behind. A total of nearly three million permanent new residents relocated to California during the decade of the 1940s, resulting in a population growth rate of 53 percent. Areas of the country that had been relatively unaffected by the Depression-era migration were likewise caught up in the reshuffling of the population during World War II. Over 12 million men and women left home for military training camps, and another 15 million (one out of eight civilians) relocated to take advantage of job openings in the burgeoning defense industry. By the end of the war, roughly eight million Americans had relocated permanently to different states, half of them to different regions.

The defense industries, located primarily in northern and western cities, were the main beneficiaries of wartime migration. Thanks in large part to Executive Order 88022, which prohibited discrimination in defense jobs or government, large numbers of Southern blacks—approximately 700,000 during the course of the war—were among the migrants relocating to the North and (for the first time in substantial numbers) to the Pacific west. Approximately 340,000 blacks migrated to California, with an estimated 10,000 arriving in Los Angeles every month during 1943. The black population of Seattle nearly tripled during the war, and that of San Francisco increased by 600 percent.

In addition to massive out-migration from the South—2.5 million southerners left the region during the 1940s—the Census Bureau recorded about 4.3 million intra-state and 2.1 million interstate migrants within the South during the war years. The great majority of the movement was rural-to-urban migration, so that the urban population in the South increased by 50 percent during the 1940s. As thousands of families left farms and small towns to relocate to larger urban areas, housing shortages frequently resulted, and many migrating families were forced to crowd into trailer camps or temporary housing units until more permanent housing could be built.

Rapid migration to urban centers during the war years left in its wake a shortage of agricultural labor. To remedy the situation, the same federal and local governments that had so recently sought to repatriate migrant farm workers back to Mexico now attempted to attract seasonal workers once again. According to the terms of the *bracero* program, created in the summer of 1942, the

Mexican government agreed to provide workers on a contractual basis. The U.S. government, in turn, agreed to provide transportation for the workers, ensure their immunity from the draft, and guarantee them work at the prevailing wage. Under the *bracero* program, more than 200,000 Mexican farm workers entered the United States to work in the fields or on the railroads. These were the legal migrants; estimates place the total number of Mexicans who entered the U.S. workforce, legally and illegally, at close to 500,000.

A wartime wedding in the 1940s with the entire wedding party in uniform.

In addition to the unprecedented tide of migration, the war also brought about a sharp increase in the marriage and birth rates. Unlike in World War I, when the number of marriages had declined, a significant increase in nuptials followed the passage of the Selective Service Act in 1940. The marriage rate per thousand women aged 17 and 29 ranged from 93 to 105 during World War II, up from 89.1 per thousand on the eve of the Depression. The increased marriage rate was accompanied by higher fertility rates as well. While the real Baby Boom would occur just after the war, the birthrate by 1943 was at its highest level in 20 years. Partly as a consequence of higher birthrates, the population during the war increased by 6.5 million, as compared to only three million during the entire decade of the 1930s.

CONCLUSION

Migration and population changes in the 1930s were quite different from surrounding years. There was less immigration, and less movement overall for jobs, despite the familiar images of destitute Depression-era transients. Fertility declined as well. The war returned these trends to more common patterns, and magnified some of them. Mass immigration resumed, fertility rose, and the American tendency of relocating for jobs rebounded dramatically. African-American migration out of the South picked up, resuming a long trend in the 20th century. In light of all this rapid change, it is not surprising that among the aftereffects of World War II came two of the better known population trends in U.S. history—the Baby Boom and the shift to the suburbs.

KATHLEEN RUPPERT

Further Readings

Balderrama, Francisco E. and Raymond Rodriguez. *Decade of Betrayal: Mexican Repatriation in the 1930s.* Albuquerque, NM: University of New Mexico Press, 1995.

Barry, Chad. *Southern Migrants, Northern Exiles.* Chicago, IL: University of Illinois Press, 2000.

Casdorph, Paul D. *Let the Good Times Roll: Life at Home in America During World War II.* New York: Paragon House, 1989.

Egan, Timothy. *The Worst Hard Time: The Untold Story of Those Who Survived the Great American Dust Bowl.* New York: Houghton Mifflin, 2006.

Goodwin, E. Marvin. *Black Migration in America from 1915 to 1960: An Uneasy Exodus.* Lewiston, NY: E. Mellon Press, 1990.

Gregory, James. *The Southern Diaspora: How the Great Migrations of Black and White Southerners Transformed America.* Chapel Hill, NC: University of North Carolina Press, 2005.

Holley, Donald. *The Second Great Emancipation: The Mechanical Cotton Picker, Black Migration, and How They Shaped the Modern South.* Fayetteville, AR: University of Arkansas Press, 2000.

Kennedy, David M. *Freedom from Fear: The American People in Depression and War, 1929–1945.* New York: Oxford University Press, 1999.

Klein, Herbert S. *Population History of the United States.* Cambridge, MA: Cambridge University Press, 2004.

Kusmer, Kenneth. *Down and Out, On the Road: The Homeless in American History.* New York: Oxford University Press, 2002.

Kyvig, David E. *Daily Life in the United States, 1920–1940: How Americans Lived in the "Roaring Twenties" and the Great Depression.* Chicago, IL: Ivan R. Dee, 2004.

McGovern, James R. *And a Time for Hope: Americans in the Great Depression.* Westport, CT: Praeger Publishers, 2000.

Nash, Gerald D. *The Crucial Era: The Great Depression and World War II, 1929–1945.* New York: St. Martin's Press, 1992.

PBS. "Surviving the Dust Bowl." Available online: http://www.pbs.org/wgbh/amex/dustbowl. Accessed October 2008.

Todd, Charles L. and Robert Sonkin. "Voices from the Dust Bowl." Available online: http://lcweb2.loc.gov/ammem/afctshtml/tshome.html. Accessed October 2008.

Uys, Errol. *Lincoln Riding the Rails: Teenagers on the Move during the Great Depression.* New York: Routledge, 2003.

Watkins, T.H. *The Hungry Years: A Narrative History of the Great Depression in America.* New York: Henry Holt & Co., 1999.

White, Richard. *"It's Your Misfortune and None of My Own": A New History of the American West.* Norman, OK: University of Oklahoma Press, 1991.

Chapter 15

Transportation

"The impulse to travel is one of the hopeful symptoms of life."
—Agnes Repplier

THE GREAT DEPRESSION and World War II were troubled times for America's transportation systems. In a time of little money, many people struggled to keep the automobiles they had purchased in the prosperous years of the Jazz Age. Even public transportation and freight haulers found it difficult to make ends meet because of reduced commerce. And although America's entry into World War II after the attack on Pearl Harbor reinvigorated America's economy, the direction of the American economy to the war effort meant that little remained to spare for civilian consumption. Very few personal automobiles were manufactured during the war years, as automobile factories were retooled to produce jeeps, tanks, and fighter planes. Even public transportation was strained to the limit carrying soldiers on deployment, and had little room for civilians.

THE FIGHT TO SAVE THE FAMILY CAR

One of the most notable developments of the Roaring Twenties was the expansion of consumer credit. Because automobiles retained their value well, and there was a lively market in used automobiles, lenders were more willing to allow people to borrow money to purchase them. As a result, many people chose to buy a nicer car than they might have had they been required to save and pay cash up-front.

A family of migrant farm workers traveled in this small truck piled high with belongings in the San Joaquin Valley of California in February 1935.

However, once the stock market crash sent the economy into a tailspin of eroding public confidence and reduced consumer spending, many people suddenly found themselves unable to afford their monthly payments. It was particularly frustrating for those who had only a few payments left before their loans were discharged, since they were just as subject to repossession as those who had bought a vehicle months before the crash and had made only a few payments. More than a few people begged and pleaded for some way to keep from having to give up the car they were so close to paying off.

At first there was little sympathy, but as the economic crisis progressed and the market became glutted not only with repossessed vehicles, but also with ones whose owners were voluntarily selling them as unaffordable, prices for used cars plummeted further. Many lenders became more willing to work with people in hopes of getting the money over a longer period of time, rather than repossessing the vehicle only to find they could not sell it for what was owed.

As a result, people down on their luck often had a car when they decided to relocate in search of work. It might not be a particularly fashionable car, and often it was an unreliable one, but with some careful nursing, it could generally be persuaded to get people to their destination. Many people learned to be their own mechanics in an effort to keep their cars going until they reached a place where work was said to be available. "Okies" fleeing the ecological disaster of the Dust Bowl traveled in great numbers along Route 66 through the mountains and deserts of New Mexico and Arizona in hopes of finding work in California, although when they arrived at the state line, many of them found an "inspection station" waiting to turn them back.

Automakers cut production in response to the economic crisis, but continued to improve new car models. In the 1930s automakers began installing radios in their cars and enhanced them with other new technologies. Galvin Manufacturing designed the Motorola, the first mass-produced car radio in the United States. In 1932 Cadillac offered automatic transmission on its models, and by 1937 automatic transmission was standard throughout the industry. In 1934 Chrysler unveiled the Imperial, the first car designed in a wind tunnel. In 1942 DeSoto made the Airstream with the aerodynamic appearance of the Imperial. The Airstream was the first car with retractable headlights. In 1936 Buick designed the Century with an eight-cylinder engine and 120 horsepower. The fastest car of its era, the Century could reach 95 miles per hour.

KEEPING THE BUSES RUNNING

The intercity bus had arisen at the turn of the 20th century as a way of connecting with smaller cities that were not served by the railroad. In addition, buses could run routes that had too small a ridership to make a train route economical. As a result, not only were there numerous independent bus companies, but the railroads had invested in buses as well. To avoid accusations of monopolistic practices, most of the railroads that owned bus lines did so through holding companies.

The 1929 stock market crash caused an immediate crisis for the bus companies. As banks began to fail as a result of the disappearance of millions of dollars of money that had existed only as figures on paper, many independent bus companies had significant difficulty paying their drivers and other employees.

Passengers boarding a Greyhound bus at the station in Harrisburg, Pennsylvania, in July 1940. The Greyhound company survived the Depression, but many smaller bus companies folded.

Combined with the loss of income as people cut back on consumer spending, including bus trips, these financial difficulties meant the end of many of the smaller bus lines.

GREYHOUND'S STRUGGLE TO SURVIVE

Even Greyhound, which by 1930 had bought up a number of smaller lines and was well on its way to becoming one of the leaders in the intercity bus industry, had to struggle to keep afloat. Its executives had by and large come up through the ranks from bus drivers, and had little or no education or experience in larger business issues such as finance and economics. Many of them had operated on the assumption that the economic boom of the Roaring Twenties was a normal economic pattern rather than a dangerous bubble, and had overextended the company with the issue of various kinds of bonds that suddenly could not be honored.

There were serious questions as to whether Greyhound would continue to operate, particularly after a large package of securities formerly held by the troubled Goldman Sachs Trading Corporation were sold to the Atlas Corporation. For the first time, Greyhound executive Glenn Traer sat down with a financial expert from Atlas, Matthew Robinson, and went over Greyhound's books in detail. They examined the cost of operating a single bus line against the fares collected on its typical run, and found an appalling $4.50 profit. However, Traer responded to this seemingly hopeless figure by reminding Robinson that Greyhound ran over 1,800 buses on a daily basis, so the seemingly hopeless $4.50 would expand to $8,100, and over the course of a year the buses would bring the company nearly $3 million.

With this evidence that Greyhound was indeed worth saving, Robinson and other executives from Atlas made key reorganizations that would simplify the company's structure and increase revenues. Subsidiaries were bought out, and stockholders were compelled to accept a reissue of their stock at much less favorable terms. In addition, less profitable routes were curtailed or eliminated altogether, while the company invested in advertising to increase ridership on those routes that were sufficiently strong to merit being kept.

The next major hurdle Greyhound had to survive was the "bank holiday" imposed by President Franklin D. Roosevelt shortly after taking office. The purpose of this forced closing was to sort out which banks were strong enough to be permitted to continue to operate and which troubled banks were in so much disarray that they could not be put back on their feet. This measure was intended to restore Americans' confidence in the banking system and break the cycle of rumors about troubled banks that led to panicky mass attempts to withdraw money, and the resultant failures that created further rumors and runs on banks.

However, the closure of all banks also meant that companies that had their operating funds on deposit could not get that money to make routine transac-

Riding the Rails

Even in the Depression, the trains continued to run. The economy might be in trouble, but it had not shut down entirely, and thus there were still goods to be shipped. As a result, people who had neither an automobile of their own, nor the financial means to ride a bus or passenger train, found freight trains a rough and ready means of getting places. Getting on was a matter of finding an unsecured boxcar on a train that was stopped or going slowly enough to jump aboard.

A close-knit subculture soon developed among the men (for the hobos were almost entirely male) who traveled surreptitiously upon freight trains. They taught one another the ways to best avoid the railroad police, who often regarded them as thieves, and to board and alight safely. Some who rode the rails looking for work later became famous, including Supreme Court Justice William O. Douglas, television personality Art Linkletter, author of western novels Louis L'Amour, and journalist Eric Sevareid.

Riding the trains was extremely dangerous because a stopped train was apt to begin moving without warning, particularly if it were on a siding well away from grade crossings. Many hobos were killed or maimed when they misjudged the speed or distance of a moving boxcar, and others died when they became trapped after railroad officials closed and locked boxcar doors without realizing there were people inside. Others were killed by "bulls" that were hired to keep hobos off trains. In one year, 6,500 hobos died while riding the rails.

Walter Ballard remembers riding the rails as a young man, admitting that he "loved it" because it got "in your blood." Ballard maintained that you could forget about all cares and "just ride." Norma Darrah, who rode the rails with her husband and nephew, did not enjoy the experience, recalling that "It was just one weary, hungry mile after another." The Darrahs were forced to survive on handouts from locals and any game they could shoot along the way. Donald Newhouser reminisces about the nostalgia that brought him to tears as he peered through a train window during Christmas 1935, "I looked down at a village below [and] saw a Christmas tree lit up in a window and children playing around it."

A couple traveling with a small child in a freight car stopped in Roseville, California, on April 19, 1940.

tions. Many could not even meet their payrolls. Fortunately Greyhound auditor Adam Sledz anticipated Roosevelt's action and created a plan of action to ensure the company would be able to pay its drivers and other employees. He sent a telegram to every Greyhound office throughout the country, instructing them to make no further deposits in banks. Instead, they were to take their money to the post office and purchase money orders, which they then mailed to corporate headquarters. The uncashed money orders were held until Roosevelt's bank holiday, at which time the corporation used them to buy money orders for the amount of each employee's salary, which were mailed to the individual employees. When the money orders arrived, employees needed only take them to the post office counter to cash them, and had money to see to the needs of their families.

Even after Roosevelt's New Deal began to stabilize the American economy, the woes of the intercity bus industry were not over. Because the surviving bus companies were still struggling to get customers, many of them tried cutting fares as a way of luring people in. However, the result frequently was pressure to lower prices beyond what was necessary to support the bus company. In an effort to stem this self-destructive cycle of price cuts, a number of leading bus companies signed a Code of Fair Competition. However, the worst culprits did not sign on, and continued to slash prices until the government finally had to intervene with the Motor Carrier's Act of 1935. This legislation not only regulated fares and safety measures, but also required that any mergers or acquisitions of bus companies would have to have the approval of the Interstate Commerce Commission.

Although steam-powered locomotives were already becoming outdated in the 1930s, these older-model steam locomotives were used well into the 1940s and beyond.

RAILROADS ENTER THE DIESEL AGE

The railroad was originally invented because early steam engines were so heavy they caused a cart running on the existing roads to bog down. The steam locomotive was key to the winning of the American West, and it became an iconic image of railroading. However, by the 1930s the steam locomotive was rapidly becoming technically outdated. Steam engines were inefficient compared to internal combustion, with much of their power potential lost as heat radiated off the firebox, boiler, and piping to the cylinder. In addition to the enormous amounts of fuel steam locomotives consumed, they required large amounts of water as a working fluid. Even locomotives equipped with a condenser to recapture spent steam still had to recharge their boilers regularly. In addition, a steam locomotive had no reverse gear, nor could multiple steam engines be linked together to provide more pulling power.

As a result, there was increasing interest in the use of diesel engines, which had proved their worth in naval and merchant marine applications during and after World War I. However, early attempts to connect diesel engines directly to the drive wheels of a locomotive through various gearing schemes proved inadequate to the demands of railroad operations, which were very different from those of ships or road vehicles such as trucks.

The solution lay in using electricity, which already powered trolleys and a growing number of electric trains that derived their power either from an overhead wire or a third rail. The diesel engines would be used to run a generator, and the resultant electricity would then be carried by cable to high-torque universal motors that would run the driving wheels. The resultant diesel-electric locomotive would not only be able to reverse direction at ease and be ganged together to provide greater pulling power, but could also provide sufficient energy to electrify an entire passenger train.

Diesel locomotives were first introduced on American railroads in the 1920s, but they were mostly confined to switch engines in railroad yards, where reversing was crucial. In 1940, the Electro-Motive Division of General Motors proved that diesel-electric engines were practical to replace steam locomotives in heavy-duty freight service. General Motors' demonstration pioneer engine, the model FT, was sent on tour on the nation's railroads, convincing executives to buy into the new technology. Diesel locomotives proliferated in the years following World War II.

THE BEGINNING OF THE TRUCKING INDUSTRY

Trucks were originally developed as substitutes for drays, heavy horse-drawn wagons that were used to carry goods from the train station to the store and from there to individual consumers. However, as larger gasoline engines became available in the 1920s, trucks became much larger than anything that could be drawn by horses. As a result, interest grew in using trucks to haul goods greater distances.

The "blitz buggy," an early jeep design, being tested on rough terrain at Fort Holabird, Maryland, in 1941.

Rolling into War

American forces in World War II had one of the best-developed logistical supply trains of all the belligerents. Almost all the materiel used by American G.I.s was carried in trucks, rather than animal-drawn wagons. Furthermore, many G.I.s were able to ride on troop transports or to hitch a ride on a truck that was carrying less than a full load. As a result, American forces were both better supplied than their allies and opponents, and arrived at battles fresher because they had not expended so much energy marching overland.

Although the manufacture of civilian automobiles had ceased, and it was difficult for civilian haulers to purchase new trucks or even repair parts for existing ones unless they could demonstrate that their work supported the war effort, trucks for the military were produced in great abundance. Many former automobile factories retooled to produce light trucks for military use.

One of the best-known of the military light trucks of World War II was the jeep, produced by Willys-Overland, and later by American Motor Company. The origin of its name was often in dispute, with some claiming that it was named after the sound made by an imaginary animal in a cartoon, while others argued for the more prosaic origin of an attempt to pronounce as a word the GP for "general purpose" painted on them. However, there was no disagreement about their ruggedness and ability to travel through all kinds of conditions that would cause the military vehicles of other combatant nations to become stuck or break down altogether.

Although the railroads had been the mainstay of long-distance hauling in the United States since the middle of the 19th century, the truck had a powerful advantage in flexibility. Not only was it not confined to a system of tracks, but it also could carry loads too small to be economical for a locomotive. The truck also benefited from the system of paved roads that had been created for automobiles with federal money, and thus did not have the railroad company's overhead in laying and maintaining tracks.

The earliest over-the-road truckers often ran on the ragged edges of the law, with shaky licensing and safety procedures, and frequent overloading of their vehicles in order to squeeze the maximum profit out of their trips. Many of them had marginal business skills, and by failing to budget for long term expenses such as loan amortization and repairs when setting prices for their services, they often ran themselves out of business. However, in the early "wildcat" days of trucking, there was always an enterprising new trucker to buy their rig and make a stab at the business. Several of those early truckers, driving rigs powered by gasoline engines, went on to found major trucking companies. Among them was C.R. England, who started in 1920 with a single pickup truck, and whose company, England Trucking, based in Utah, eventually grew to include over 4,500 drivers and more than 3,600 company-owned trucks. Carl Moyer, an early driver with the England firm, later established his own company, B&C Truck Leasing, while cousins of C.R. England's wife Maude Knight would go on to form Knight Transportation.

As the trucking industry grew, various supporting industries developed to take advantage of the money that was there. Most obviously, truckers needed fuel and maintenance for their rigs. In addition, those who drove long distances would need meals while they were on the road. Thus gas stations on truck routes began to specialize in serving the needs of truckers and became the earliest truck stops. In addition to selling gas, servicing trucks, and offering cheap meals, truck stops began to offer a selection of consumer items that truckers might need on the road, creating the earliest version of the convenience store. By the end of the 1930s all the major parts of the trucking industry and its supporting infrastructure were in place. Even the semi-tractor trailer had made its appearance, with the all-important fifth-wheel connector that allowed trailers to be hitched and set off with ease.

HARD TIMES FOR A FLEDGLING INDUSTRY

Since its invention in 1903, the airplane, like the automobile, had grown in popularity. Airplanes of the early 1930s, the Ford Trimotor for example, offered no respite from the roar of the engine or the smell of engine oil. Flying at lower altitudes than modern planes, the Trimotor was beset by turbulence, much to the discomfort of passengers. Eager to fix these shortcomings Donald Douglas designed the DC-1 in 1933. It had a soundproof cabin to protect passengers from the clamor of the engine, and ventilation ducts for

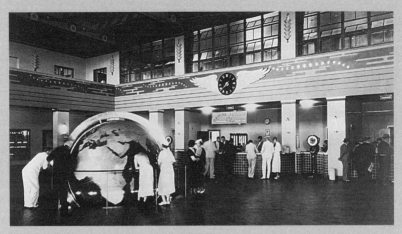

The Pan American Airways seaplane terminal at Dinner Key in Miami around 1940. It served as a hub for travel between the United States and South America.

Early Air Travel

In the early days of flight the experience of flying required a sturdy tolerance of discomfort. Airlines did not adequately heat cabins with the result that temperatures sometimes dropped below 50 degrees Fahrenheit. Noise and vibration were constantly rattling one's nerves. Poorly ventilated air contained exhaust and engine fuel fumes. Each passenger received bags and a box in case he or she became ill, but some passengers did not use these contrivances but instead vomited out a window. Under these circumstances pilots kept disinfectants at the ready.

Space was at a premium, requiring passengers to carry mail on their laps. (In the early days of flight airlines carried mail. Passengers were a secondary source of income for airlines.) Noise was so great that passengers could not talk to one another. Instead they passed notes. Airlines, seeking to improve the experience of flight, hired stewardesses to entice passengers with coffee and food. In 1928 Western Air Express hired 15 stewardesses and in 1930 United Air Lines hired eight. Stewardesses were required to be registered nurses and, likely to satisfy male passengers, were assessed for age, height, weight, and attractiveness.

By 1950 a variety of entertainment and news made the experience of flight more enjoyable. Passengers could select among movies, music, comedy, current newspapers and magazines, and radio broadcasts. Passengers could choose among alcoholic beverages and more sobering options: coffee, tea or soda. It may be difficult to believe in the current era of austerity, but in the mid-20th century airplanes had bars, lounges and even pianos. Smokers congregated in the back of an airplane and had a variety of brands of cigarettes to choose.

the circulation of air. In 1934 Douglas built the DC-2 and in 1936 the DC-3. The biggest of the trio, the DC-3 could hold 21 passengers, whereas the Trimotor could hold only 10.

Thanks to new levels of comfort and service, flight became an experience in its own right, rather than a means of shuttling peopled between locations. In 1929 airlines experimented with showing motion pictures to passengers, and in 1934 Transcontinental and Western Air made cinema standard on flights. In 1929 a radio transmitter first guided planes to their landing pads, and in 1930 Cleveland Hopkins Airport was the first to build an air traffic control tower. By the 1930s passengers could buy tickets by phone, obviating the need to go in person to the airport to purchase a ticket.

In spite of these improvements, the airplane was in many ways still a new technology when the stock market crash hit, and was not yet deeply entrenched in American society. The Great Depression hit the airline industry hard. Although the airplane had gone from inventor's plaything to useful implement in the skies of World War I, and it had earned its keep hauling high-priority mail during the boom years of the Roaring Twenties, it had still not made itself a necessity. There were no regular passenger routes linking cities across the country, and the airplanes of the time were not yet so fast that they could offer a good tradeoff of speed for expense for travelers who needed to be somewhere quickly.

Even before the United States entered World War II, military interest in the potential of the airplane was growing. Fighters and bombers had already proven their worth as weapons in World War I, but the military was also interested in the possibility of using airplanes in supporting capacities. Although by far the vast majority of material necessary to maintain modern industrial warfare would have to travel by surface transportation, there would be many times when the speed of an airplane could allow vital cargos to be delivered to a contested area swiftly enough to turn the tide of battle. In the end it would be air power that brought the war to a stubbornly isolationist America, in a lightning-swift dawn raid on America's military and naval bases in Hawaii. By the end of the war, airplanes and air travel had become much more familiar.

ON BLOCKS FOR THE DURATION

Keeping a car going during the tight times of the Great Depression had often meant making sacrifices in other areas in order to afford the necessary gas and repair parts. However, America's entry into World War II posed a different set of challenges entirely. Even in the worst part of the Depression, America's automobile companies continued to produce cars. Some of the smaller companies, particularly those that produced luxury cars, had gone bankrupt, but companies such as Ford and General Motors had not only stayed afloat, but even found a way to prosper amidst privation.

Not so after the Japanese attack on Pearl Harbor. Fighting so vast a war would require the lion's share of America's industrial resources, leaving nothing to spare for consumer consumption. Although the government never went to the point of forcibly nationalizing industries, they made it very plain to the automobile manufacturers that if they wished to stay in business, they would turn their production capacity to the war effort. As a result, the last automobiles for private purchase rolled off the assembly line in early 1942. In addition, the manufacture of spare parts for automobiles ceased, meaning that Americans were not only unable to replace their existing automobiles, but would find it very difficult to repair anything that broke down. As a result, many vehicles ended up spending most of the war in the garage simply because it was impossible to get them fixed.

Even people lucky enough to keep a car running throughout the war found it difficult to drive very much. Because petroleum was a vital resource for the modern military, its availability to civilian use had to be rigorously restricted. However, the previous two decades had seen such a severe decline in trolleys and other forms of mass transit for commuters that it was simply not possible to shut civilian gasoline off entirely. People needed to be able to buy enough gas to get themselves to work and to do essential chores, but no more. As a result, gasoline was one of the first consumer goods to be rationed by the Office of Price Management. Each car was given a lettered sticker according to its owner's role in the war effort, which entitled that person to purchase a set amount of gasoline per month. Once that amount was used up, the person simply had to do without until the next month's stamps were issued. If they could not get to work or shop for groceries, that was their misfortune. Most people did not blunder twice.

In order to conserve both fuel and tires, which were made from much-needed rubber, a Victory Speed Limit of 30 miles per hour was imposed throughout the nation, even on the open road. This slow speed also discouraged unnecessary driving simply because it took so long to get anywhere. Many families who might otherwise have visited relatives for the holidays spent them at home.

This government poster exhorted commuters to share rides and conserve resources for the war.

A 1940 Studebaker coupe. A number of luxury car makers failed during the Depression, and few consumer automobiles were made during the war.

IS THIS TRIP REALLY NECESSARY?

If travelers thought to get around the severe limits on civilian gasoline consumption by taking the train or intercity buses, they were sorely disappointed. Although World War II marked the absolute high-water mark in passenger rail service, it was as a result of the vast number of soldiers and sailors the railroads were moving about the country. Whole trains were filled with men in uniform, with some of them even crouching in overhead baggage racks in an effort to squeeze in one more desperately needed unit that needed to get to the port for an overseas deployment.

As a result, civilians were strongly urged to avoid any unnecessary travel by rail in order to keep the seats free for servicemen. Many railroad stations had large posters admonishing civilians to consider the relative importance of their trip in the war effort. Excursion trains had been eliminated altogether, and many people so foolish as to try to take a vacation by traveling the regular lines subsequently found themselves stranded somewhere along the way, unable to continue to their planned destination, but equally unable to find a seat on a train returning home.

Those whose business unavoidably took them on out-of-town trips found the railroad a far less congenial place than it had been in the prewar era. Not only were the passenger cars hideously overcrowded, but service had been greatly reduced in an effort to give at least something to everybody. Once deferential porters and other servers had become gruff and impatient, primarily concerned with keeping things moving as rapidly as possible. Meals aboard the trains had been reduced to a few menu items, and diners were restricted to a single cup of coffee, a consumer good that had been strictly rationed because shipping tonnage that would have been used for its import was instead needed to carry war material to the fronts.

Passenger rail service was not the only way in which the railroads were affected by the war effort. Fighting a two-ocean war required enormous logistical efforts in moving material across the country. Weapons and ammunition, as well as supplies such as rations, uniforms, and spare parts, all had to be moved from factories in the American heartland to ports on the coasts. Doing so required enormous numbers of boxcars, and could only be accomplished because all the nation's railroads made a conscious effort to use its rolling stock as efficiently as humanly possible. Even locomotives and cars that had been on their way to the scrap heap were often pressed into service in a desperate effort to stretch America's ability to transport vital freight.

LIBERTY SHIPS

America's wartime transportation system did not stop at her shores. Because the transportation of vital material was an essential part of maintaining the Allies' fighting "teeth" on the front, Allied shipping tonnage had to be not only maintained, but increased. At the same time, the Germans recognized the same factors and sought to destroy as many Allied cargo ships as possible. During the height of the Battle of the Atlantic, German U-boats were destroying British merchant ships at three times the rate British and Commonwealth shipyards could build replacements. As a result, there was a real possibility that Britain could not continue to hold out.

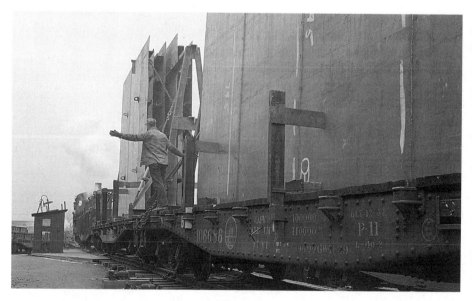

Flatcars hauling prefabricated sections of Liberty ships six miles from a former railcar factory to the Bethlehem-Fairfield Shipyards in Baltimore, Maryland, in the early 1940s.

However, the beginning of the 1940s saw U.S. shipbuilding capacity at a low point. Although American shipyards had produced a large number of ships in response to the necessities of World War I, during the Depression construction of cargo ships had almost completely ceased. As a result, there was little reserve building capacity that could be quickly activated. Even before the United States actually entered the war in December 1941, Britain approached America with requests to buy additional shipping. After America's formal entry into the war alongside Britain, it became even more vital to support the British ability to continue fighting if there

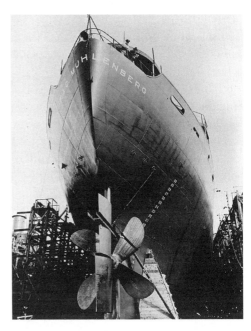

A completed Liberty ship ready for launching at a West coast shipyard around 1942.

was to be any hope of successfully invading the Continent and taking the war to the Nazis.

President Roosevelt's response to the crisis was to set industrialist Henry J. Kaiser to creating an entirely new way of building ships in order to greatly increase the speed with which they could be completed and launched. Kaiser's response was to reorganize the way in which ships were constructed to take advantage of mass-production techniques developed in the automotive industry. Previously ships had been constructed in place, much as a house might be built, with raw materials brought to the dry dock in which they were assembled.

In order to reduce the amount of time any given ship occupied the dry dock during construction, Kaiser's methods removed much of the construction process to factories elsewhere, and brought pre-assembled sections to the dry dock for final assembly. As a result, construction time was reduced from 200 days to a mere 40, and more than 2,700 ships were constructed over the course of the war.

The resultant ships were known as Liberty ships. Although they were built as cargo ships, because they were built during wartime to cross seas infested with submarines, they were equipped with guns and carried navy sailors to crew those weapons. However, the ships continued to be operated by members of the Merchant Marines.

CONCLUSION

By the end of World War II, there was an enormous pent-up market for consumer goods, particularly for automobiles. Although Americans had endured privations, those were almost entirely in order to free up resources for the fighting fronts. The American homeland had seen almost no direct enemy action, only the misadventures of spies and some ill-aimed balloon bombs, all of which was kept out of the papers in order to avoid alarming the public. Furthermore, high wartime salaries and a lack of consumer goods upon which to spend them meant people had money to buy much better products than they could have before the war. Along with wartime technological advances, such as improved four-wheel drive and radar, all of this meant that transportation in the decades after World War II would be very different. The automobile's influence would continue to grow, and commercial air travel was about to take on a much bigger role in American life.

LEIGH KIMMEL

Further Readings

Brady, Tim, ed. *The American Aviation Experience: A History*. Carbondale, IL: Southern Illinois University Press, 2000.

Elphick, Peter. *Liberty: The Ships that Won the War*. Annapolis, MD: Naval Institute Press, 2001.

Goddard, Stephen B. *Getting There: The Epic Struggle Between Road and Rail in the American Century*. New York: Basic Books, 1994.

Heppenheimer, T.A. *Turbulent Skies: The History of Commercial Aviation*. New York: John Wiley, 1995.

Jackle, John A. and Keith A. Sculie. *The Gas Station in America*. Baltimore, MD: Johns Hopkins, 1994.

Jackson, Carlton. *Hounds of the Road: A History of the Greyhound Bus Company*. Bowling Green, OH: Bowling Green University Press, 1984.

Kowalke, Ron. *Moving the Goods: A Nostalgic Reflection of the Rigs that Rolled the Roads of America in the Glory Years of Truck History*. Iola, IA: Krause Publications, 1995.

Schwantes, Carlos Arnaldo. *Going Places; Transportation Redefines the Twentieth-Century West*. Bloomington, IN: Indiana University Press, 2003.

Siddiqi, Asif. "Pan American's Flying Boats." Available online: http://www.centennialofflight.gov/essay/Commercial_Aviation/china_clipper/Tran5.htm. Accessed November 2008.

Uys, Errol Lincoln. *Riding the Rails: Teenagers on the Move during the Great Depression*. New York: Routledge, 2003.

Chapter 16

Public Health, Medicine, and Nutrition

"How can you frighten a man whose hunger is not only in his own cramped stomach but in the wretched bellies of his children?"
—John Steinbeck

WHEN PEOPLE THINK of health, they often think first of medical care: physician's appointments, prescription drugs, surgical procedures, and hospitalization. But at least three major factors affect everyone's health: nutrition, public health, and medicine, and among these three medical care may be the least important. This equation may not be obvious in 21st-century America, where a wide variety of foods and nutritional supplements are available to people at most income levels, and where important public health provisions such as clean drinking water and a functional sewage system are taken for granted. But less than a century ago most Americans could not take any of the three factors for granted: many Americans suffered from nutritional deficiencies, basic sanitary provisions were far from universal, and effective medical care was not available for many common diseases, nor was care necessarily available to people who could not pay for it or who lived in rural areas.

THE SANITARY MOVEMENT AND PUBLIC HEALTH
Of the three main factors influencing health, public health was the most advanced in the United States of the early 20th century. While technological advances or new discoveries in medicine may receive more headlines, simple

improvements in the quality of life of ordinary individuals have a far greater impact on the sum total of morbidity and mortality (illness and death) in a nation. In fact, the Centers for Disease Control and Prevention (CDC), the principal agency responsible for safeguarding public health in the United States, estimates that the average lifespan of Americans increased by about 30 years between 1900 and 1998, and that approximately 25 of those years are due to improvements in public health. The success may also be seen in the shift from infectious to chronic diseases as leading causes of death in the first half of the 20th century. In 1900 the leading causes of death in the United States were tuberculosis, pneumonia, diarrheal diseases, and enteritis; in 1946 the leading causes were heart disease, cancer, and injuries.

The roots of modern public health lie in the "sanitary movement" of the 19th century, led by reformers such as Lemuel Shattuck and John Griscom. The sanitary movement led to the establishment of local and state boards of health and the creation of many city services now taken for granted, including municipal water supply and sewage systems, garbage removal, and housing inspections.

Provision of basic medical services for the poor, including care for expectant mothers and infants, was also included in these early reforms. Of course, these benefits were not evenly distributed. While even the poorest city dweller in 1930 had access to basics such as clean drinking water and rudimentary health care, impoverished people living in rural areas were largely left to their own devices.

EXPANDED GOVERNMENTAL ROLE IN PUBLIC HEALTH

The federal role in public health greatly expanded in the 1930s due in part to New Deal programs intended to improve the welfare of the average citizen, as well as reforms necessary as the nation prepared for and entered World War II. Federal and state expenditures for public health doubled in the 1930s, and many local public health departments were established with funding provided by the Social Security Act of 1935. County health departments became the mainstay of local public health delivery. In 1934 only 541 counties out of 3,070 in the United States had public health service, while by 1942 1,828 counties had a full-time public health office.

In preparation for American entry into World War II, the Selective Service Board conducted physical and mental examinations of 16 million young men of draft age. While this should have been a particularly healthy group of individuals, the examination results revealed a shocking level of health that threatened the ability of the United States to field an army and to support civilian war efforts (such as staffing munitions factories). Over 40 percent of the young men examined for service were physically or mentally unfit. Leading reasons for rejection included bad teeth, vision problems, tuberculosis, venereal diseases, impairment from polio, hernia, and nervous and mental diseases.

A washstand in a farmhand's house near Dickens, Iowa, in 1936. Improved sanitation, which reached urban areas sooner, helped life expectancy in the United States rise by about 30 years between 1900 and 1998.

These results spurred even greater federal investment in public health, as the Public Health Service expanded grants to state and local communities. In addition, concerns about public health emergencies resulting from rapid urbanization encouraged passage of the Community Facilities Act, which provided over $300 million for construction of health and sanitation facilities in communities experiencing large increases in population due to expansion of war industries or military camps.

The Discovery and Development of Penicillin

Alexander Fleming (1888–1955) is usually recognized as the discoverer of penicillin, one of the first antibiotics, and a drug still widely used today. However, the sequence of events that led from Fleming's almost accidental discovery of the mold that yielded penicillin, to the development of an effective process to produce and purify the drug in the large quantities needed for therapeutic use, is less well-known but equally important. The story of penicillin is also a story of international cooperation in science: important roles in the development of penicillin were played by Alexander Fleming, a Scot; Howard Florey, an Australian; Ernest Chain, a German (and a Jewish refugee from Naziism); Norman Heatley, an Englishman; and John Sheehan, an American.

In 1928 Fleming was studying staphylococcus, a type of bacteria that commonly resides on the skin but which can also cause many diseases, including wound infections, septicemia, and pneumonia. During a short vacation, he left several Petri dishes with staph culture uncovered in his London lab and found, upon his return, that a mold had invaded and destroyed some of the staph colonies. In 1929 Fleming published a paper on the mold, *Penicillium*, and the drug penicillin which was derived from it, but did not pursue the subject further due in part to the difficulties of culturing and purifying penicillin.

The story of penicillin picks up again at Oxford in 1938, when the research team including Howard Florey, Ernest Chain, and Norman Heatley began investigating the curative properties of penicillin in mice. They were successful in developing methods to grow, extract, and purify penicillin efficiently enough that it could be useful as a drug to treat human disease. The outbreak of World War II in 1939 created an increased demand for antibiotics, and American as well as British laboratories became involved in penicillin production. Over 1,000 scientists in the United States alone were involved in this effort. The final step in the effective mass-production of penicillin was completed in 1958, when John Sheehan of the Massachusetts Institute of Technology announced that he had successfully synthesized the penicillin molecule.

Ironically, the "miracle drug" of penicillin has one great weakness: the microbes it kills are able to mutate into forms that are not killed by penicillin, part of the more general and growing problem of the development of antibiotic-resistant organisms. The first penicillin-resistant bacteria were identified in 1943, only a few years after mass production of penicillin began, and the problem has become much greater in recent years due in part to the wider use of antibiotics worldwide. This ability of microbes to develop resistance to antibiotics means that continuing research is necessary to develop novel types of antibiotics to which microbes have not yet become resistant.

MEDICAL CARE

Medical care in the United States in 1929 was as good as was available anywhere in the world, providing you had the means to pay for it. Medical education in the United States was the equal of that available in Europe, having been professionalized and modernized according to the recommendations of the 1910 Flexner Report. The short-term proprietary schools of the 19th century had been replaced by professional schools, often university-affiliated, which required two years of college-level science for admission, and four years of study (two years of basic science and two years of clinical studies) before graduation.

Although these reforms greatly raised the quality of medical care provided by American-trained doctors, and helped make the United States the world leader in scientific medical discoveries, it also sharply reduced the number of medical schools and medical graduates and restricted entry for many potential students who could not meet the new entrance requirements. This left many people without access to regular medical care. Rural areas, which had often been served by graduates of the proprietary schools, were particularly hard-hit in this regard. Between 1910 and 1935 89 medical schools in the United States closed and the number of physicians per capita fell from 173 to 125 per 100,000 people.

Several federal surveys carried out in the 1930s revealed the inequality of health enjoyed by Americans according to their economic class. The National Health Survey, carried out by the U.S. Public Health Service in 1935 and 1936, was a groundbreaking study of more than 730,000 U.S. households, including

A basal metabolism machine from around 1940. Military needs during the war led to new medical techniques such as the underwater weighing technique used to measure body fat.

over three million people from 21 states. This survey revealed that illness and disability were higher among the poor and unemployed than among the well-to-do. For instance, individuals from families on relief were 57 percent more likely to have a disabling illness than families with incomes of $3,000 or more, and 87 percent more likely to have a chronic illness. A contemporary survey by the Department of Labor, on over 14,000 families living in 42 large cities, revealed that the amount and quality of health care received was proportional to family income.

THE ANTIBIOTIC REVOLUTION

The greatest medical advance of the first half of the 20th century was the development of antibiotics, which provided physicians with effective treatments for common diseases and allowed them to replace a therapeutic repertoire that formerly included traditional methods of unproven efficacy such as bleeding and purging (one estimate is that in 1900, a patient had only a 50 percent probability of benefiting from an encounter with a physician) with one that promised rapid and efficacious treatment.

The first modern antibiotic was arsphenamine (Salversan), discovered by Paul Ehrlich in 1909. It rapidly replaced mercury compounds as the treatment of choice for syphilis. The second was penicillin, discovered by Alexander Fleming in 1928, but not exploited for its potential in treating human illnesses until the 1940s. However, the first widely available and widely effective antibiotics were the sulfa drugs based on the antimicrobial properties of sulfanilamide, a chemical formerly used in the dye industry.

Protonsil, developed in Germany in 1932, was the first sulfa drug. It proved highly effective in treating infections caused by streptococci, including childbed fever and bloodstream infections. Many other sulfa drugs were developed in the 1930s and 1940s, and they became a staple of both civilian and battlefield medicine. American soldiers were supplied with sulfa powder, which they were instructed to sprinkle on open wounds to prevent infection, and sulfa drugs were also credited with saving the life of both Winston Churchill (from pneumonia) and Franklin Delano Roosevelt, Jr. (from strep throat).

The efficacy of antibiotics gave a huge boost to pharmaceutical manufacturers, which were subject to only minimal government regulation or oversight. This changed after the

Glass pharmacy bottles bearing labels from the Merck corporation. Drug companies thrived with the introduction of antibiotics.

Malaria in the United States

Americans today rarely have occasion to think about malaria unless they are traveling to a country where it is endemic. Yet little more than 50 years ago it was still a substantial threat to life and health in parts of the United States. The eradication of malaria in the United States was only achieved in 1951 after significant, long-term devotion of resources by federal, state, and local health agencies, and is a good demonstration of the effectiveness of public health measures in eradicating a disease for which no cure is available.

Malaria is a parasitic disease spread by mosquitoes and causes one to three million deaths annually, mostly in children. The World Health Organization ranked it as the eighth highest contributor to global disease burden in 2001, and the second highest killer in Africa (after HIV/AIDS). It has been known to humans for over 4,000 years; it was described in ancient Chinese writings in 2700 B.C. and was recognized as a cause of the decline of many Greek city-states in the 4th century B.C.E.

Scientific advances in the late 19th century helped establish the cause of the disease and the means by which it was spread. The malarial parasite was identified in 1880, and transmission by mosquitoes was established by 1898. Prevention and control of malaria focused on public health measures that prevented mosquitoes from breeding, including drainage, brush removal, and application of oil or larvicide to sources of standing water that could not be drained. These lessons were applied by the U.S. Public Health Service to combat malaria in the United States. One impetus was to allow the construction of military bases for year-round use in formerly malarial regions in the southern United States. The Tennessee Valley Authority, whose primary job was to harness the Tennessee River for hydroelectric power and develop the surrounding countryside, also played a role in malaria eradication. When the Authority began work in 1933, 30 percent of the population in the Tennessee River valley had malaria. By 1947, after elimination of breeding grounds and insecticide use, the disease had essentially been eliminated in the area.

The roots of the Centers for Disease Control and Prevention (CDC) also lie in anti-malarial activities. The CDC began as the Malarial Control in War Areas program of 1942–45, whose purpose was to control or eliminate malaria around southern military bases, and prevent re-introduction of malaria into the civilian population by soldiers serving or training in malarial areas. In 1946, with the end of World War II as well as the success of the malarial control program, the CDC broadened its focus to include other diseases.

The final blow against malaria in the United States was struck by the Malarial Education Program, an undertaking of the CDC and the state and local health departments of 13 southern states, which began operation in 1947. In that year, 15,000 cases of malaria were reported in the United States. By 1950 that number had dropped to 2,000, and in 1951 malaria was declared eradicated from the United States.

Elixir Sulfanilamide disaster of 1937, in which over 100 people died after taking a sulfa drug including the toxic compound diethylene glycol. Public reaction to this tragedy led to passage of the Food, Drug and Cosmetic Act of 1938, which formed the basis for modern federal oversight of the pharmaceutical industry.

The pace of antibiotic discovery increased in the 1940s. Variants of sulfa drugs discovered during this time include sulfadiazine, used against urinary tract infections and toxoplasmosis, and sulfacetamide, used to treat conjunctivitis. Streptomycin, discovered in 1943, was the first drug effective against tuberculosis, and also the subject of the first published randomized controlled trial (conducted in England in 1947), a type of research now considered the gold standard for establishing the effectiveness of medical treatments. Other important antibiotics discovered in this period include chlortetracycline, of the tetracycline family of antibiotics; neomycin, commonly used in topical antibiotic ointments; and chloramphenicol, the first antibiotic to be manufactured synthetically on a large scale.

PAYING FOR MEDICAL CARE

As more effective medical treatments became available, demand also rose, and with it the issue of how to pay for medical care, particularly hospital care. Although national health insurance had been proposed periodically since the turn of the century, it did not become a reality. For individuals who were not destitute, particularly those who were employed, a different approach became popular: purchase of private health insurance plans. Early insurance plans such as Blue Cross began small and were often offered to members of particular occupational groups or people who lived in particular areas. These plans operated on the principles still used today, which was that individuals would pool their risk and their resources by paying a small amount regularly into a general fund, which would be used to pay the expenses of members who required care.

Private health insurance coverage expanded greatly from the 1930s onward. For instance, in 1933 there was only one Blue Cross Hospital service plan, with an enrollment of 2,000. By 1953 59 percent of the civilian population had some type of health insurance. However, these plans still left almost 40 percent of the population without insurance, and the plans were not comprehensive in the sense of covering all types of medical expenses.

THE VETERAN'S ADMINISTRATION AND WORLD WAR II

The Veteran's Administration (VA) system provided another means by which many Americans, particularly men, received access to health care. The Selective Service Board examinations were the first experience some young people had with organized medicine, and enlistees were provided with free medical and dental care, something many had never before experienced. In addition, expansion of VA services to encompass all disabilities, not just those which

The Donora Tragedy and Clean Air Legislation

The Donora Tragedy struck the southwestern Pennsylvania town on the banks of the Monongahela River in late October of 1948. Donora had a population of 14,000, and was home to two plants run by the U.S. Steel Corporation: the Donora Zinc Works and American Steel and Wire. Both plants had been operating in Donora for years, and had already been linked to air pollution. The company had settled several legal claims in the 1920s, but most Donora residents simply considered the problem a nuisance. A weather phenomenon, known as inversion, would turn that pollution into lethal smog from October 28 through 31, 1948.

Inversion occurs when a warm air mass traps cold air near the earth's surface. Heavy metals dust, carbon monoxide, sulfur, and other pollutants from the Donora plants were thus trapped at ground level, creating a toxic smoke that eventually became so thick that visibility was reduced to almost nothing. The Zinc Works continued operating for several days after the problem had been identified, until people began to realize the seriousness of the situation. Local newspapers carried headlines announcing the growing death toll, alarming Donora residents.

By the time doctors issued recommendations that people with breathing difficulties should evacuate the town, the smog was too thick to drive through. People had already begun complaining of various nose, throat, and respiratory symptoms, including sore throats, eye irritation, headaches, breathing difficulties, nausea, and vomiting. Doctors worked day and night as fire department members traveled throughout the town administering oxygen to the victims. The deadly smog would claim 20 victims, with thousands more sickened or hospitalized.

After several days of smog, rain helped clear the air and the Zinc Works reopened the following day. The victims of the "Donora Smog" were the first documented deaths from air pollution in the United States. The Donora Tragedy drew national media attention, including from noted news anchor Walter Winchell. The tragic deaths brought the realization that air pollution was not just a nuisance, but also a potentially lethal danger.

The Pennsylvania State Department of Health, U.S. Public Health Service, the United Steelworkers labor union, and the Donora Borough Council all launched investigations into the tragedy, marking one of the first cases in which the health hazards of air pollution were documented in the United States. The results were the 1949 creation of the Pennsylvania Division of Air Pollution Control, and numerous state and federal regulations to control air pollution.

were service related, meant that many for the first time could receive regular care after demobilization.

Important medical advances were made by military doctors during the war that then became standard practice in the provision of health care to civilians. These innovations include the use of DDT to combat disease-bearing insects, development and use of new antimalarial drugs, large-scale clinical trials and the first widespread use of antibiotics including penicillin, development of specific centers to treat burn patients, and development of large-scale systems to collect, distribute, and use whole blood. The underwater weighing technique used today to measure body fat percentage was developed by the military to allow them to distinguish between overweight due to muscular development and overweight due to excessive fat.

MENTAL HEALTH

Modern psychiatric and psychoanalytic theories and treatments became well-known in United States in the 1930s, aided in large part by the emigration of many European scholars and practitioners fleeing the Nazis. Psychoanalysis in particular became known through representations in popular media, although few Americans actually underwent any type of psychiatric treatment. The self-help/support group model of mental health treatment has its roots in the 1930s due to the success of Alcoholics Anonymous. Other psychiatric techniques developed in this period include the controversial prefrontal lobotomy, popularized in the 1930s and 1940s by the American physicians Walter Freeman and James Watts, and electroconvulsive therapy (ECT) or electroshock, developed as a replacement for insulin shock therapy and still used today.

World War II spurred interest in psychiatric evaluation of average citizens. The condition of "shell shock," which is now called post-traumatic stress disorder (PTSD), was identified among soldiers who experienced anxiety attacks, flashbacks, and recurrent nightmares after suffering traumatic experiences. The phrase "passive-aggressive" was developed, initially to describe soldiers who passively resisted or simply failed to obey commands, and then applied to the general public in cases where individuals chose covert methods to avoid complying with figures of authority such as parents or employers.

EUGENICS

The pseudoscience of eugenics, which called for selective breeding of human beings to produce what its proponents deemed a superior race, had roots in anti-immigrant sentiments and social Darwinism in the early 20th century in the United States. Among the many groups thought less desirable by eugenicists were immigrants, African Americans, Hispanics, and Native Americans; those considered less intelligent; those convicted of petty crimes; the mentally ill; alcoholics; and even those with poor vision.

Bill Wilson and Alcoholics Anonymous

Alcoholic beverages have been part of the regular diet of many Americans since the Colonial period. Despite this long history, America has had a somewhat uneasy relationship with alcohol consumption. This is best exemplified in the so-called Noble Experiment of Prohibition, which banned the production, sale, or transportation of alcoholic beverages from 1920 to 1933. Prohibition reinforced the prevailing attitude of the time that alcohol consumption was disreputable at best, and that excessive consumption represented a moral failing. Today, it is understood that people have differing reactions to alcohol, and many regard alcoholism as a disease that may require a combination of psychological and medical treatment. That change in attitude may be traced in large part to the influence of Alcoholics Anonymous (AA).

Bill Wilson (1895–1971) was a Wall Street broker whose heavy drinking eventually endangered his career. In 1933 he sought psychiatric treatment for alcoholism, and in 1934 he joined the Oxford Group, an evangelical Christian organization that had developed a spiritual approach to treating alcoholism. Through the Oxford Group Wilson met Bob Smith, a physician also struggling with alcoholism, and together they co-founded Alcoholics Anonymous (AA), a self-help group to help alcoholics stop drinking. AA started small: by 1939 Wilson and Smith estimated that they had helped 100 alcoholics get sober. That year they also published the first edition of *Alcoholics Anonymous*, known colloquially as "The Big Book," which described the now familiar 12-step program used in AA. Since then, over 20 million copies of *Alcoholics Anonymous* have been sold, and the 12 steps have been adopted for numerous self-help programs for everything from gambling to sexual compulsion.

The 12 steps detail a process members embrace to aid them in their struggle with addictive behavior. There are multiple versions of the 12 steps, but most share the following emphases: admitting one is powerless over the addiction, accepting the assistance of a higher power (sometimes specified as God), making a moral inventory of oneself, admitting past wrongs and seeking to make amends or restitution when possible, and endeavoring to help other addicts in their recovery process.

Although AA and other 12-step programs have helped many individuals, and some of their tenets (such as treating addiction as a disease) have become commonplace, they have also been criticized. The insistence that alcoholism (or other addictions) is a disease is controversial, as is the very definition of what constitutes an addiction. The AA principle that alcoholics should never again consume alcohol has also been challenged. The effectiveness of AA has been questioned because AA members are self-selected, and may be receiving other treatment. The spiritual component of AA has also drawn criticism; it has sometimes been likened to indoctrination and does not permit rational examination of its belief system.

The "scientific racism" of eugenics had also spread abroad from the United States, with horrific consequences during World War II. According to author Edwin Black in *War Against the Weak*, a significant amount of American corporate and institutional support for German medical research in the decades before World War II was part of an international movement promoting eugenics. The movement's ideas were picked up by Adolf Hitler, who took eugenics to its ultimate end with the extermination of millions of Jews and others who did not fit his Aryan ideal.

Campaigns by powerful supporters in the United States had led to the introduction of state laws beginning in 1907 that prohibited interracial marriages and authorized forced sterilization. Despite some opposition, the laws remained on the books in the 1930s and 1940s and deprived many people of the opportunity to have children. While exact numbers are still not known, it is thought that more than 40,000 people underwent involuntary sterilization under state laws through 1944. The practice was not halted until the 1960s, by which time another 22,000 people are thought to have been sterilized against their will. The governors of several states, including California, where as many as 20,000 of these sterilizations occurred, issued public apologies to the victims in 2003.

NUTRITION

Relative to many other nations, the United States in the 20th century enjoyed a bountiful, safe, and varied food supply. Many new food products were introduced in the 1920s and 1930s, including cold breakfast cereals, mixes for baked goods and puddings, and processed cheese. Wonder Bread in 1930 was the first commercially sliced bread to be sold in the United States. Within five years sliced bread became more popular than unsliced bread. Purchasing shifted from foods bought primarily in bulk, to those sold in labeled packages such as cans or boxes, a change that also favored the development of brand-name packaged foods, and introduced many Americans to "foreign" foods such as ravioli and chop suey. Home kitchens became smaller in part because of the greater use of "convenience foods" such as canned and frozen foods, and had more modern appliances including iceboxes or refrigerators and electric mixers.

This simple stovetop toaster from the 1940s required no electricity.

Canned ham was introduced by the Hormel Company in 1926, followed by spiced ham and pork luncheon meats. Their most famous product, Spam, was developed in 1937, but only became popular after the advent of World War II, when canned meats became a staple used to feed members of the armed forces. The army alone consumed over 150 million pounds of processed pork luncheon meat during the war. Spam remains popular in many countries today because of its distribution during World War II, and it remains the best-known among processed meat products sold in the United States as well.

The modern fast food business in the United States got its start in the 1920s with the success of the White Castle hamburger chain. Walter Anderson and Billy Ingraham, who founded White Castle in Wichita, Kansas, made it the leading national chain through perfection of the formula adopted by many successors: limited menu, low prices, and emphasis on take-out food. Many imitators followed, but poverty during the Great Depression and food shortages during World War II inhibited growth of the fast food industry until the late 1940s.

The Volstead Act (Prohibition) brought many changes to American beverage consumption. Soft drink production increased and American taste in (now illegal) alcohol consumption changed. Cocktails became popular as home-brewed spirits were mixed with fruit juices and other flavorings, and illegally imported Canadian and Scotch whiskeys became popular. Another result was the closing of many breweries and vineyards. The American wine industry did not recover from Prohibition until the 1970s. Many luxury restaurants also closed when Prohibition became law, but when it was repealed in 1933 the culture of fine dining was revived along with a consumerist culture, which led to the creation of fine food magazines such as *Gourmet* (founded 1941).

POVERTY AND NUTRITION

Of course, discussion of American nutrition must acknowledge that vast differences existed between rich and poor during this period. This contrast is nowhere more obvious than in the case of pellagra, a nutritional deficiency disease characterized by the "4 D's" of dermatitis, diarrhea, dementia, and death. Pellagra caused thousands of deaths annually in the United States in the early 20th century. Because pellagra occurred primarily in the American South and in group quarters such as prisons and mental hospitals, it was originally thought to be a contagious disease until Joseph Goldberger demonstrated its basis in nutritional deficiency.

Pellagra is associated with a corn-based diet, which was the cheapest food available in the South in the early 20th century. This explained both why inmates or patients contracted pellagra while wardens and physicians did not, and why economic downturns were reflected in increased incidence of pellagra among the mill workers and tenant farmers, who in periods of economic necessity consumed a diet composed almost entirely of corn. By 1925 Goldberger had demonstrated that pellagra could be prevented and cured by the addition of protein foods or brewer's yeast to the diet. However, because of continued poverty, pellagra continued to be a regular presence in the South until the 1940s, when the War Food Administration mandated the addition of niacin to bread, thus supplying the missing nutrient and making pellagra largely a disease of the past.

The economic hardships of the Great Depression also heightened awareness of how many people lacked basic nutrition, and several New Deal programs included a nutritional component. The need to prepare for World War II also sparked interest in improving nutrition among the general population, since large numbers of able-bodied people would be needed to serve in the military and in war industries. Government programs that aided nutrition include the federal food stamp program in 1939, which supplied low-income people with basic foods; free school lunches beginning in 1940; and War Food Order No. 1 of 1943, which mandated the addition of vitamins and minerals to staple foods such as margarine and flour.

PRODUCTION AND RATIONING DURING WORLD WAR II

World War II brought many changes to American food production and consumption patterns. Because food was needed for American soldiers as well as to distribute to the Allies overseas, increased production (the annual food production of American farmers was 50 percent higher during World War II than during World War I) was accompanied by food rationing and price controls. "Victory gardens" appeared in many backyards, and community canning centers were created as Americans were encouraged to grow and preserve their own fruits and vegetables, since commercial production was largely reserved for the war efforts.

In the 1940s, the War Food Administration mandated the addition of niacin to bread to eradicate the disease pellagra. This early advertisement for packaged bread emphasized that it was "enriched for better nutrition."

Gardeners show off their victory garden produce around 1943. That year, victory gardens produced more than eight million tons of produce—more than half of the nation's total output.

Sugar was the first product to be rationed, in May 1942; coffee, meat, fats, and processed foods soon followed. For sugar and coffee, each family was issued stamps that allowed them to purchase a given amount of the product, while for other products a point system was used that allowed consumer choice, while also preserving equity in the distribution of scarce products.

CONCLUSION

While many changes in public health, medicine, and nutrition in the 1940s and beyond can be traced to the vast mobilization of resources and technology during World War II, other improvements were the result of long-term trends or campaigns in the 20th century. Improvements in sanitation and access to nutritious food that had begun even before the war helped increase life expectancies, and were reinforced by the introduction of antibiotics. The war accelerated these improvements, and led to greater government involvement in public health. The prosperity of the postwar years would mean that later problems would be different—chronic diseases in an aging population, and health problems associated with overconsumption were on the horizon.

SARAH BOSLAUGH

Further Readings

Black, Edwin. *War Against the Weak: Eugenics and America's Campaign to Create a Master Race*. New York: Four Walls Eight Windows, 2003.

Etheridge, Elizabeth W. *Sentinel for Health: A History of the Centers for Disease Control*. Berkeley, CA: University of California Press, 1992.

Furman, Bess. *A Profile of the United States Public Health Service, 1798–1948*. Washington, D.C.: Government Printing Office, 1960.

Gehlbach, Stephen H. *American Plagues: Lessons from Our Battles with Disease*. New York: McGraw-Hill, 2005.

Leavitt, Judith Walzer and Ronald L. Numbers, eds. *Sickness and Health in America: Readings in the History of Medicine and Public Health*. Madison, WI: University of Wisconsin Press, 1978.

Levenstein, Harvey. *Revolution at the Table: The Transformation of the American Diet*. New York: Oxford University Press, 1988.

Ludmerer, Kenneth M. *Time to Heal: American Medical Education from the Turn of the Century to the Era of Managed Care*. Oxford: Oxford University Press, 1999.

Root, Wverly and Richard de Rochemeon. *Eating in America: A History*. New York: William Morrow, 1976.

Rosen, George. *A History of Public Health*. Baltimore, MD: Johns Hopkins Press, 1993.

Rothman, Sheila M. *Living in the Shadow of Death: Tuberculosis and the Social History of Illness in American History*. Baltimore, MD: Johns Hopkins University Press, 1995.

Shorter, Edward. *The Health Century*. New York: Doubleday, 1987.

Smith, Andrew F., ed. *The Oxford Companion to American Food and Drink*. Oxford: Oxford University Press, 2007.

Starr, Paul. *The Social Transformation of American Medicine*. New York: Basic Books, 1984.

Stone, Michael H. *Healing the Mind: A History of Psychiatry from Antiquity to the Present*. New York: W.W. Norton, 1997.

Warner, John Harley and Janet A. Tighe, eds., *Major Problems in the History of American Medicine and Public Health: Documents and Essays*. Boston, MA: Houghton Mifflin, 2001.

Wheatley, Steven C. *The Politics of Philanthropy: Abraham Flexner and Medical Education*. Madison, WI: University of Wisconsin Press, 1988.

Index

Index note: page references in *italics* indicate figures or graphs; page references in **bold** indicate main discussion.

sports
  baseball 6, 30, 148, *148*, 149
  golf 30
  horse races 6
  skiing 6
  See also entertainment and sports
Spruance, Raymond 196
Stalin, Joseph 176, 202
Stanwyck, Barbara 52
State Fair (1945) 28
Steelman, John 176
Steel Workers Organization Committee (SWOC) 173, 175
Stein, Gertrude 141, 148
Steinbeck, John 10, 205, 214
Stephenson, D. C. 153
Stevens, Wallace 10
Stewart, Jimmy 9, 23, 139, 147, 195
Stimson, Henry 185–186
Stimson Doctrine 186
Straussmann, Fritz 130
streptomycin 86
Studebaker *231*
suburbs 38
sulfa drugs xi, 240, 242
Sullivan, Arthur 141
Sullivan, Louis 33
Swing Era 143
syphilis 240
Szilard, Leo 130, 131

T
Talmadge, Eugene 170
Taylor, Myron Charles 175
Taylor, William 50
Tchaikovsky, Peter 140
technology. *See* science and technology
telephones 31
television 28, 39, 45, 148, *148*
Temple, Shirley 138, *138*
tenant farmers 77

Produced by GOLSON MEDIA
President and Editor   J. Geoffrey Golson
Layout Editors   Oona Patrick, Mary Jo Scibetta
Managing Editor   Susan Moskowitz
Copyeditor   Ben Johnson
Proofreader   Mary Le Rouge
Indexer   J S Editorial

1/11   1   5/10
   12/14   ②   11/14
  6/16   ②   11/14